The Adventures of KungFu Mike and the Magic Sunglasses

The Adventures of KungFu Mike and the Magic Sunglasses

A CONFESSION BY
MICHAEL BOULERICE

—ɯ—

ISBN: 0692469850
ISBN 13: 9780692469859

Table of Contents

An Unfortunate Halloween

—ᏜᏜᏜ—

WHEN I WAS SIX YEARS old, my elementary school class celebrated Halloween by letting us dress up as our favorite characters from books. I was then obsessed with the Gingerbread Man, and my mother made my costume from scratch with a bolt of brown felt, oversized black buttons to act as the chocolate chips and – the piece de resistance – brown shoe polish on my face. I went to school that day and partied it up with cupcakes, Dixie cups filled with room temperature soda and our eccentric first grade teacher who always demanded that we call her "Barbara" and not Mrs. Bertrand. Everyone else had store-bought costumes that looked incredible, but Barbara privately told me she liked mine because, "Someone put real time and effort into it."

When I got home from school that day, I immediately began shedding my costume to get ready for trick-or-treating. I couldn't make up my mind between two conflicting costume ideas, so my mom finally gave up and told me I could be two things that year; the Gingerbread Man for school and Johnny Appleseed for trick or treating. I participated in the Johnny Appleseed play that Little Harbor Elementary had put on at the beginning of the school year, and I was still infatuated with the character by the time October 31st rolled around.

I threw my felt Gingerbread Man costume on the floor, put on a blue button-up chambray work shirt, overalls and one of my mother's straw gardening hats before rushing downstairs to get my picture taken with my sister and her friends. I was in such a rush that I forgot all about the shoe polish on my face. As soon as Mom snapped the picture, we all headed out to beg our neighbors for candy together.

And that is the story of how I accidentally spent the Halloween of 1986 in blackface as an African American slave.

That's Shitty

—⚍—

I WOKE UP THAT MORNING with the restless feeling you get when you immediately remember that you have an exorbitant amount to accomplish that day.

As I slipped out of bed to shut the alarm off right before it started to beep, I felt it -- the most urgent need to shit I had ever felt in my life. It wasn't your normal, "Oh, I should try to sit on the toilet at some point this hour" kind of need, but more the "If you don't launch yourself into the bathroom right now, you are going to spackle the lower half of your body with viscous, off-colored feces" kind of need. Apparently all of the running and horrible-tasting health food eating was starting to make my normal morning poopy time an anxiety causing, explosive, browner-than-usual jihad.

I squeezed my cheeks together and tiptoed through my bedroom door, my head lowered and my breathing heavy in concentration as I made my way to the cold-tiled purgatory a few steps away. Just as I was about to turn the knob, I heard the shower running. Then I heard my roommate coughing in his bedroom, which made me realize that my worst nightmare was coming true; I had to shit, and my roommate's girlfriend, the girl who will stand in the shower until her skin begins sliding off her bones, was in my bathroom. This meant I had to wait at least another thirty minutes before I would be able to evacuate my bowels. I tiptoed back into my bedroom and shut my door.

I turned on the TV, hoping that it would distract me from the boiling turd monster that was attacking my sphincter with a sledgehammer. Scooby Doo was whining about something to Shaggy as I dropped to the floor in the fetal position, literally holding my ass cheeks together to keep the flood from breaching the dam. My butthole was simply too tired to do it by itself. I squirmed and moaned on the carpet, chanting "no, no, no, no, no", waiting to hear the metal on metal sound of the shower curtain rings against the rod, signaling that I could finally stop torturing myself. I waited.

And waited.

And waited.

Finally, as a last ditch effort, I decided to get up and ask to use the bathroom in my roommate's bedroom. When I stood up, I realized I couldn't control myself in that posture anymore, and a walnut sized amount of poop came out of my ass. I moved my hands from pinching my ass cheeks to cupping my actual asshole to keep any more from coming out. My stomach was killing me, and I was sweating like a Swede in a sauna. I had tears in my eyes, and there was no holding it in any longer. That was it -- I had to shit right then and there.

Acting quickly, I flung my closet doors open and grabbed three t-shirts and a Vons plastic shopping bag that I was using for a waste paper basket. I laid two of the t-shirts on the ground on top of each other, ripped my boxer shorts off, squatted over my makeshift puppy pad, and exhaled for the first time in what seemed like hours. It took about seven seconds for me to take the dump, and when I looked down, I saw a neat, almost too perfect pile of coiled shit, its only inconsistency was that it was yellowish and that it didn't even smell as bad as I thought it was going to. "This must be what vegan shit looks like!" I chuckled to myself. Relief quickly turned into shame as it dawned on me that I had just taken a shit on my bedroom floor like some kind of corn-fed mongoloid who broke into Grampy's Citrucel.

I quickly wiped my ass with the third t-shirt, threw it on top of the shit along with my boxers, and tied it all up like a hobo's bindle before jamming it into the Vons bag, finally tying it in three knots to seal Pharaoh Poopy into his recycled plastic tomb. I opened my panoramic bedroom window to bring in the fresh ocean air, threw some clothes on, and ran outside with the shit bindle as fast as I could. After touchdown spiking the bag in the green BFI dumpster outside of the condo and running back inside, I sat down at my laptop and laughed to myself, as I turned back to the TV and saw Scooby Doo and company being chased by some brown, muddy monster through a haunted house.

Raiders of the Lost Aunt

—⚏—

THE SUMMER I MOVED HOME from Wisconsin, my dad and I drove up to my grandparent's place in Vermont to visit for the weekend. My grandmother had recently passed away, and even though it cut into his gambling and boozing time significantly, my dad liked to go up and visit as much as possible to check up on my grandfather, who we all called Pop Pop. I didn't mind much. When I wasn't being force-fed ice cream sundaes, I was in Pop Pop's workshop attached to the side of the house making ninja weaponry out of broom handles, electrical tape and box cutters. Vermont was awesome.

When we arrived, I hopped out of the car and ran to give Pop Pop a hug. He was sitting on the front porch in a green lawn chair waiting for us, drinking a glass of warm Golden Anniversary beer and listening to a Red Sox game on an AM radio. His thick French Canadian accent welcomed us.

"Oh it's good to see you, bub. He's getting big, isn't he?"

"Yeah he is." Dad lit up a cigarette. "How have you been, Pop?"

"I been alright. Laura's not too hot though. Go in and say hi, bub."

My great aunt Laura lived with my grandparents in Vermont since well before I was born. I was never close with her growing up, but she was there for every holiday, every vacation, and every unfortunate traveling birthday that I would spend with my father while my mother was going to grad school during the summer. She was there for everything, but she wasn't really there. I never got one birthday present, one Christmas card or even held an actual conversation with Aunt Laura the entire time I knew her. My dad always said that she had been notoriously shrewd her whole life, but other family members said that she was so nuts that she just forgot about that kind of shit.

Aunt Laura came over to the states from Canada after retiring from her lifelong career as an elevator attendant. As one would suspect of a lifelong elevator attendant without ever seeing one, Aunt Laura had a hunchback. She didn't just have bad posture. She was pretty much shaped like a candy cane; her spine taking such a severe u-turn that positioned her head very close to her belly button. Her condition wasn't so bad when I was younger, but it progressed considerably over the years to the point that her stride was reduced to a shuffle, and she lived in constant pain. It was this combination of old age, chronic suffering, and forty-five years of going up and down in a metal box that made Aunt Laura lose her grip on reality.

If she wasn't sitting at the dinner table clumsily feeding herself the turkey that Dad cut into bite size pieces while she spat half-garbled Québécois at us, she was either losing herself in an episode of *Murder, She Wrote* in the living room, or snatching my Nintendo game instruction manuals out of their boxes. No one in my family ever believed me when I tried to tell them that my delusional aunt was robbing me of the 8-bit equivalent to James Bond's microfiche. I was always "careless" and "unappreciative of expensive gifts." Fucking Aunt Laura.

Of all the delusions a senile elderly woman could have, I always wondered why she consistently saw Baby Michelle Tanner from Full House wandering around the house. Maybe it was because Aunt Laura never got married or had kids, and some subconscious lack of fulfillment placed a familiar child in front of her eyes as a way to pacify her before she passed. Or maybe she saw all sorts of crazy shit, but she only publicly acknowledged seeing that one thing.

Dad and I walked inside and there was Aunt Laura; sitting in her leather armchair, fifteen throw pillows on the back cushion supporting her hump, watching an episode of Full House on the wood-paneled television in the living room. It was July, and the heat inside was still cranked all the way up.

"Hi Aunt Laura!" I ran over to her and gave her a gentle hug. Despite how weird she was, I really liked her.

"Did you know that they used to boil babies like that in oil?"

Aunt Laura pointed to the television. Michelle Tanner was sitting in her high chair, being spoon fed by Uncle Jesse.

"Uhhhh, no. I didn't know that, Aunt Laura." Her gaze returned to the show.

She had a strange fixation with babies being boiled in oil. This first came up when my brother brought my newborn niece up to Vermont to visit. Aunt Laura held her in her arms lovingly, looked up my brother, and just said it out of nowhere. It would be the last time Aunt Laura was allowed to hold an infant.

Dad said hello to Aunt Laura in his customary way; kissing her on the forehead and rubbing her back in a circular motion, coaching an "Oooh, that's nice. Rub the hump, bub." out of her.

"How are you, Aunt Laura?"

"Oh, not so hot, bub. The doctor says he wants to see some samples."

"Really? What kind of samples? Does he need some blood drawn or something?"

"Oh no, bub. He wants some of the tinkle. I have to bring it to him."

Aunt Laura was visited by home health nurses for years. If a doctor said that he wanted a sample of something, he would have collected it there. On top of that, her physician was a woman. Dad became suspicious.

"When did he say that he wanted the sample?"

"Tomorrow. It's waiting in the bedroom."

Dad and I looked at each other, stood up and walked slowly over to Aunt Laura's bedroom. It smelled terrible. There, sitting on the iron radiator, were two Vlasic pickle jars, both filled halfway with a dark orange fluid that was undoubtedly urine.

"...Jesus fucking Christ, Laura. Mikey, go get a trash bag."

I sprinted into the kitchen, grabbed a Hefty bag out from underneath the sink, and ran back into Aunt Laura's room. Dad took the trash bag from my hands. As he was loading the hot jars of piss inside, I looked around the room. I realized when I was in there that I had never actually been in Aunt Laura's room before. One of the wood paneled walls was covered with picture frames. I walked over to examine one of them. It was an old black and white photo of a man in a casket at a wake. I looked at the frame to the right of the man in the casket, that one contained a picture of an old woman, again in a casket. I stepped backwards, and realized that every picture on the wall was of the same subject. The only decoration in her room was a gigantic wall of sepia tone death.

"Dad, have you seen this before? It's all dead people."

"Yeah, Mikey. Aunt Laura is getting old, and sometimes old people get a little loony. She still loves you though. Here, take this to the trash out back by the workshop."

I held the bag as far away from my face as possible as I walked out of the room, through the kitchen to the workshop, where I dumped the bag in a trashcan. When I came back, Dad was explaining to Aunt Laura how she didn't need to keep those kinds of things in the house.

"Don't do anything with those samples, the doctor needs those. He also wants some of the stool."

"...what?"

"The stool. He says that he needs to see the stool, bub."

"Dad, what's stool?"

"It's shit, Mikey. Stool is shit. Laura, what are you talking about?"

"He needs the stool, bub. He told me to keep it nice and cool."

Dad kind of looked at her for a bit, trying to figure out what she meant. I stood there and watched him, Full House still playing in the background.

With the Sox game over, Pop Pop finally shuffled back in from the front porch and sat down in his chair. Dad asked him if he knew anything about a doctor needing samples. He didn't know anything about it. After a few more minutes of interrogation, Dad gave up and went to the fridge to grab a Golden Anniversary for himself.

I followed behind, hoping to convince him to make me an ice cream sundae. He opened the door, stared inside for a few seconds, reached inside, and pulled out a white envelope that read "doctor" on the front. He opened it and started gagging.

Inside the envelope was shit. Aunt Laura was shitting in envelopes and storing them in the refrigerator.

Dad ran to the bathroom and puked. I remember that very specifically because I had never seen him puke before. I looked in the fridge, and sitting next to a carton of Egg-Beaters and a six pack of Golden Anniversary beer was a stack of envelopes, all with "doctor" written on the front of them in well-practiced cursive.

We spent the next several hours throwing away all of the food in the fridge, bleaching the inside of it until our eyes stung, and driving to the A&P to pick up all new groceries for Pop Pop and Aunt Laura, who spent the rest of the night in her chair with the fifteen throw pillows, watching the TV intently, waiting for Baby Michelle to come back on.

—w—

When I was fourteen, Aunt Laura fell down the stairs and broke her hip during one of her attempts to find Baby Michelle, who she thought was hiding in one of the rooms on the second floor. The doctors at the hospital said she was too feeble to recover on her own, and since nobody in my family could take the time to be with her consistently, we made the call to relocate her from the hospital to a nice full-time hospice facility a few miles from my grandfather's house where she would be looked after.

A few months into her stay, my older half-brother Marty and I went to visit Aunt Laura together. Walking through the hallways of the hospice really freaked me out. Old, forgotten grandmothers and grandfathers shuffling around in warm bathrobes and slippers to destinations unknown even to them, crowds slumped over in front of a single television lulling them into sedated submission, or stuck in wheelchairs, shoved to the side of a busy corridor, moaning and grunting for something nobody would or could get them, even if their lamentable attempts at communication could be deciphered.

And there was the smell; the musty, sterile smell of the hospice that can never truly be described, but can only be equated with slow, comfortable death. This was the first hospice I'd ever been to, but I knew even then that when it came time for me to make the same decision that my family had to make with my Aunt, I would never have it in me to put someone there. I kept very close to Marty as we winded through the facility.

Aunt Laura lucked out and had a room all to herself. Normally rooms were situated for two people, but Aunt Laura's bunkmate passed a few days into her stay, and the hospice administrators never found someone to take her place.

Even though the room was all hers, Aunt Laura remained in the bed closest to the door and farthest from the sunny window that looked out onto a big grassy field just underneath the picturesque Green Mountains. Aunt Laura never removed the thick curtains from her bedroom the entire time I had known her, only living by the light of one dim lamp next to a bed smothered in chiropractic pillows to soothe her hunchback just enough for her to fall asleep. Even there, bedridden in that facility, counting down the days before she expired, she wanted nothing to do with the outdoors or natural light in general. She was so comfortable in the dark that any attempt to make her understand why light was nice, especially so close to the end, was futile.

Marty and I walked over to Aunt Laura, kissed her on the forehead and pulled up chairs next to her bed so we could relax. She was sitting with her back propped up by a half-dozen uncomfortable foam hospital pillows. They had given her a haircut; a cute little white bob a little below her ears. It made her look much younger than usual. She was wearing her favorite grey pullover sweater, the one I rarely saw her out of my entire life. Her mouth was open, exposing the few bottom teeth she had left, and her bottom lip was glistening with fresh drool. She never answered our hellos. She just stared at us with her big blue eyes, cloudy with age behind her giant, rose tinted glasses. I hadn't seen Aunt Laura since before her tumble down the stairs, but it was obvious that the recent trauma coupled with heavy medication had finally pushed her all the way through the rabbit hole to a place from which she was never coming back.

Aunt Laura continued to stare through us while we did our best to fill her in about life outside of her room; how I was doing in school, how interesting Marty's life was now that he had moved to the west coast, anything we could think of. She never responded. It was almost like we were talking for no other reason than to make an uncomfortable situation more comfortable for ourselves.

Marty looked over at me and saw that I was visibly shaken by what I was seeing. He blotted her chin with a napkin left over from her lunch, and left the room for a minute to talk to her regular nurse about how she was doing, and if there was anything that we could help out with before we took off.

I sat next to Aunt Laura for a few minutes silently, just watching her, listening to intermittent screaming and groaning echoing from the corridor beyond the door. I sat there and fidgeted with my sweaty palms, alternating glances between my aunt and the open doorway, screaming inside for my brother to come back. I couldn't keep the one sided conversation going by myself. ***Please Marty, get back here.***

Suddenly, Aunt Laura turned to me out of nowhere, looking at me with her big, confused eyes.

"Daddy, I'm scared. I don't like it here, Daddy. Can we leave soon?"

My heart dropped into my ratty skateboard sneakers. Aunt Laura's mind had regressed back into that of a child, and thought that I was her father who had been dead for at least thirty years.

I remembered hearing somewhere that it was dangerous to correct someone who was that delusional, and I didn't want to confuse her further, so I just went with it, hoping that I wouldn't have to do it for long.

"Yes, Laura. We're going to get you out of here soon. We need you to get healthy first, though. Can you do that for me? Can you be strong?"

I stammered a little as I said it. I almost felt like she was going to laugh and make me feel stupid for falling for some insane prank. My eyes welled up. I refused to blink; I didn't want her to see me crying.

"I can, Daddy. I really don't like it here, but I'll stay until I'm better."

Marty, almost on cue, came back into the room just as Aunt Laura stopped talking. We stayed for a few minutes longer, kissed her on the forehead and took off.

I held back tears all the way to the front doors of the hospice, finally breaking down as soon as I sat down in the front seat of Marty's car. I never felt close to Aunt Laura before, but seeing her in that bed, in that innocent, naked state of existence; pangs of guilt turned my stomach in knots. I felt guilty for never really knowing her, never having a relationship with her and knowing that I would never have the chance to rectify my mistakes weighed heavily on me. We stayed parked in the lot for a few minutes. Marty rubbed my back and reassured me that everything was ok while I hunched over in the front seat, crying until my head hurt.

Growing old never bothered me before, but the thought of Alzheimer's taking over my brain and putting everyone I ever cared about through uncomfortable bouts of psychosis made me want to jump out of a plane without a parachute on my sixtieth birthday.

That was the last time I saw Aunt Laura. She died a few weeks later.

A few months passed, and Marty and I found ourselves in Vermont again to hang out with Pop Pop for a few days. As far removed from reality as Aunt Laura was, she was his only steady companion since my grandmother died, and our family knew we needed to increase the frequency of our visits.

When we stayed in Vermont, we would help out around the house. Mowing the lawn, tending to Pop Pop's garden, waxing the old linoleum kitchen floor - anything we could do to help out, we did. This particular visit, Marty and I decided it would be a good idea to start cleaning out

Aunt Laura's room so that we could use it as a guest bedroom when family would stay over in the future. Pop Pop was taking a nap and we didn't have anything better to do that day, so I decided to head into Aunt Laura's room to get it over with.

Save for a few jackets lying on the bed, Aunt Laura's room hadn't changed one bit. Her bed was still unmade from when we rushed her to the hospital months earlier. Knick-knacks, pill bottles, picture frames all sat in their usual places - it was like she never left. The hairs on my neck stood up as I made my way to her closet. I knew she was a pack rat, so I figured I should start where she probably stashed most of her stuff.

The closet was packed to capacity. Jackets, boxes, Catholic iconic candles, more boxes and trash bags filled with God knows what were jammed into the closet in such a chaotic yet orderly way that it reminded me of exposed organs in a human body during an autopsy. I thought about how weird it was for me to make that kind of correlation. Then I realized I was in Aunt Laura's room; the dismal museum of all things macabre. I mean, she had a wall filled with nothing but black and white framed photos of loved ones in caskets for Christ's sake. The room's dark power must have been rubbing off on me.

I started pulling things out, examining them, and tossing them on the bed. An hour later, I had all but emptied the closet, finding nothing of any significance. I yanked the last trash bag full of clothes out, revealing an old, green metal lock box on the floor.

Intrigued, I picked it up. It was pretty heavy. I placed it on Aunt Laura's dresser to examine it further. It was about the size of a desktop computer tower, with two key-holes to the left and right of the front face.

I searched her room for the keys for another hour. I was dying to find out what she would have hidden away under significant security. Knowing Aunt Laura, it was probably a urine sample from the 1970s, or better yet, even more photos of dead people. I finally gave up on the search, and brought the box out to my brother, who was sitting on the couch in the living room with a beer, watching the Red Sox game.

I put the box on the living room table and sat down in a chair opposite Marty. We both stared at it, trying to figure out the best thing to do with it. Because it was old, Marty thought it might be worth some money, so he wanted to hold off on taking a hacksaw to the hinges until we spent more time searching for the keys. He was gone for about an hour before he walked back into the living room, exasperated and sweating from shifting around heavy antique furniture in her room trying to find them.

"Fuck this. Mikey, bring the box into the workshop. We're cracking this thing open."

I spent a lot of time as a kid in that cramped work-shop in Vermont. On lengthy visits, it was a great place to escape the oppressively cold hands of my fidgety, hypochondriac grandmother sliding down the back of my shirt to check my temperature, or being forced to watch Aunt Laura eat. During my "I think that I'm a ninja" phase, I fabricated supremely authentic Shinobi weaponry out of broom handles, rusty box cutters and barely adhesive electrical tape that I would whip around in the backyard, decimating legions of imaginary enemies until I nicked my thumb and gave up for the day. My dad and I once made a functional crossbow that shot U-shaped wire nail projectiles during an exceptionally long visit. We were so proud of its success that we hung it above the one window in the workshop for display, but now that I'm older, I think he did that so I wouldn't go on patrol through the rough streets of Bennington in search of wrongs that needed righting.

Later on in life, I realized that the workshop was a sanctuary for members of the family other than me. My dad also liked to hang out in there, but more because it was a secluded place for him to burn a pinner before one of our famous rounds of Old Maid than to craft instruments of death. My sister would sneak in there from time to time to crank cigarettes without our grandparents noticing. When I was fourteen, I would help my older brothers piece together makeshift weed pipes out of discarded plumbing materials, and my own alternative smoking devices that I could smuggle home when I was a sixteen-year-old skate punk. We would congregate in the workshop while our grandparents were napping in their individual living room chairs -- just to escape for five minutes and talk. It eventually became a place for all of us to escape the acute fear of growing old that would inevitably set in during our stays in that sleepy town in Vermont, and I was always glad it was there.

Vintage tools hung on weathered nails and lined the baby blue walls of the workshop, right above countless unlabeled coffee cans filled with screws, nuts, bolts, and anything else that was found around the house after countless old man DIY projects over the years. For how little the workshop was actually used, it was surprisingly clean. It was almost like the ghost of my neurotic grandmother was vacationing from the astral plane to nervously make sparkle anything that was exposed to air, just as she did in life.

Marty and I brought the green metal lock box in, set it down on the lead paint-spackled worktable and scoured the walls for appropriate safecracking utensils. Chisels. Ball peen hammers. Hatchets. We discussed strategy.

"Let's smash the locks with a hammer." I pulled one off of the wall.

"What if there is something fragile in there?" Marty was scratching his head. "Maybe we should take a hacksaw to the hinges."

"Will a hacksaw even cut through metal? Dude, let's bash this fucking thing open. It'll be quicker. Who cares if there's something fragile in there? Do you really want to hold on to Aunt Laura's long lost porcelain clown collection?"

"Yeah Mikey, that's a great idea. Just get the friggin' hacksaw."

"I don't know if that's such a hot idea, bub."

We both started laughing. There is nothing like an Aunt Laura impersonation to break tension.

I grabbed a dusty hacksaw off of its nail, and we both took turns assaulting the hinges of the box, trading hilarious Aunt Laura quotes to pass the time.

"Oh bub, you know they used to boil babies like this in oil."

"The night ain't complete unless you eat something sweet, bub."

"Ohhh, that's it, bub. Rub da hump."

The lock box just didn't want to give up its innards. About an hour into it, Marty and I were sweating, which was making the metal shavings stick to our hands and forearms, irritating the skin. One of the hinges was successfully split, but the hacksaw blade was starting to dull, which made work that much more difficult. We tried putting the saw down and prying the box open with our fingers, but it wouldn't budge. Finally, we came up with the idea of using a crowbar. With a groan and a vibrating metallic snap, the lid flew off of the lock box and fell to our feet.

Marty and I stood back and stared at the contents of the box. On the top was a legal size yellow envelope.

Marty picked it up and opened it. It was a collection of Aunt Laura's medical records from decades ago.

"Awesome. Fucking awesome." Marty was pissed. We both knew the chances of Aunt Laura having anything of value in there were laughable at best, but it was inevitable that somewhere in that hour worth of grunting and perspiring our hopes would grow.

Marty kept flipping through the stack of papers in the envelope while I examined the remaining contents of the box. There were envelopes - lots of them, all unmarked. I picked one up and opened it. There was $200 in $20 bills tucked inside.

I handed Marty the envelope. His eyes widened.

I dug through the box, pulling out envelopes and ripping them open. Each one of them had cash in them. $200. $300. $500. Every envelope held a tiny little fortune inside.

Never in my life had I seen cash like that. My family always struggled with money while I was growing up. Things like this just didn't happen to people like us. Marty started feverishly tearing through the envelopes with me. We were so excited that we could barely speak.

Crazy Aunt Laura had been socking money away into a paranoia fueled secret stash for years without anyone knowing...and we found it.

"Holy shit, dude. What do we do with this? I mean... HOLY SHIT, DUDE!" I was having a hard time spitting out sentences. There were hundred dollar bills and shredded envelopes all over the worktable.

"There must be thousands and thousands of dollars in here, Mikey. This is serious; we need to have a long talk about this before we do anything."

"Before we do anything? What do you mean?! Look at all of this money. You know nobody knows about this. I mean, fuck. Do you remember her buying anything ever since you've known her? As far as everyone else is concerned, Aunt Laura didn't have a cent to her name."

"Well, she did have a bank account, but we used that money for the funeral. It barely put a dent into the flowers."

"There you go, dude. Everyone else thinks that she's all tapped out. This could be ours, Marty. All of - "

I was startled by a car pulling into the driveway. Not just any car, a rusted out silver Chevy Caprice Classic wagon; my dad's post-divorce "See judge, I don't have any money" car.

"SHIT. Mikey, put the money back in the box and hide it in your room. I'll stall Dadoo."

With all of the excitement, both of us forgot that Dad was driving up from Massachusetts to spend the weekend before taking me back home to Mom in New Hampshire. Without even speaking about it, we both knew Dad couldn't find out about the money. He would make some argument about how he deserved to keep it all, and if we argued, he would tell Pop Pop about it and guilt us into handing it all over to him. My dad could throw a hundred mile-per-hour guilt trip fastball at you like nobody's business. There was no way my greedy little teenage mind was going to let that happen. I had to work fast.

I frantically stuffed cash by the fistful back into the lockbox, looking out the window every two seconds to make sure Dad wasn't going to come in. He was rummaging through the back seat of the station wagon for a couple of grocery bags, undoubtedly filled with steak from his favorite local butcher, and plastic handles of Fleishman's whiskey.

Marty went outside to greet Dad in the hopes that he could buy me some time. I kept fumbling. Bills and envelopes were falling all over the floor. I looked up again. Dad and Marty were both carrying grocery bags, and heading for the front door. I finished cleaning up, sprinted for my bedroom, and hid the box under my bed just in time to hear the front door open.

Pop Pop, Marty, Dad and I all sat down for dinner that night. Dad had, in fact, brought steaks, and after he was done piling food on our plates, sat down at the table sporting his signature evening attire – tighty whities, stained v-neck undershirt and black socks. Pop Pop and Dad sat on opposite ends, leaving Marty and I to shoot troubled glances across the table at each other throughout the entire meal. We were mulling the situation over in our heads. *How would we find time to count the money without Dad finding out? What would we do with the money? Should we even do this? Was that the only box in Aunt Laura's room? Was she going to crawl out of the grave and strangle us in our sleep for orchestrating such a depraved plot?* The suspense was killing me; what happened a few hours prior was the equivalent of coming downstairs on Christmas morning to find that Santa brought you the BMX bike that you always wanted, but the card on the handlebars read "Ho ho ho! If you tell your parents about this, the bike will self-destruct and I will never visit you again. Hugs and kisses, Santa." I could barely maintain my composure.

Dad went to the fridge and cracked a beer to go with his food. And another. After the third beer, Marty and I looked at each other at the exact same time thinking the exact same thing - we would wait until Dad fell asleep, and then we would count the cash and split it between us. We both impatiently piled food into our mouths.

After dinner, Dad retired to a couch in the living room with an orange Popsicle in tow to watch some Kojak. Pop Pop followed. Marty and I crossed paths while cleaning our plates in the kitchen and reaffirmed in whisper what we were going to do. Sure enough, after twenty-five minutes and a few more beers, Dad was sawing logs with a half-eaten Popsicle melting on his chest. Knowing from past experience that removing the Popsicle stick would wake him up, we left it there and casually stepped into my tiny bedroom to count a mountain of Aunt Laura's money.

Marty and I sat across from each other Indian style on my twin bed and dumped the contents of the box between us. We emptied each envelope and organized the bills by denomination, making a separate pile of discarded envelopes in the corner. Keeping a hurried pace while trying to stay accurate, Marty would count a pile of bills, write the total down on a notepad, and then hand me the pile to recount. Every couple of minutes or so we would burst out laughing. Both of our hearts were racing as the total kept rising.

I thought about the Sony Walkman I always wanted, the yellow sports edition one with the water resistant clasp that all of my friends had but me. I thought about all the times that I begged and pleaded for my friends to let me borrow theirs for a few days at a time to make my lengthy bus ride into school more tolerable. "Why don't you just buy your own?" they would always say. I couldn't just tell them that my family didn't have enough money. That was something I always hid from people. I loved finally having a great set of friends, but I was insecure and I didn't want to jeopardize that feeling of belonging by making them feel like they were hanging out with a loser poor kid like in Wisconsin. I thought about how I wouldn't have to miss another snowboarding field trip because I couldn't afford a lift ticket, and how I would be able to buy Subway for lunch like all the popular kids from then on, instead of sitting down in the cafeteria with a molded tray sloshing full of school gruel.

Thirty minutes later we completed our count. There was a little over $13,000 lying on my quilt.

As we were splitting the pile up evenly, we talked about what we were going to do with the money. All Marty knew he wanted to buy was a word processor so he could start writing again. Then he started talking about paying off some old bills that had been racking up interest over the years. I had no idea what I wanted to do with my cut. I was fourteen-years-old with over $6,000 in cash that my parents had no idea about, and I was two years away from getting my driver's license, so buying a car I couldn't even drive really wasn't an exciting idea. What was I going to do? Buy a Jetta and sit in it in my driveway on the weekends? I was too young to even get a bank account to put the money in. The only thing I could come up with was buying a safe to put the money in, something that would be a lot harder to break into than Aunt Laura's lock box.

"Guys, what's going on? Why is your door closed?"

Dad was up, and he was knocking. Fuck. I threw a blanket over the money just as the door swung open, barely covering half of it.

There was Dad, standing in the doorway with a Popsicle stick plastered to his undershirt, staring at Marty and I, who were sitting on a bed covered with thousands of dollars in cash.

"Guys, what are you doing? Wait...what? What is all of -- WHAT THE FUCK?!"

Caught red handed, Marty and I frantically searched each other's eyes trying to conjure up a way to correct the situation. I can't imagine how awkward it must have been for Dad when he woke up to two of his sons wading in a massive pile of money in his childhood bedroom.

He shut the bedroom door behind him, sat down on an antique radiator, and rubbed his eyes while we explained everything to him. Marty and I were both afraid that this was going to play out with Dad guilting us into giving all the money over to Pop Pop. My dad may have done a lot of shitty, underhanded things in his life that directly impacted his family, but he always went out of his way to treat his father like a king. He'd want to pay tribute to the king from Aunt Laura's Arc of the Convalescent, making sure his pockets were lined in the process, of course. After all, the court jester needed to pay rent too.

"You know we need to give this to the old man, don't you?" Dad tossed his first guilty knuckleball over the plate - strike one.

Fuck, was Dad right? Were we being ridiculously selfish about Aunt Laura's treasure?

"You guys found this in his house. You can't just keep this for yourselves. I didn't raise you two like this."

Steeee-rike two. My stomach started to turn. I felt like a scumbag. What the hell was wrong with me? That money was stashed away year after year by my recently deceased aunt for Christ's sake, and all I was worried about was not being able to keep it for myself.

I couldn't believe that it was over, just like that. No Walkman, no snowboard, nothing. The reaper of hopes and dreams came to me in the form of a middle aged, saggy underwear-clad man with a Popsicle stick adhered to an orange stain on his shirt. I was crushed.

Marty snapped to his feet and pointed at Dad with a determined look on his face. "Look, if you shut the fuck up, we'll split it three ways."

Not knowing what to do with myself, I shifted around on the bed out of pure discomfort and shock. Stacks of bills crinkled under my ass. Dad and Marty stared at each other, not saying a word. I thought about how Dad might react to the offer. Why would he take a third of the money when he could take the whole thing right then and there? I didn't realize the genius in Marty's thinking until later.

Dad reached for a pile of hundreds on the bed. "How much money is here? Did you guys count all of this yet?"

"It's...uh...$9,000." I almost choked when Marty shamelessly low-balled the father we shared by over four grand. I wiped the sweat from my palms on my cargo pants. Marty and I stared at Dad, while he squinted and thumbed through the bills. You could see the gears grinding in his head.

I sat silently on the bed and mulled the situation over -- If Dad took all of it from us and skimmed off the top before presenting it to Pop Pop, he ran the risk of Pop Pop somehow finding out that his son had taken some for himself, ultimately making Dad lose face. If he took Marty up on his offer, he had three thousand dollars in his pocket, no questions asked. Dad had to know that if he went with the former, there was a distinct chance one of us disenchanted children could "accidentally" let slip that we found $9,000 in Aunt Laura's box. The only surefire chance of Dad walking away from this both unscathed and in the black was to go with the latter.

"Alright fine, but not a fucking word of this, not to anybody." It worked. Marty was a fucking genius. Dad walked out of the room to hide his cut, while Marty and I split the remaining $10,000 between us, giggling like little girls flipping through an issue of Tiger Beat magazine at a slumber party.

The three of us crafted a fallback story, just in case family or friends had questions about why we had money on us, which was very probable, considering Marty and I never had any kind of expendable fun money our entire lives. We decided to tell people we hit the jackpot on a $5 lotto scratcher that we split the cost of at a local gas station. I actually told people that same story until I was about twenty-three, before I finally confessed to friends about the shameless pilfering of dead Aunt Laura's life savings.

The next day, my dad drove me back to my mom's house in Stratham, New Hampshire with $5,000 in cash tucked away in my backpack. On the way, my dad and I stopped at a Wal-Mart to pick up a little safe for me to keep my stash in. I remember standing in line at the register with him, thinking how fucking cool my dad was to let his fourteen-year-old son wander around with thousands of dollars to do with as he pleased. Then I thought about how most dads would want their kid to lock it up in a savings bond or something, so they wouldn't blow it all on useless shit, like a fourteen-year-old was bound to do.

As we shuffled through the line, I halfheartedly wished Dad would have taken the initiative and done what was right, something that I just didn't have the maturity or the resources to do by myself at that age. I knew that saving the money for when I really needed it--like for college tuition or a down payment on a house--was the right thing to do. As lame as it sounds, I desperately craved structure in my life. It was something my single mother just couldn't provide a young boy all by herself. I needed my dad to sit me down and teach me how to be a man. This would be one of those moments that would stack the delicate house of cards that is my current ability to discern right from wrong.

The first thing I did when I got home was look around for a place to stash the money. I couldn't hide it in my room, as my mother was known to do some private investigation from time to time. I certainly couldn't bury it in the backyard, because I would need to dip into it on occasion. I ended up finding a little space in the loft of our garage, nestled in exposed Pink Panther insulation. It was the perfect place to hide a briefcase-sized fireproof safe, and there was no set of stairs or a ladder to reach it easily. You actually had to open the breezeway door and use the handle as a foothold in order to monkey yourself into the rafters, which was something I knew Mom would never do.

A few weeks after I returned home, Mom took me out to dinner to celebrate my fifteenth birthday. We went to my favorite restaurant, Abercrombie & Finch (a British pub/restaurant, not to be confused with the clothing store that smells like a whore convention). After our meal, she handed me a card with $50 in it, which was a big deal because I knew Mom really struggled financially to take care of my sister and I. I knew I didn't need the money and I wanted to give it back to her, but I couldn't - it would have looked far too suspicious for me to turn down cash on my birthday. On the other hand, I couldn't just tell her about the money, because she would have taken all of it.

I knew that Mom could have used that $5,000 for a lot of important things, but I just couldn't give it up. I couldn't give up the electric feeling of having something so important, something that would finally afford me the opportunity to live like all the other kids. I fiddled around with a rolled up $500 wad in the pocket of my shorts while I ate a slice of cheesecake, my mother looking on and smiling the entire time.

A few weeks later, Marty picked me up at my house to spend a weekend at Dad's place while he was still in Vermont with Pop Pop. We talked about what we'd spent our money on since we last spoke. He picked up that Brother word processor he had his eye on, and spoke about it like it was the greatest technological achievement Mankind had ever produced. I, on the other hand, hadn't spent a dime. I wanted to, but I needed transportation to get to stores, or the mall, in order to do so. Hitching a ride with my mother wasn't an option, and springing for a taxi in rural New Hampshire was more expensive than fabricating a set of makeshift rollerblades out of shellacked $100 bills and skating to the mall.

We decided to spend some of our money together at the mall the following day. I was ecstatic; it was the first time in my life that I would be able to buy what I wanted and actually enjoy a shopping experience. Before that, my experiences as a consumer revolved around August school shopping with Mom at Marshall's, begging and pleading for the newest Five Star First Gear organizational supplies, but settling on dusty, two-year-old girly Trapper Keepers designed by Lisa Frank that had been mistakenly placed in the tube sock discount bin.

I broke my rich man cherry at Radio Shack, where I picked up the biggest, baddest Sony Sports water resistant Walkman that I could find. Big, yellow, clunky. It was awesome. After that, I wandered into Strawberries to buy some cassettes. It was amazing. I remembered all the times that I flipped through those little Columbia House membership pages, tearing off the album stamps that represented the music that I was dying to hear, and pasting them on the wall next to my bed. I tore through each aisle, picking up each and every album whose cover I used to stare at before I went to sleep every night. Black Flag's *My War*, Slayer's *Divine Intervention*, Ozzy's *No More Tears*...I was fucking psyched.

After that, I went to Foot Locker and bought four pairs of shoes without even trying them on. When we were done shopping, we decided to take a limo down to the then-brand new Fleet Center to catch a Celtics game, first making the driver pull into a gas station so that we could split the cost of an entire roll of scratch tickets, out of which we won another $750 each. I was quickly learning that spending money was a whole lot of fun. I came back to New Hampshire with about a dozen shopping bags, and an untamed penchant for buying useless shit.

I walked into my first day as a freshman in high school with an unusual lack of social anxiety and a wad of cash in my front pocket. After going through a few rounds of "meet your new teacher and pick up your new textbook." I sat down with a handful of friends to eat our bagged lunches in the cafeteria. As I was about to tear into a mediocre turkey sandwich, I longingly looked up to the lunch counter just in time to watch someone walk away with a six inch Italian Subway sub. I was about half-way through my soggy prison food when I remembered that I brought money with me.

I walked over to the counter and ordered myself a sandwich. While I was waiting, I turned around and watched my friends at the table eating their equally dis-appointing meals. When the lunch lady came back with my sandwich, I ordered seven more and threw them all on the table.

"THROW THOSE SHITTY LUNCHES IN THE FUCKING GARBAGE, FRIENDS!"

Everyone's eyes lit up as they thanked me and tore through the wax paper. I felt like a fucking king, not be-cause I had a ton of money to toss around, but because I realized I could make people happy with it. It didn't seem like a waste to me, especially if I could enjoy the spoils with friends.

My spending got more and more outlandish as the months went by. If someone would hit me up for lunch money, I would hand them a $20. If my buddy had a birthday coming up, I would buy him the expensive video game that he wouldn't shut up about for weeks prior. On the weekends, I would go to Wal-Mart with friends and buy ridiculous remote control cars, which we would set on fire and launch off of ramps, spattering the driveway with burning plastic until they stopped working. I bought a gas powered remote control helicopter, taped fireworks to it and purposefully made it climb to an altitude at which it would lose radio signal, just so we could watch the rotor cut out, sending it spiraling to the pavement and exploding, after which we all laughed and screamed "AIRWOOOOLLLFFFF!!!" I brought my best friends to an arcade and gave them $100 each to blow on Killer Instinct and Skee-ball. There was no amount of teenage boredom that money couldn't cure, and there was no amount of money that I wouldn't spend to cure it. Fuck responsibility, we were having the time of our lives.

A few months down the road I was finally running out of money, so I started returning some of the useless shit I bought at Wal-Mart for refunds. Hell, I even returned shit that I didn't buy at Wal-Mart. At Wal-Mart, I found out, it was possible to bring the charred remains of my Airwolf helicopter--without a receipt, box or instructions--to the customer service counter and get my money back. They didn't even have a SKU number for a toy that came remotely close to the description of the one I brought in, but some knuckle dragger just handed me cash and I walked out the door. When I got into my friend's big brother's car, I realized I had actually purchased the helicopter at Toys-R-Us. I started visiting Wal-Mart weekly to make returns, clinging to the dwindling remnants of false security that was the few hundred dollars left in my little safe.

The day finally came when I was forced to spend the last $5 of Aunt Laura's fortune, which I reluctantly handed over to the lunch lady in exchange for one more delicious Subway sandwich and a frosty can of Coke. When I sat down to eat, I accidentally knocked my soda over onto my sandwich. Even a sloppy brained fifteen-year-old kid could catch the irony in that set of events.

I could almost hear Aunt Laura cackling in the distance, partly because the defeated look on my face must have been priceless, but mostly because she knew she had taught me a valuable lesson from the grave that I would take with me to mine.

"Don't be an asshole with your money, bub."

Mike Loses Virginity;
Self Respect

—ɯ—

Pᴇᴛᴇ ᴡᴀꜱ ᴀ ʟᴀɴᴋʏ ᴋɪᴅ of Irish descent, who originally hailed from Texas, where he lived with his mother, father and younger sister. At some point during his childhood, Pete's father became an abusive, belligerent alcoholic and flew the coop on the family after an incident, the details of which I was never told, but have been assured are horrific. Pete's grandmother, after hearing about what happened, invited her daughter and grandchildren to live with her in Maine until they could get back on their feet, both financially and emotionally.

Pete's grandmother was a widow who became impossibly wealthy after her husband's passing, and lived in a huge, multi-million dollar mansion right on the rocks of York Beach. To call this place palatial would be grossly inadequate. It was a sprawling seaside estate worthy of any episode of *MTV Cribs*, complete with ornamental gardens impeccably maintained by a year round staff of landscapers, an investment wine cellar, imported marble everything, enormous rooms filled with laughably expensive art, a library filled with ancient first editions, and a number of bedrooms and bathrooms that could only be deemed reasonable if there was a Four Seasons sign posted at the end of the rose colored gravel driveway. When describing Pete's grandmother's house to friends, I can only say "The place was so nice that it made you feel bad about yourself."

Until Pete arrived in Maine, his grandmother had been living in this monstrous display of money all by herself, and you'd initially think would make her happy to have family living in it with her, but that wasn't the case at all. Pete's grandmother was a wretchedly tempered, elitist old cunt, who spent the bulk of her golden years tricking herself into believing she had earned her fortune instead of inheriting it after a lifetime as a pandering trophy wife. She took great pleasure in letting everyone to the left of her tax bracket know just how little they mattered to her. From the minute Pete put his bags down in what would become his bedroom; his grandmother did her best to scare him and his family into being lock-step with her way of life.

Pete and his sister were immediately enrolled in an expensive private school on the grandmother's dime, and even though tuition wasn't even a drop of water in the ocean that was her portfolio, Pete's grandmother used her grandchildren's schooling as guilt leverage in nearly every conversation she had with her daughter, along with the prototypical "I told you not to marry that man, re-member?" jabs. They did everything she asked, no matter how ridiculous or mundane, and tip-toed around her for fear of incurring her explosive Mother Dearest "NO MORE WIRE HANGERS!" wrath.

Despite their best efforts, including the children doing well in school and Pete's mother starting a successful interior design business, Pete and his family rarely rose to the grandmother's lofty expectations. She was so sickened by them that she spent the bulk of her time travelling overseas to do whatever rich old cunts do, leaving the mansion to what remained of her bloodline.

Pete, being a teenager in need of an outlet for everyday teenage angst, regularly offered his mansion on York Beach to us as a place to party while his grandmother was away buying art at international Sotheby's auctions or hobnobbing with other terrible, ascot-wearing sociopaths in foreign lands. We would be on our skateboards trying to ollie a set of stairs at the Kittery Outlets, when Pete would randomly decree that we were all going to his house to get wasted when we were done. He was never a kid that was desperate for friendship or acceptance, but he knew he had a very special, sought after thing that most kids our age had no access to, so he offered up his absurdly picturesque estate as casually as a stick of gum.

Being your average teenager who was normally reduced to police-doomed house parties, seasonal beachfront property break-ins and improvisational woodland bonfires for partying, an elegant seaside compound devoid of adult intervention that you could mask as an innocent, supervised sleepover was incredibly attractive. We didn't even really appreciate the lavishly adorned, incredibly baller surroundings. We could have partied inside the rotting asshole of a beached sperm whale if it meant we could do so without a flashlight being shoved in our faces, but there we were; a handful of lower-middle class road-rashed teenage skate rats getting obliterated in the lap of extreme luxury, and it was all thanks to Pete's grandmother.

The emotional straightjackets Pete's grandmother clapped on her family created more than one party animal, however. Despite her successful interior design business and the fact that she had just escaped certain death by fleeing Texas for the posh home of her mother, Pete's mom loved to party, and she loved showing people a good time. While our respective mothers were garnering their parenting advice from an issue of Redbook at the gynecologist's office, Pete's mom was buying us cases of Olde English 800 malt liquor, cartons of cigarettes, and stacks of porn magazines. She not only encouraged us to throw huge, underage drinking parties, but also enjoyed laughing along with us as we blew up propane tanks and hair spray bottles on the private beach behind the estate.

I specifically remember waking up at Pete's house to regularly find his mom enjoying her usual breakfast-- a Marlboro Red and a glass of Johnny Walker Red Label on the rocks. I look back at all of this as an adult, and a part of me is compelled to think Pete's mom was wantonly delinquent in her responsibilities as a supervising adult (the porn being the weirdest, now that I think about it), but thinking about what she escaped and what she was then enduring under the constraints of her mother, I get it. Not brilliant, but I get it.

When I was seventeen, we decided to throw a party to celebrate Pete and I successfully managing to jimmy open the unimaginably well-stocked investment wine cellar with a miniature crowbar. Picture your typical underage drinking party, but substitute double-fisted bottles of Mad Dog 20/20 and Natural Ice with magnums of Perrier Jouet and Krug Clos du Mesnil--the movie **Home Alone** and a rap video had a baby. It was a phenomenal waste of thousands upon thousands of dollars' worth of highly expensive wine, and our cat burglar tactics would end up being one of the deciding factors in getting Pete and his mother thrown out of the house upon his grandmother discovering it when she returned from her vacation.

Earlier that summer, Pete bought a Hi-8 camcorder, which we used to record all of our antics. Blowing up propane tanks, executing skateboard tricks, vomiting; the whole shebang. Every morning, we would groggily pry ourselves off of whatever swatch of carpet we had passed out on, congregate in Pete's room, and review what we had recorded the night before. The night of the party was no different, and the Hi-8 was being passed around the crowd, catching every minute of disjointed, drunken teenage flirtation and amateur hour alcohol intake.

I was in the kitchen swilling the last half inch of Bollinger out of a bottle and popping some pizza rolls into the toaster oven when she walked into the room; a beautiful, sun-kissed sixteen-year-old girl with blond hair, sporting a tank top and flower-print booty shorts. Her name was Rachel, and I got a socially devastating boner every time she was within fifty feet of me that summer.

I offered her some of my pizza rolls, and we hung out in the kitchen and talked about high school, plans for college and anything else that kids that age talk about for an hour or so before she suddenly grabbed my hand, led me into one of the many guest bedrooms of the estate, and told me that she wanted me to be her first. I was thrilled, because I was also a virgin, and I couldn't even manage to ask this girl out on a date the entire summer, let alone tell her that I wanted to try and stick my teenage cock inside of her for twenty seconds. I wasn't sure how or why this was happening to me, and I didn't care. This was it; I was finally going to have sex.

Awkward kissing led to awkward groping, awkward groping led to awkward clothing removal, and awkward clothing removal led to awkward, fumbling manual stimulation. I was nervous to the point that I had beads of sweat on my forehead, and so was she. We laid down on the guest bed and spent the next fifteen minutes alternating between making out and trying to figure out how to put a condom on my pensive, harder than diamonds erection. I was so embarrassed; I so wanted to look like the cool, experienced guy, but there I was--playing Mr. Wizard's Experiment Hour with a three pack of Trojans and a girl who knew as much or less about the act of fucking than I did.

Once we managed to sheath my sword, I climbed on top of her and attempted penetration for the first time.

And the second time.

And the third time.

After the fifteenth time I tombstoned my dick into her taint, she finally grabbed me and guided me in. Well, she guided the head of my cock into her, because that was all that would fit. It was like trying to fuck a pair of vice grips. I spent the next twenty-five minutes gyrating my hips like I was trying to become the fifth member of Menudo after Ricky left, thinking that I could pry myself inside with a little finesse.

I looked at Rachel's face, hoping to see it frozen in boundless pleasure, but what I found was a facial expression that showed nothing but pure, unfiltered pain. I asked her if she was OK, and she grunted back, "Yeah, I'm OK. It kind of feels good. Keep going." So I did, until I finally managed to sink myself balls deep into her. It felt amazing. I did it! I finally did it! I looked down to see it, as that was the first time my penis was ever inside of a vagina, and I wanted to take a mental Polaroid.

That's when I saw the blood. Lots and lots of blood. It looked like I had murdered a kitten with some bed sheets and a ball-peen hammer. I was just about to tell her that we should probably stop when all of a –

"YOOOOOOOO!!! LOOK AT MIKE HAVING SEX FOR THE FIRST TIME!!! HE'S A FUCKING STUD!!! WHOOOOO HOOOOOO!!!"

The door to the guest room burst open, the lights came on and two-dozen people poured into the room, all led by Pete with his Hi-8 camcorder in front of him.

I whipped the comforter over both Rachel and myself, and Rachel pulled some of the bed sheets over her head in some kind of hilariously futile attempt to mask her identity. I screamed and screamed for them to leave the room, but nobody budged. They just stood there, drinking champers and giggling at us.

I started to laugh back; I was drunk and the ridiculousness of the situation was starting to sink in, but I was also figuring that they would start to feel bad after a while and take off, leaving Rachel and I to finish what we started. Pete zoomed in with his camera and caught the blood on his guest bed.

"Jesus Christ, Mike. What are you, fucking her with a table leg?! LOOK AT ALL THE BLOOD!!! HOLY SHIT!!! Guys, seriously, look at the blood!! This girl is going to need

*a transfusion!!! Ladies, get in line to fuck KungFu Mike.
Apparently he's packing a cock the size of a baby's arm!"*

That was it; the final nail in the coffin. Rachel started
crying, my dick started to go limp, and I was sitting naked in a bed covered in blood, tears, and broken dreams.
The party guests left the room, Rachel threw her clothes
on as fast as she could, and knowing that there was no
way that I was going to be able to squirt any Fix-A-Flat
into the flaccid tire that was my entrance into manhood,
I walked into the kitchen to grab a drink, just in time for
Pete to dump a bottle of Moet on my head as the rest of
the party reviewed the new footage on a big screen TV in
the piano room.

California

—ɯ—

THERE'S A POINT IN MOST New Hampshirite's lives when they realize they absolutely, positively must move away. This realization is typically derived from a grab bag of cruelly unpredictable weather, anciently puritanical town governances, latent New England racism, and a state economy with dwindling employment opportunities. 100% of young people in New Hampshire grow up with dreams of moving to California or Florida, and maybe 50% of them actually achieve that goal. The funny thing about the statistics I just made up is that less than 5% of them don't end up moving back home after a year or two, and that's usually due to a mix of homesickness and the inability to make ends meet in a new place.

For me, it was writing that ultimately forced my hand and sent me west. I was sick of embellishing resumes and sweet-talking managers into offering me jobs I really didn't want, and I wanted to take a stab at becoming a rich, full-time writer instead of a poor, part-time blogger. I called my brother Emmett in Los Angeles, and asked him if I could crash at his house until I landed on my feet. He agreed immediately, and prepared his guest bedroom for me to say in.

I sold everything I owned until I was in possession of nothing but two bags of clothes and a computer, bought a one-way ticket to LAX, and gave my notice at my job as a recruiter in biotech/pharmaceutical industry. My boss, who was actually the brother of a good friend of mine who had moved to San Diego a couple years prior, told me I was making a huge mistake and that I would never make it as a writer. It was a cruel attempt to scare me into staying under his employ, but all it did was propel me further into my plans. I knew even if I didn't leave, or if I left and wound up moving back home for some reason, I'd still be much better off working for someone who wasn't an irredeemable piece of shit.

When I landed at LAX and reached the baggage claim conveyor, I realized I was standing next to David Carradine. He was on my flight and I didn't even know it! He was much taller than I imagined he would be, and much older looking. I grew up watching reruns of both Kung Fu and Kung Fu: The Legend Continues almost religiously and spent the bulk of my life thinking of Mr. Carradine as a God. That coupled with the fact that I was a naïve New Englander who hadn't spent much time around celebrities compelled me to say something to him.

"Mr. Carradine?"

He turned and faced me. "Yeah?"

My heart froze. I hadn't been in Los Angeles for more than ten minutes, and I was already having a conversation with my childhood hero. I was star struck, and my mouth betrayed me.

"I...I...I was on your flight."

He cocked his head and gave me a questioning look, saying nothing.

"I...I'm a huge fan of your work." Christ, I felt like such an idiot saying that. Before taking off, I prepped myself for how I would act if I was ever put in front of a celebrity. *Act cool. Act like you've known them forever. That way they won't know you're a loser.* All of that went out the window.

He picked up his compact black luggage from the conveyor and said "Yeah, great" with dripping condescendence. With that, he was out the automatic sliding doors and gone forever.

I stood at the baggage claim conveyor, waiting for my two bags of clothes, and kicking myself for blowing my chance to have a decent conversation with David Carradine, and maybe even getting him to sign my plane ticket stub. It wasn't until I got in a car and headed to my brother's house in the Valley that I realized several things about that encounter. For starters, David Carradine was picking up his own luggage, and was probably walking out to his own car. No assistants, no bodyguards, nothing. He was even on a commercial flight with me; certainly not the baller movie star status I expected.

Secondly, he was kind of a dick. Granted, I was a blubbering fan boy in front of him, but after decades of being in the spotlight, you would think he could have drummed up a little more congeniality for someone who was clearly a huge fan.

It was then that I created a logic loop in my head. Celebrities were real people. Most real people are dicks; therefore, most celebrities are dicks. It was an obviously sweeping generalization, but in the years that have passed since my chance encounter with David Carradine, I've come to learn that logic loop is 100% infallible. For the most part, celebrities make their living by trading their privacy for money. Somewhere along the way, most of them forget that, and look at their gawking fans like oozing lepers who want to paw through their pockets and finger their wives, instead of appreciating them for being the sole reason they were able to fulfill their youthful dreams of stardom.

Within forty-five minutes of the plane's wheels touching down on the tarmac, I became a jaded Angelino, which ended up helping me fit in quite well, because most residents outside of the entertainment industry share the same sentiment. They hate celebrities, but without them and the people who flood the city for a chance to see them or become one of them, Los Angeles would be ghost town and they know it. I found similarities between how the average Angelino viewed celebrities and how the residents of coastal New Hampshire viewed the littering, horn honking, money hemorrhaging tourists that wholly supported our town's economy every summer.

Emmett lived in a blue, three-bedroom ranch style stucco rental with his expectant wife Angela in Reseda. He worked as a producer/editor for a cable company's commercial department, and Angela was an editor tacked on to numerous "Real Housewives of [name of city here]" projects. She was an extremely pale, stocky woman who dressed stylishly, and had shockingly dyed hair that reminded me of the character Rogue from the X-Men comics, which was in stark contrast to my brother's defiant New England worn jeans and button up short-sleeved shirts.

Angela was a quiet, standoffish woman with whom you could have nothing other than surface level conversation. She originally hailed from upstate New York where she grew up in a house that also served as the headquarters for the family's funeral home business. One night when Emmett and I were having margaritas at a bar in Burbank and the topic of his wife's rather distant personality came up, he told me about how, when they were at capacity in the basement, her parents used to wheel freshly embalmed corpses into Angela's bedroom when she was a kid. She literally slept in a bedroom with dead people. I was completely mortified by that story and I hoped he was joking about it, but it did more to explain why Angela was the way she was, as well as Emmett's relationship with her than anything else could have.

Emmett and Angela slept in separate bedrooms due to their dueling issues with flailing insomnia, placing me in their third bedroom, which doubled as their home office, satellite closet and storage area. I slept on a full-sized futon bed, and kept my clothes folded in the luggage they came in because there was no room to put them anywhere else. I spent my days attending job interviews and my nights writing, reading in bed or hanging out with Emmett. Angela typically spent her time outside of work hanging out with her own friends and was rarely at home.

One Friday night while Angela was out doing whatever pregnant vampires do in Los Angeles, Emmett and I decided to watch old home movies and drink Manhattans as an homage to our father. We ended up drinking an entire bottle of Maker's Mark, and there was a lot of hugging and crying involved. It was one of the most touching, bonding moments I've ever had in my life, and with men, sometimes it takes a truckload of booze to get there. Angela came in around midnight to the two of us blubbering sappy gibberish, and was immediately furious with us. She stormed into her bedroom and slammed the door. Emmett followed her in there, and a massive argument ensued. I took that as a queue to go to bed, so I cleaned up after us and did exactly that.

I woke up around 8:00 am the next day to the mechanical whine of a vacuum and the sobs of a woman. I stumbled out of bed and looked at myself in the mirror. My hungover eyes were yellowish and bloodshot. I opened my bedroom door to find Angela vacuuming in the living room, bawling her eyes out while she did it. I asked her what was wrong. Never turning the vacuum off, she told me Emmett and her got into a huge fight again that morning and he took off to hang out with some of his friends in Eagle Rock.

"I'm really sorry about that. Is there anything I can do around here to help?" Seeing her pregnant, sobbing and cleaning at the same time forced that second part right out of me, despite my state of exhausted sickness.

Angela bared her whitened teeth at me like a snarling badger caught in a Havahart trap. "No. You've done quite enough." Three minutes later, I was scouring Craig's List for apartment rental listings in Los Angeles.

Unsurprisingly, Emmett came home later that night and told me I needed to find another place to live. He was incredibly apologetic about it and you could bet he was serving as a messenger rather than a decision maker, so I told him not to worry about it, that I was already on the hunt for an apartment and would be out of his hair as soon as possible.

A woman named Tammy ended up sending me a response after I had inquired about a roommate situation in Burbank and asked me to come down to see the place. The apartment complex was called the Kenwood Mews and sat a few hundred feet away from the Warner Brothers studios. Any Angelino who had spent enough time in the city would have told you it was kind of a dump compared to other places, but to a poor kid from New Hampshire, the place looked like Eden. It was a huge beige complex, built out of that stereotypical southern Californian stucco and adorned with palm trees, a swimming pool with cabanas, and incredibly attractive aspiring starlets walking this way and that.

I walked through the gates, past the pool and knocked on Tammy's door. She was a middle-aged woman of a hearty stock, with silvering hair and sun-weathered skin. I was really apprehensive about finding a roommate on Craig's List, but she seemed harmless enough with tie-dyed t-shirt, jeans and yellow rubber Crocs, so I walked in and checked the place out.

It was a small, two-bedroom apartment with wall-to-wall carpeting and piles upon piles of her junk contrasting against the stark white, undecorated walls. Framed artwork, battle-worn cardboard boxes, and tchotchkes of every conceivable size, shape and denomination were scattered everywhere.

"Did you just move in?" I asked Tammy, hoping to Christ her answer would be a yes.

"Oh no, I've lived here for years. I just keep my stuff where I keep my stuff." Her answer was so aloof that it was almost endearing. "I work so much that I barely have time to organize."

Tammy then showed me the bedroom for rent, which was miraculously clear of her hoarding. It was roughly 15' x 15', with the same carpeted floor and white walls, one window that faced a rather menacing looking alley-way, and a sliding, mirrored door closet space that was entirely too big for the five pairs of pants and two dozen t-shirts I had to my name.

"There's a cable hookup right there," she pointed to a corner of the room "So you can put a modem in here if you're one of those Internet people. I have cable hooked up, but I never watch it."

We got talking and I learned Tammy was a baker at an establishment in Toluca Lake. She was originally from Arizona and spent her life moving around and working at local bakeries with her girlfriend who she recently parted ways with. Her lifelong goal was to open up her own bakery in Los Angeles, which deposited her squarely in Burbank, only a few hundred yards or some-thing other than a common expression, especially an old one from Toluca Lake. Tammy seemed nice, and de-spite my reservations about her clutter and the fact that I knew next to nothing about her, I offered her a check for the deposit and rent right on the spot, which she accepted. Normally I would have shopped around a bit longer, but after the conversation I had with Emmett, beggars couldn't be choosers unless they wanted to be-come actual beggars.

The next several months were a blur of geographi-cal acclimation, social interaction, and work. I ended up taking a job with Maxim (the medical staffing agency, not the magazine) in Pasadena, and was frequently on call for nursing job placements via pager when I wasn't in the office.

If I wasn't getting lost going to or from work on Los Angeles's glorious knitting knot of freeways, I was sleeping on the futon mattress I brought from Emmett's house, drinking, or attempting to get my dick wet. I regularly frequented the White Horse (the bar, not the heroin) in Hollywood, hoping I would garner a woman's affection. In a lot of ways, LA isn't anything like it's depicted in the movies, but in a lot of ways, it is. I regularly managed to weasel my way into parties in Beverly Hills, where girls would offer you a line of coke off of their glorious bolt-on tits before leading you into a bathroom for a world class blowjob despite your being in an obviously lower caste, and swallowing with a smile. Admittedly, I complain about California a lot, but it's the only state I've lived in where girls aren't made to feel like whores for exploring their sexuality and doing as they please without the fear of retribution, unlike New Hampshire, where every girl who gets her rocks off is branded as a harlot.

With the first several months of my life in California being as busy as they were, I barely spent any time at the Kenwood Mews apartment, and because of that, I wasn't aware of Tammy's mental decline. Whether she was always crazy or her instability was a recent onset was beyond me, but I started to notice things weren't right at home.

It began with me regularly waking up to find my bedroom door cracked open. This was something I blew off as a random occurrence, having grown up in poorly constructed apartments where doors would blow open and closed with the slightest breeze. Then I started noticing that the bathroom door would be open just a crack after I got out of the shower, which didn't make sense because it never popped open while I was taking a leisurely, hour-long shit.

The theory that Tammy was watching me while I slept and bathed slowly pieced itself together, and forced me to recognize the other strange happenings taking place that I was previously unaware of. There was no artwork on the walls after years of her living there, despite the accumulation of it scattered around every usable corner the apartment. The shades in the apartment were always drawn. She spent all of her time in her bedroom, and rarely left it when she was home. I spoke with her maybe five times in the seven months I'd been living there, and when we did speak, she was always upset that I'd brought a guest in. Food I placed in the fridge would go missing, but everything else was labeled with Post-It notes as "Tammy's: Do Not Touch," bizarrely contrasting with the lesbian-hippie vibe she originally put on for me.

I started visualizing Tammy watching me in the shower, munching on my Trader Joe's spinach nuggets while using her free hand to rub her drooping labia. That is no way to live.

Not wanting to move back to New Hampshire and not wanting to spend another $1,400 per month living with Misery's Kathy Bates, I called Seth, who was living in Carlsbad, a seaside community two hours south of Los Angeles. At first it was a general "Hey, how are you, man?" conversation, but it quickly led to "Do you have a spare bedroom for a sexual abuse victim?" Seth had a spare bedroom and was thrilled to have me as a semi-permanent houseguest. I hung up the phone, and began to drum up fashionable ways to quit my terrible job at Maxim, and get myself out of the awkward and possibly dangerous situation I'd put myself in.

Several days later, I sat down with Tammy at the apartment and told her I was going to move out at the end of the month. We were on a month-to-month basis with no contract involved, and I told her I was willing to list the room on Craig's List for her to help her fill it after I left.

"WHAT DO YOU MEAN YOU'RE LEAVING?!? YOU ARE A FUCKING ASSHOLE!!! I CANT BELIEVE YOU'RE LEAVING ME!!! YOU ARE A SCUMBAG!!! SCUUUUMMMMMBAAAAAGGGGGG!!!"

After her frothing rant, Tammy flipped the chair she was sitting on, ran to her bedroom, and slammed the door. I wiped her spit from my face, grabbed a steak knife from the kitchen, and went into my bedroom to sleep, making sure to leave a piece of Scotch tape connecting the door and the frame. When I woke up, the tape was hanging from the door.

I walked into work the next day fully prepared to give my notice, but by boss was away on vacation. At the end of the work day, I sat down in front of my computer, typed out a resignation letter, printed it out, left it on her desk, and told all of my co-workers that I was never coming back. I loosened my tie in the elevator on the way down to my car in the parking garage, called Seth, and set a move-in date.

The following evening, I came home to find several items of my clothing lying on the living room floor. Tammy's door was closed, and she was watching a movie at a really high volume, which was totally unlike her. I walked into my room and discovered my closet door open, clothing strewn about the floor and my bed, which I had made the previous morning before work, unmade. Tammy had clearly been rummaging through my shit and doing unspeakable things in my bed, and that chilled me to my core.

I texted Seth and told him I was going to move in that night, and he told me to come on down. I began packing my clothes back into the two luggage bags they came in, and listened to the blaring audio of the movie Tammy was watching. It was clearly a foreign film and the voice speaking German sounded familiar, but I couldn't quite place it.

With her door closed, I quietly began walking load after load of my belongings into my car. I threw the futon mattress I was sleeping on, as well as my particle-board Target computer desk in the parking garage dumpster.

Just as I was about to disconnect my computer and throw it into the car, I threw a line I heard from Tammy's movie into a Google search. I knew I had heard that voice before, and I wanted to know where so I wouldn't have to mull over it in the car the entire way down to Carlsbad.

SEARCH RESULT: Adolph Hitler: Germany's Declaration of War Against the United States -- Hitler's Reichstag Speech of December 11, 1941

With that, I bundled up my desktop computer, carried all of it down to the car at once, and sped to Carlsbad as if my life depended on it.

POST SCRIPT: It took six months of badgering from lawyers to get Tammy to give me my security deposit back. She told me in one of our emails that she was let go from yet another baking position shortly after I moved out, and ended up vacating the Kenwood Mews. Her whereabouts are currently unknown, but I still have an aversion to slightly cracked open doors. All the way open is fine and all the way closed is fine, but if a door is open just a crack, there's a split second where I sense somebody on the other side of it, watching me.

Several months after living with Seth, I moved back home to New Hampshire because I couldn't take California for another minute, and now I fit comfortably within the confines of my imaginary statistics from the first paragraph of this story. I'm the guy who couldn't hack it out west, and I couldn't be happier about that.

Paradise Lost

—⚊—

WHEN I WAS FOURTEEN, I spent the bulk of my free time with Seth and Matt. I was living in Stratham, New Hampshire with Mom and Gen, and attending Exeter Junior High School (not to be confused with the ritzy Phillips Exeter Academy). Gen was seventeen, and running around with kids her age doing God knows what. Mom was either working her tail off as an unappreciated, underpaid social worker in the oncology clinic of a local hospital, or busy trying to cobble a busy single mother's social/love life together, so I found myself alone at home a lot. At the end of every school week, I'd pack a back-pack full of clothes, strap my skateboard to my back, and ride my bicycle eight miles down Route 33 to sleep over Matt and Seth's houses for the weekend.

Matt and Seth lived in adjacent houses on the same street in Rye, New Hampshire, a quiet little wooded com-munity bordering the bulk of the state's paltry eighteen miles of rocky coastline. Rye Beach is famous for the wealth of its residents, and a drive down the winding Ocean Boulevard yields dazzling views of the Atlantic Ocean, and extravagant mansions you could only dream of affording while simultaneously freebasing bath salts and huffing aerosol keyboard cleaner. To me it was, and still is, the most impossibly beautiful place in the entire world. Being able to spend my days away from school riding around that seaside utopia searching for adventure with Seth and Matt is the backdrop of the fondest memories I have of childhood, and probably one of the few reasons I didn't end up devolving into a frothy mouthed, dead skin mask-wearing serial killer as an adult.

Matt was a freckled, redheaded boy from a British couple who came over to the states in the 1970s along with Matt's grandmother. His father ran a bustling HVAC engineering business out of the basement and worked eighty hours a week down there, long enough to develop carpal tunnel in both hands and put an immense amount of stress on his congenitally weak heart. His mother was an executive at a local real estate company and was also very successful. They all lived in a big, four-bedroom Tudor style house that Matt's dad designed, complete with a huge, flawlessly manicured lawn and a big in-ground swimming pool. Most of my family's friends were either in the same dreary fiscal state that we were in or were oleaginous, leather elbow patch intellectuals who trumped up the historical value of their worthless antique furniture to guests at wine and cheese parties in order to inflate their perceived net wealth. Going over to Matt's house was one of my first experiences being accepted by a financially stable, well-adjusted family, aside from my wealthy aunt and uncle...who didn't count. You're forced to hang out with family until you're old enough to keep the relationships with relatives you truly enjoy, and let the others expire from neglect.

Matt's family was happy, successful, friendly and fun, seemingly without any scary, dark baggage tucked away. My family was poor, dysfunctional and struggling in almost every conceivable way. I looked at Matt's dad as the financial keystone of their awesome life, and I wanted to be like him. It was the first time that I viewed someone other than my brothers as a fatherly role model. Hell, I wanted him to *be* my dad. I remember shopping for clothes in Goodwill with my mom and asking her to buy me a dusty old copy of TurboCad I found on a shelf with the other electronics, with the idea that I could practice using it, become a wildly successful engineer and make enough money to not only pull my family out of poverty, but be able to start a family of my own and have them be as comfortable as Matt's family.

My parents and Matt's parents were best friends, even before I was born. My mom and Matt's mom had a little sewing business together and were actually commissioned to sew a flag for Wimbledon one year. While they sewed and Matt and I crawled around on the carpet in our diapers, my dad and Matt's dad would get hammered on the golf course together and laugh at each other all day. One year they were responsible for a local country club creating a new rule: "EFFECTIVE IMMEDIATELY: YOU MAY NOT BRING KEGS OF BEER ON YOUR GOLF CART." When I was six and my parents divorced, the dads kind of grew apart due to mine moving two hours away, but my mom and Matt's parents remained very close and are still close to this day.

Seth's family moved to Matt's street from upstate New Hampshire shortly after I moved to Wisconsin. When I came back three years later, they had become close friends. Seth's older brother as well as Seth's mom and dad lived in a two-story house that was kitty corner in relation to Matt's.

Seth's family was very religious. Seth and his brother spent a lot of time working with the local youth group at Bethany Congregational Church. They were both home schooled by their stay-at-home mother while their father worked as a security guard at a small New Hampshire university during the week and only came home on weekends.

Seth's mother was incredibly nice, almost to the point that it didn't seem real. She would drop whatever she was in the middle of doing to drive us somewhere or prepare a snack for us if we were hungry, ranging from something as simple as a chili dog to as complicated as popovers. She was completely devoted to serving her two sons and her husband in an almost manic way and rarely took any time for herself. This was about as foreign as foreign got for me, as my mom took *all sorts* of time for herself – her morning cup of coffee during which we weren't allowed to speak to her (a concept I now find brilliant in my thirties), enjoying a glass of Chardonnay through an episode Masterpiece Theater or retiring to bed early to curl up with a good book. Mom knew how to take care of herself when she was off the clock, and we grew up knowing adults needed private time. Seth didn't.

During our early teenage years, Matt, Seth and I were inseparable. We'd spend all day building makeshift skateboard parks in driveways, riding our bikes to the miniature golf course down the street (donning aqua socks and jumping in the water hazard to collect balls, effectively turning a thirty minute game into a five hour game) and having sleepovers every night. When the parents had been snoring for hours already, we'd regularly sneak out of the house in the middle of the night and roam the streets of Rye in search of adventure. Streetlights in the sleepy seaside community were few and far between, so we would navigate by moonlight alone. We would explore partially constructed mansions, steal the chrome air stem caps from the tires of parked cars and hide in the woods that tightly insulated the sides of the road anytime a stray vehicle careened down it and bathed our paths in piercing halogen brightness. Sometimes we would bolt super quiet rollerblade wheels onto our skateboards and silently glide down the winding rural roads to meet up with girls from school on the other end of town.

We were in that comfortable sweet spot of an age where you were too old to be an angel, yet too young to cause any real damage. We were incredibly lucky to have a town in which we could experiment with misbehavior without getting hurt or arrested, which after some introspection, I can largely credit for molding the three of us into the considerate, law abiding, somewhat responsible citizens we are today. We were able to get it out of our systems. At fourteen, I was already seeing the catastrophic results of hyper-conservative parenting in the kids that bucked against it by getting expelled and arrested, which made me appreciate being able to spend time in the perfectly safe, homogenized snow globe that was Rye even more.

Once, while another preposterously gorgeous summer sun set over the Atlantic, Matt, Seth and I were playing a game we called "Rock Hop" out on a jetty in Rye Harbor State Park, a large grassy area complete with a large pavilion and picnic table seating, situated right on the water, and was completely unoccupied aside from us. Essentially an amalgamation of HORSE and parkour, Rock Hop required one person to jump from one jetty boulder to another, and the other two of us having to make it to the same boulder. You got a point every time you made it without losing your balance and falling off. A different person would start on the next round, and the game would eventually evolve into us launching ourselves toward boulders farther and farther away in order to thwart our opponents, and a winner would be crowned at the little navigation tower at the end of the jetty, most likely bleeding from an elbow or knee. We'd typically play one game on the way out to the tower, and another one coming back to the shore.

When we hopped off the jetty and started walking over to where our bikes were parked, we were approached by a middle-aged man. He wore a Boston Red Sox baseball cap with a violently curved brim, dark sunglasses, a polo shirt tucked into his denim shorts and black sneakers with white mid-length tube socks sprouting out of them. Put a road map in one hand and a camera in the other, and he would have looked like your average out-of-state tourist flocking to the seacoast from parts unknown every summer.

"Hi guys! Having fun out there today?" The man stopped about ten feet away from us and knelt down to pull one of his tube socks back up.

"Yep." Was our collective answer. Fourteen-year-old boys aren't exactly known for their conversational skill set.

"Good, good. That's good. Hey, listen. I have a proposition for you boys."

"...OK?"

"See that lady at the picnic table over there?" The man pointed to a picnic table underneath the shaded pavilion, which was roughly a hundred feet from where we were standing. Sitting at the table was a woman who looked to be in her late twenties. She had curly brown hair and was wearing a floral print dress that billowed in the warm ocean breeze. She waved at us. I was the only one of us to wave back, more because of the politeness reflex that was beaten into me growing up than a genuine desire to communicate with a total stranger.

"Uh, yeah?"

"Well that lady over there is my wife…and she screwed up." His face went from friendly to serious. "She screwed up real bad. She's in a lot of trouble with me, and she needs to be punished."

Matt, Seth and I said nothing in return, only exchanging nervous glances with each other. This was getting very weird, very fast. Between us and our bikes and the roads leading back home was about a hundred feet of grass and this unfamiliar man, whose face became more dark and grave with every passing second.

"If you guys go over there, you can do whatever you want to her, touch whatever you want. You can do whatever you want to her, and make her do whatever you want to you. She knows why I came over here to talk to you, and she's waiting for you guys to come on over. I'll just stand back here and let you guys do your thing."

We exchanged silent *what the fuck do we do?* glares at each other for the third time, not uttering a single word in response to the man's offer.

As a fourteen-year-old, I had only the thinnest idea about what sex was. I knew what the act of coitus entailed, but everything else surrounding the act – foreplay, what felt good and what didn't, how to perform well – enveloped my concept of sex like a grey mist. My mom caught me reading her copy of *Our Bodies, Ourselves* when I was eight, which made her feel like I knew enough to forego having "The Talk" with me.

Dad never had "The Talk" with me either. The only two lessons about women I got from him were "Don't ever get married." and "I'm serious, don't get married. It's terrible."

Both of them were completely OK with me watching the most violent movies imaginable, but the minute nudity popped into a scene, the tape was slapped back in the case and returned to the rental store, still warm from the player.

With both parents not up to the task, I ended up being responsible for my own sex education, so I was reduced to the tattered remains of nudie magazines we'd occasionally find in the woods, overhearing kids talking about it on the school bus and treating scrambled cable channels like Magic Eye images which occasionally yielded a wavy, disembodied nipple for reference material.

I stumbled into masturbation only a year earlier, when I was watching the six o'clock CBS News in my bedroom and Dan Rather announced that a segment on Internet pornography would start after the commercial break. Not only did we not have residential Internet access because it was so new, but there was no hidden porn in my home either, so I was immediately aroused by this unexpected delivery of erotica. Rather's commentary about the prominence of Internet porn and its implications became a distant drone in the background as I hypnotized by the grainy, pixelated images of women with black "censored" bars covering certain parts. After some concentrated effort, I finally figured out the mechanics of the act, which left me paralyzed and twitching on the bed, reeling from the sensory tidal wave that is the first orgasm. Of course, not knowing anything about the physiology of the act, I tried to keep going, thinking you might be able keep feeling that for hours and hours if you didn't stop. This resulted in a bolt of pain that forced a quick blip of a high-pitched scream out of me.

"Mike? Is everything OK up there?" My mom called up.

"…Stubbed…toe…" I couldn't even speak.

"What's that?"

"Toe stub. Toe…I just stubbed my toe."

"Be careful up there, will you?"

I didn't respond. I just climbed back on my bed, wishing my dick came with an instruction manual like one of my Nintendo games.

That was the extent of my sexual awakening up until the age of fourteen, when my best friends and I had our chance encounter with an anonymous sexual deviant looking to subject "his wife" who was "in trouble" to the fumbling awkwardness of a handful of children in the name of… what? Voyeurism? Cuckoldry? Pedophilia? At our age, we had no idea any of that stuff existed. They certainly didn't teach us about the fetishist subcultures in health class. As far as we knew, the man genuinely wanted us to help him punish this woman (is that something adults do?), whose smiles and waves and eye contact really didn't fit the mannerisms of a grown woman who felt so guilty about something, so desperate for forgiveness that she would allow herself to be ravaged by the Burger King Kid's Club.

Still, despite the thick layers of creepiness that surrounded the situation, there was a glimmer of allure to it. This wasn't a sun-bleached issue of Nugget magazine found next to a dumpster at the mall, the bra section of the Woolworth's catalog or a muted episode of Kiana's Flex Appeal: this was a real girl. Not just a girl, but an actual adult woman, with whom we could do anything. Anything. My heart thrummed and my pubescent mind raced with the possibilities. *I don't want to have sex with this woman. That would be way too weird and I don't want my first time to be like that. But what if I touched her boob? I could just touch her boob really quickly, get on my bike and ride home. I could say I touched a real adult boob, and kids at school would think it was awesome. I could —*

"Uh, we have to go." "Thanks anyway, mister." I was snapped out of my trance as Matt and Seth forked left and right around the man, almost speed-walking to the bikes ahead.

I sighed, resigned myself to the fact that Matt and Seth were ultimately right, and followed their lead. The man said nothing else.

We couldn't help but stare at the woman sitting at the picnic table. We couldn't really tell further back, but as we drew closer, we realized the woman was actually very attractive. Stunning, even. She smiled at us again, but the smile waned as she realized we weren't stopping. She clasped her hands in her lap and looked down at the grass in front of her feet as we passed by.

Without saying a word, we tapped our kickstands up, mounted our bikes and hightailed it back to Seth's house while the twilight slowly ebbed behind the opaque inland pines. As soon as we put enough distance between us and Rye State Park, the rest of the ride home was filled with "HOLY CRAP, GUYS!!", "WHAT THE HECK JUST HAPPENED?!" and "THAT WAS SUPER CREEPY!!!" It seemed like the farther we rode, the weirder and more uncomfortably real the encounter at the park became, almost as if distance and perception were momentarily proportional to each other.

That night, tucked into a sleeping bag on the floor of Seth's basement while Matt and Seth snored away, I lay awake thinking about how my previous notions of Rye being a nurturing safe haven in which to hide from the reality and consequences of life had been shattered that day; how no physical location on Earth – no matter how picturesque and comforting - could ever be that haven. It made me feel cold, but somehow more adult and aware.

I drifted off to sleep shortly after that. In my dream, I touched the boob.

Stevens Point

—⚏—

IN JUNE OF 1990, I lived on 586 Broad Street, a nice residential neighborhood in Portsmouth, New Hampshire. I was ten years old and Gen was twelve. Mom and Dad got divorced when I was six, so I was oblivious to a lot of the struggle that went along with that. At that point, all I knew was that they argued a lot. Mom yelled at Dad, and Dad yelled at Mom in return. It was an endless volley of shouting; the score to the movie being filmed inside my mind as I played with plastic action figures on the carpet of our living room or out in the backyard. Dad moved a few hours south to a really rough neighborhood in West Springfield, Massachusetts. He lived in Edgewater Apartments, in a one-bedroom that was under one of his employers' names so he could avoid paying income tax.

Mom drove down to and lived at Smith College every summer to work on her masters in social work, and my sister and I would spend our school vacations with Dad.

He worked as a depilatory wax salesman by day, and as a bookie with the alias "A.B." by night. We would accompany him on his sales route about once a week, but for the most part, we stayed in his sweltering apartment to watch cartoons while he was working, and weren't allowed to open the door for anyone or leave the apartment for any reason while he was out. When he came home, we'd go out for dinner at the Pizza Shoppe in Springfield or the Blue Eagle in East Longmeadow, where we were allowed to order whatever we wanted and we would laugh until we were blue in the face.

We'd stop for dessert on the way home, after which he would begin his second job, usually in nothing but an undershirt and his skivvies. Every now and again he would let me answer the phone as "A.B. Jr." and take bets from people with aliases that ranged from "John Doe" to "Razor". Once the bets were in, we'd watch the horse races and basketball games on Dad's black box and record the scores. I didn't care much for sports, but I really enjoyed hanging out with my dad and being useful. Dad would make us call Mom every other night or so. She would ask us how we were doing and we'd rush though our conversations with her so we could get off the phone and eat candy or play cards. Dad's house was a no-holds-barred vacation land where we were allowed to do anything we wanted, and at the end of every summer, we would sulk the entire car ride back to Portsmouth, which seemed like an every-hold-barred, barren-cupboarded torture chamber after being so spoiled for so long. I'm pretty sure that's what Dad had in mind. If he couldn't have physical custody of us, he would surely have emotional custody. That's how we spent every summer vacation until I turned ten years old and Mom finally graduated from Smith. That was the end of summers with Dad.

My mom rented the house we lived in. Mom and Dad had plans to buy the house from the owner when they had saved up enough, but that plan was put on hold when Dad took off. Mom didn't make a lot of money and wasn't very good with the family finances, and with Dad's contribution to the coffers reduced to a minimum monthly child support payment he would only occasionally pay, we became very broke, very fast.

One day while I was at elementary school, my mom held an impromptu garage sale on our front lawn and sold a large amount of my toys at it. I came home and bawled into my pillow until you could see a vague wet likeness of my face in it. My Construx building blocks, my M.U.S.C.L.E. man set and matching wrestling ring, my He-Man action figures – all gone. My Mom told me that we needed the money and she thought I didn't play with them anymore. She said if she had known I still wanted them, she surely wouldn't have sold them, but it was more like she was trying to convince herself than convince me. I was upset with her for a while after that, but like most children that age, I couldn't stay mad at my mom for long. The concept of everlasting hate is most assuredly reserved for adults.

When Dad left, he took with him the only other male presence in our house. The main influences on my young life were my mother and my older sister. Instead of playing catch out in the backyard and going to baseball games like most boys do with their fathers, I watched Luke and Laura's wedding on General Hospital with my sister and went through the motions with Mom when she put in one of her Body Electric workout VHS tapes. There was never a football game, or sport of any kind on our television. The manliest man in Mom's life, my uncle Stephen, convinced her to enroll me in judo classes at the community center in downtown Portsmouth to "learn the values of discipline, honor and integrity," but only after she discovered there was no kicking and punching involved. I thought it was totally normal for a guy to blow-dry his hair until I was well into my teenage years. My childhood home was completely devoid of testosterone. Evidence of this can be found in a second grade school paper I wrote about toxic shock syndrome. When my second grade teacher asked me why I chose that topic, my response was "I read about it on the back of a box when I was on the toilet. It's really serious." Most mothers would have made their sons sign up for the football team after an incident like that, but Mom, the eminent feminist, Smith College graduate, and proud owner of a well-worn paperback copy of Our Bodies, Ourselves, suffered only mild embarrassment.

My dad bought me the most amazing BMX bike for my eighth birthday. My first bike. Before that, I was subjected to riding my sister's oversized "Big Girl Bike" up and down the sidewalk of Broad Street. As if an eight-year old didn't look ridiculous enough riding an adult-sized bike, Big Girl Bike came complete with the slanted bar that designates a woman's bike, hologram unicorn stickers that glimmered in the sun like gay desert mirages and pastel colored plastic spoke beads that would click-clack as they rolled and alert the neighborhood children that it was time to point and laugh.

The BMX bike my dad got me was the perfect antithesis of Big Girl Bike; black and red paint job, awesome motocross Velcro padding on the frame and pegs on the front AND the back. It was as if he pulled it right out of my dreams. When he sent me back home to Portsmouth with it, he slipped the receipt in my front pocket and told me to bring it to the store if I needed to trade it in for a bigger or smaller one after I was done adjusting the seat bar, definitely a big boy job. Dad got back in his car and took off, and instead of going inside to say hello to Mom after not having seen her for a whole weekend, I wheeled my amazing new bike to the driveway and rode it in circles around Mom's blue Honda Civic sedan. Riding the bike felt good; it felt normal, and normal felt good. It felt like the thing boys my age were supposed to be doing, and it was pure freedom. I had a real boy's bike, and it was the greatest thing that ever happened to me. I pedaled faster and faster around the driveway, sometimes lifting my hands off the handlebars for a split second, mimicking the older boys in the neighborhood when they would ride with no hands down the middle of the street. Mom eventually came out to see me, took one look at the bike and asked me if Dad gave the receipt to me. I said he did and handed it to her. The next day when I came home from school, the bike was gone. "We need the money, Mike. Your father doesn't give us enough money to live right now. You can use your sister's bike until we have enough money to buy you a new one."

Not too long after, Mom started dating a guy named Bob. Bob was nice. He was a professor at a college in Maryland, then taught at the junior high school in Rye, a quiet seaside community next to the city of Portsmouth. Mom and Bob met because he taught my half-sister Chrissie, who was off at college at that time. He stopped teaching for a while to work as an architect for a small building company. Once the housing crash came and small builders were out of jobs, so was Bob.

Bob was from Rye, where his parents still lived in the little beach house he grew up in. His parents were also very nice, and they always baked me brownies and cookies anytime I came over to visit them. Bob didn't live with us, but he was over our place all the time, staying over every few nights or so. Mom eventually put Gen and I in one bedroom so Bob could have an office to work in while he was over.

The new man dating Mom was very tall, and he had wavy, brown hair and a big mustache. He always wore tweed jackets with leather elbow patches. Bob had a really deep, booming voice, and two daughters from a previous marriage. They were very sweet to my sister and me. They were older than us by at least a decade, and they lived in NYC pursuing careers in fashion and journalism respectively. We thought they were gods; so cool.

I had just finished third grade and was enjoying my muggy New England summer by sitting on the cool dirt underneath the big oak tree in our backyard, dismembering G.I. Joes that I had doubles of when Mom called Gen and I over to the lawn chairs her and Bob were sitting in. Mom told us that Bob got a job as a professor at the University of Wisconsin, and that we all going to move there to a town called Stevens Point. Stevens Point was where one of the UW campuses was. The plan was that we would stay there for two years and move back to New Hampshire. Gen started crying immediately. She didn't want to leave her friends and not be able to go to Portsmouth Junior High, as she had been looking forward to it all through elementary. I didn't know why Gen was so upset. We had been living in Portsmouth for as long as I could remember, and I was excited. We were going to pick up and move thousands of miles to a new place, with new people and new buildings and a new school. I saw Wisconsin as an adventure. Plus we were going to be living with Bob, and Bob was fun.

One day before we moved, Bob, Mom, Gen and I went to the beach on an overcast day. I picked up a piece of driftwood and went to throw it into the ocean, but it slipped out of my hands and crashed straight into Bob's head. Bob screamed at me for the mistake. It was the first time he ever yelled at me, and I was terribly frightened by it. He said that I did it on purpose, and that I was a "really bad person," as if I was a fully mature adult that willingly attacked him. I cried, my Mom did her best to explain it away as an accident, which it was, and he eventually forgave me later that night. The driftwood left a bump on the corner of his forehead, and it never went away.

The sky turned green and purple during our first night in Stevens Point. Tornado warnings were all over the TV and radio. As we drove our U-Haul to our new place we saw houses with windows and doors all boarded up. Bob was fascinated with Midwestern weather patterns, and stayed on the porch while we all ran inside and into the basement. The first three nights I lived in Wisconsin, I slept under our dining room table in the unfinished, damp basement of our house. We ate from cans, and I was only allowed to go upstairs when I had to go to the bathroom.

We didn't have a lot of money, so we moved into an old house that Bob found through one of his colleagues. It was being sublet by another professor that was away on sabbatical for a year. It was cheap and we hoped that a year would be enough time for us to establish ourselves, but the house was absolutely beautiful; polished old wood everywhere, and decorative stained glass windows that send rainbows cascading across the floors on sunny days. A couple weeks after moving in, Mom started work as an oncology social worker in a local hospital, and Bob started working at the university. Gen and I were quickly registered for school, and I began fourth grade at Emerson Elementary, while Gen started sixth.

My first day of fourth grade at Emerson Elementary School was the first time in my young life that I experienced genuine isolation from my peers. Before I moved to Wisconsin, I was very sociable and was always at friends' houses after school to play Nintendo or for weekend sleepovers. My mom had to pry me out of play dates. After I moved, all socializing stopped, and for reasons I couldn't understand. All the boys had bowl haircuts and wore the same clothes; t-shirts and Umbro shorts with spandex underneath them in the summer, and tight rolled jeans, fleece headbands and Columbia jackets with "Bugaboo" stitched into the collar in the winter. It was like the Village of the Damned and I was Christopher Reeve; the outsider.

Aside from not being able to connect with kids in Stevens Point through sports like football and hockey that they were obsessed with, we were stretching every penny we had to make ends meet after spending most of our savings on the move, so we and couldn't afford to keep up with the fashions like other families. I wore any hand-me-down clothing from my sister that could be deemed remotely unisex, whether it fit or not. The oversized pastel B.U.M Equipment sweatshirts and pink winter jackets sent up bright red flags in the court of public opinion, but the jeans actually worked out pretty well after I realized once you tight-rolled them, most jeans ended up looking the same if you rip the leather Mudd or L.E.I. patch off the back. Underwear and socks would be sparingly purchased at Marshall's during annual school shopping trips. I never cared about what I was wearing back in New Hampshire, but I was a boy trying to make new friends in an unfamiliar place where a trendy wardrobe was deemed absolutely imperative, so having to settle for thrifty, popularity-suffocating rags was really tough for me.

The worst was the shoe shopping. The only place we could afford to buy a decent pair of sneakers for me was at Payless. Mom bought me the same pair of shoes every time; white Lower East Side high tops. They were supposed to be Payless' answer to Adidas, but they had an extra stripe and were made out of pleather and Styrofoam. I would grab a marker and color in three out of the four stripes in an attempt to mask their provenance, but it was painfully obvious that they weren't Adidas, and the kids at Emerson Elementary missed no opportunity to laugh at them. Almost immediately, I became the most unpopular kid in school.

Our tight budget got even tighter. Shortly after we moved to Wisconsin, my dad stopped paying child support as a way to get back at my mom for moving Gen and I so far away. My mom filed paperwork with the court to begin the process of forcing the government to make him pay, but they told her it could take years to get the case in front of a judge. As if that wasn't enough, Mom lost her job at the hospital a few months later and struggled to find work after that. She filed a wrongful termination suit, and her lawyer said it would help her cause if she had little to no income to report, so thinking it would be resolved in a few months, she simply didn't look for a new job. As it turned out, the case went on for well over two years before it was settled. We didn't have enough money saved up for a decent rental property by the time the travelling professor returned from sabbatical, so we had to move out of the house and rent a run-down two-story place on the other side of town. It was white with grey shutters, and the paint was peeling. I remember wanting a tree house very badly at that point in time. Something about a tree house seemed so relaxing; a place that adults would never bother to climb into. A little guy Fortress of Solitude. A place to hide. Our new house had a yard, but no trees.

Around this time, I began to suffer my first bouts of depression. I felt so alone and hopeless. School was a relentless nightmare, and coming home wasn't much better because Mom was too busy looking for jobs to be burdened with my little kid problems, and while Bob was OK, I definitely wasn't close enough with him to talk about serious stuff. It became harder and harder to wake up in the morning and live. I pretended to be sick a lot in order to stay home from school. Mom rarely forced us out of the house if we said we were ill, so I would feign a flu, wait until she left for work and I'd spend the day curled up in bed with a book. I thought about killing myself, feeling nothing seemed like a much better option than enduring the wrecking ball of anxiety in my chest as it relentlessly battered my consciousness into submission, but I knew that I was too much of a baby to go through with it. I cried a lot. Mom eventually put me in front of a child psychologist. He was a bald guy with hairy knuckles who asked me to draw a lot of pictures for him.

We started eating the same meals every day. Breakfast was All-Bran and skim milk. Lunch was either leftovers from dinner or cold cuts on old bread. Baked chicken or fish, boiled spinach and a dry baked potato for dinner. Mom explained this by saying it was really healthy food and that we needed the nutrition as growing children, but in reality Bob decided that he did not want to pool his money with my mothers' when it came to groceries. He didn't want to pay for our food; only his, which left my mom with an extremely limited food budget. She still fed us the best she could, though. The only other food items in the house were Triscuits, sardines, coffee beans and glass gallon jugs of Carlo and Rossi chardonnay, and we weren't allowed to touch any of those.

The kids in Stevens Point hated me. They hated everyone that wasn't from Stevens Point, especially when they were different. I was teased relentlessly. They used to call me "The Cow" because of the "bull" sound in Boulerice, or "Fat Albert." I wasn't fat, but they found out my middle name was Albert, and I probably don't have to describe the line of logic used in the creation of my unwanted nickname. "Do you smell cow shit? Oh, hi Mike" or "HEY LOOK, IT'S FAT ALBERT!!! HEY HEY HEY!!!" I was ridiculed for my generic clothing, non-bowl haircut and the Lower East Sides that were all but falling off of my feet by the eighth month. Girls would hand me notes in class pretending to want to be my girlfriend, and they would ask to talk to me privately during recess. At recess they would loudly announce that they thought I was gross and poor and wanted nothing to do with me. Their friends were always in on it, pointing and laughing every time. I was so desperate for companionship that I allowed it to happen, hoping the constant viciousness would eventually evolve into something even borderline amicable.

When they found out that Emerson Elementary was filled with crumbling asbestos insulation, they built a brand new school for us; Jefferson Elementary School. The school board decided that, instead of paying movers to bring the contents of the library over to the new school, they would have the students fill their backpacks with books and lug them three blocks over to Jefferson. While I was hunched over with a backpack full of encyclopedia volumes, a classmate decided to take his pack off, swing it around like an Olympic hammer and slam it into the side of my head as hard as possible. I flew sideways and my face hit a no parking sign, leaving me with a painful lump on the side of my head and two black eyes. Kids would follow me on my walk home from school and throw rocks at me. I stopped going home immediately after the bell and hid in the Stevens Point Public Library. I knew the kids would never find me in there, but there was adult supervision even if they did. I was safe. I would spend a couple hours a day in the library, reading Choose your Own Adventure books, graphic novels, newspapers, National Geographic and a bunch of classic American authors. Poe was my favorite, especially after Mom helped me understand his use of allegory. I really clung to the idea of hiding a story within a story. I also loved Piers Anthony and Dan Simmons. I would leave after the streetlights came on with a backpack full of books. The library became a very important place for me. It was my tree fort.

We tried everything to make kids stop picking on me. Parent teacher conferences, parent/parent conferences, principal/teacher/parent conferences; nothing worked and we were out of options. I couldn't change schools because it would have cost too much. One day, Mom and Bob sat me down in the living room. Bob told me that this was going to be a problem I was going to have to solve myself. Bob said that I had to beat up David, the most popular kid in school. He was the leader of the bullies. Bob said that they were OK with me getting suspended if that's what it was going to take, and Mom reluctantly agreed with him. She was averse to violence, and through osmosis, I was as well. I had never been in a fight before. I had taken those Judo classes before we moved to Wisconsin, but I never needed to use them in real life. I was the youngest child of my family, and up until then, I hadn't experienced a schoolyard brawl or any violence, save for what I saw on television when the A Team was on. I just wasn't a violent kid.

The next day, I was in the locker room getting changed for gym class. David was a few lockers down from me, and I had butterflies in my stomach. The anxiety building up in me as I mentally prepared myself for starting the first fight in my life was intense. I almost abandoned the whole idea. Finally, I walked up behind David, put my right arm around his neck as I learned in Judo class and began choking him. At first he started laughing, thinking it was one of his friends fucking with him. I tightened my grip. Both of his hands latched onto my arm as he tried to pry away. I tightened my grip more. My whole body tensed up. I was a bear trap; I would not let go. I quickly surveyed the locker room. All of the kids were standing there, watching. Nobody tried to break it up. One kid ran out of the locker room to grab the gym teacher. That didn't sway me. I looked at the side of David's face. It was bright red. My arm was covered in drool and scratches from his finger-nails. His hands left my arm and flailed straight out, reaching for something, anything. Nothing was there. David's legs started to buckle and he was on his knees. I remained on my feet, never letting my grip slip for a moment. The locker room door burst open. The gym teacher and her assistant ran over and pulled me off of David. I let go. David slumped to the floor unconscious. The gym teacher grabbed me by the back of my t-shirt and asked me what was what wrong with me. I don't know if it was the anxiety leaving my body or genuine hysteria, but I started laughing. She brought me to the principal's office and the assistant revived David. He left school shortly after to see a doctor and I left school with a five-day outside suspension.

Steve was David's best friend, and second in command in all things related to my bullying. He had a blond bowl cut and an impish upturned nose. He approached me on the chain link bridge in the playground the day after my suspension was up, and told me he was going to "Make me beg for mercy." I grabbed him by the front of his oversized Wisconsin Badgers t-shirt and punched him in the face five times. When I let go, he fell onto his ass, got up and ran away. I never got in trouble for that.

That afternoon, Steve and David's other friend Keith stopped me when I was riding my bike home from school by standing in front of the sidewalk and not moving. Keith was a brutishly strong, massive kid. He picked up my bike with me still on it and threw us both to the ground. He told me he was going to beat me up because I beat up David and Steve. I kicked him in the balls and punched him in the face, and he lay on the ground crying. I accidentally ran his hand over with my bike as I tore down the street, leaving him there. That was the last time I ever had to fight in Wisconsin, and it was the last time I was bullied by anyone at Jefferson Elementary. Violence worked. Bob was right after all.

Bob started to change after our first year in Wisconsin. Mom had no money coming in and he didn't contribute anything to my sister and I. Weeks would go by without Bob acknowledging our existences unless there was something to blame on us, at which point we would get an earful from him. We did our best to steer clear of him and not do anything that would upset him and incur his wrath.

Bob and Mom started having lots of discussions about money, and when they were in the middle of one, Gen and I had to leave the room. The discussions would get heated and would sometimes last an hour or more. We were used to parents fighting from growing up with Mom and Dad, but those fights were tame in comparison. They would fight, but there was rarely screaming, and for the most part, always made up after and were amicable with each other. Bob would get really mad and bellow at Mom, and sometimes Mom would cry. During the times that Gen and I were excommunicated from the public living quarters while Mom and Bob were arguing, I would read a book while Gen would keep her ear to the bedroom door and listen, sometimes cracking it open to hear better. You didn't need to open the door to understand what Bob was saying in his big, booming voice, but Mom's voice was meek and muffled. After a while, the conversation would end. They would go about whatever they were doing before the argument started and we'd be allowed to roam wherever we wanted to.

Bob started devoting a lot of his time to disciplining us. Whenever anything was out of place, he'd yell at my sister and me and send us to our rooms. As time went on, the severity of infraction that would earn us a timeout upstairs became lower and lower. If we left a fork unwashed in the sink, if we listened to the TV too loudly, if we took a book from the bookcase and didn't return it to the proper position – there was yelling and there was a timeout. It got to the point that my sister and I did our best to hide from Bob during waking hours.

In fourth grade, I joined the school orchestra (all students of Jefferson Elementary had to back then). The music teacher sat all of us down and showed us all of the instruments involved in an orchestra and asked us to pick out one we wanted to learn how to play. I chose the cello and was able to borrow a used one from school for a while so I could practice at home. Mom, positively beaming at the thought of being the mother of a great concert cellist, somehow managed to scrounge up enough money to buy me a beat-up used cello from a pawnshop. She made me play it for three hours every day, both after school and on the weekends. I was just a kid then and kids don't normally see things like this in their parents, but there was something manic about Mom's eyes anytime the cello was brought up; something desperate. I think her watching me play was a way for her to escape our hopeless situation. All that practice ended up turning me into a halfway good cellist, and I was selected to play in a special quartet at a holiday concert at school. We played Sabre Dance, and we received a standing ovation at the end.

I also went on to play the cello solo in Pachebel's Canon at a different school concert. At that same concert, a female cellist in I had a crush on was playing a part in the chair directly in front of me. I discreetly lowered my bow and flirtatiously began tapping the tip of it against the back of her foot. I thought I was careful enough to make sure nobody saw it, but apparently everybody in the audience witnessed my awkward courting ritual and got a good chuckle out of it. That is, everyone except for Bob. Bob was furious. He turned to Mom, who was still laughing, and said he was disgusted by my behavior and lack of respect. Bob screamed at me the entire way home, and sent me to my room for the rest of the night. Mom and Bob spent the rest of the night fighting, and I listened to Bob's muffled baritone voice rattle the old wood paneled walls until I fell asleep.

I played the cello until I hated it. I'd sit there, flipping through notated sheets on my rusty music stand, and stare longingly out the window watching the neighborhood kids play a game of street hockey, or flag football with tube socks tucked into their jeans instead of official Velcro flag belts. I couldn't stand it anymore. Mom was so adamant about making me play that I began fantasizing about throwing the thing down the stairs. It got to the point that she had to bribe me with the trendy clothing I so desperately wanted to wear so I could fit in with kids at school. She told me that she would buy me one pair of Umbro shorts every time I played in a school concert, and that actually worked for a while until I realized the kids at Jefferson Elementary hated me no matter what I wore, or did, or said, because I was an outsider. When clothes stopped working, the deal became "you play in that concert or you're grounded."

One day after Mom told me I couldn't go outside and play because I had to practice, I lost it and actually did throw the old cello down the stairs, snapping the neck and splintering the body into a tangle of strings and an irreparable pile of wood. I felt guilty for doing it almost immediately after, because we were poor and I knew she spent a good amount of money on it, but her fantasy of me becoming a world renowned cellist was not mine, and with everything else going on at home, it was something I couldn't bear to do for another minute. I never played the cello again.

Bob's aggressive behavior ramped up considerably by the time I was in fifth grade. Ultimately, we were only supposed to stay in Wisconsin for two years and then move back to Portsmouth, but Bob was having a hard time finding a job back East. He almost landed a job as a professor in Savannah, though. We were all set to move down there, but they gave the job to someone else a few weeks after they had given him an offer letter. Bob started drinking more, and he started to turn even more verbally abusive. Screaming all the time, at Mom and at my sister and me. He never got physically abusive with Mom, but his words were almost worse. His voice was so loud and booming, which made his tirades that much more effective.

I knew better than to make Bob angry, so I started tiptoeing any time I was inside the house. Sometimes when Mom wasn't home, he would corner me for no reason and scream until veins popped out of his neck and his eyes watered. He would grab me by the collar of my shirt, throw me into my room and slam the door so hard it vibrated. He would tell me how much he hated my sister and me, how we were terrible children and how he wished he could sent us back East so he and Mom could live in peace. When he yelled at me, I would try to cover my face and hide from him but he was too close for me to get my arms up. I just held them at stomach level and flinched until he finished. His breath smelled like anchovies and wine. I would wipe Bob's spit off of my face, and either run outside or upstairs to my room to cry.

One day, Gen and I decided that we had no other choice but to take care of Bob ourselves before things got worse. Mom wasn't going to leave Bob, Bob wasn't going to leave Mom and we couldn't just move in with Dad back East because Mom had custody of us, and also because we didn't feel right leaving Mom alone with Bob.

After much deliberation, we decided that we were going to kill Bob, and that we wouldn't get in trouble because we were just kids and they couldn't prosecute us for murder.

The thought of killing someone scared the brains out of me, but Gen was steadfast and brave, and convinced me that it was the only way to make things better. Gen and I snuck into Mom and Bob's bedroom at two in the morning one night. I was armed with a little Swiss Army Knife that Dad got me for my birthday. Its two-inch blade folded out. We crept over to the left side of the bed where Bob was sleeping, shirtless and face up. Mom was on her stomach facing the other way. The room was so quiet that I could hear my pulse in my ears as I held my breath. I looked at Gen. She was breathing heavily. It was dark, but I could still see her face, and the anger held in it that I recognized; it was the Boulerice temper. I was too young to have inherited it yet, but almost every male on Dad's side of the family possessed it, and I grew up hearing all sorts of crazy stories about how my stepbrother Martin beat up three guys and threw them all through a plate glass window, and about how Dad was the guy everybody feared in high school because he would fly into a Viking rage while fighting and wouldn't stop until everybody had to go to the hospital. I didn't possess the legendary Boulerice temper at that age, but I squeezed my eyes shut called upon it as I raised the knife above my head, preparing to drive it into Bob's naked chest. It was heaving with long, slow sleeping breaths.

I must have stood there for thirty seconds but it felt like hours. Gen didn't say a word; she just stood and looked on. My knees felt weak and my hands were shaking. I had never fainted before, but my half-sister Chrissie did once at a David Bowie concert. I felt exactly how she described feeling before it happened; blurred vision, erratic breathing, and a feeling of immediate weakness. My breath came in tight gasps, and I starting seeing little white flashes in my eyes. I was paralyzed with fear. Before I could stave it off and finish what we went in there to do, Bob grunted, flipped over onto his side, and started snoring. Gen and I bolted out of the room.

Something changed in me after that night with the knife in Mom and Bob's bedroom. I stopped flinching when Bob yelled at me. My hands stopped involuntarily moving to my face to protect myself. I still didn't look him in the eye when he was doing it, because I knew it would provoke him and make him scream for longer. I could only bring myself to look at the lump on the corner of his scalp, where my piece of driftwood him that day on the beach. It was like I started stepping out of my own body when he would lace into me, and I would step back into it when he was through with me. It was the same trick I developed as a little kid when Mom and Dad would argue; I would slam the doors of perception shut, and transport myself somewhere else. I wished Mom could step out of herself when Bob yelled at her, but I knew she couldn't. She couldn't protect herself, and I couldn't protect her because I was only twelve years old. We couldn't move because we had no money. Bob had everything, and he had us sucking at his teat for a pittance, which kept us tethered to him. I think that's how he wanted it.

Gen did Mom's budget for her once because Mom was never very good with money, and found out that we were spending too much on wine. Gen was old enough to know that what was going on in our house wasn't normal or good, and young enough to not be complacent about it. That launched the argument to end all arguments, and before you knew it they were fighting all the time, about money, about Bob and about living in Wisconsin. They would argue, the argument would turn ugly and sometimes it would turn into a physical altercation, complete with screaming, clawing and wrestling. One day when Mom and Gen were going at it, Gen accidentally tumbled down the stairs. She ended up being all right and Mom was immediately horrified and apologetic even though it was really just a freak accident, but you could tell something had changed between them.

Shortly after that, Gen ended up getting shipped to Northfield Mount Herman, a boarding school, when she was fourteen because she and Mom couldn't stand each other, and Bob wanted her gone. Mom was able to pay for it by calling Dad and telling him he could either pay Gen's tuition or pay child support. Gen left shortly after, but she would call every other week or so to check in on me. Then I was all alone.

Gen told Dad about how awful Bob was to us all the time. Dad called once and Bob answered the phone. Dad told him that if he ever yelled at me or Gen again that he would fly out with five friends, the "Guido Boys," and make sure he never walked again. I never met them personally, but Mom had told Bob plenty of stories about Dad, and how he used to do bookie collections with a Louisville Slugger and a pair of friends he only referred to as The Guido Boys. Bob was nice for a good month after that, but the yelling eventually started back up, and it became more aggressive than ever after Gen left. Mom was powerless to stop Bob from tearing into us, and we spent our days and nights walking on eggshells.

One Saturday morning, I walked into our garage after breakfast and rummaged through all of the stuff that Bob and Mom picked up over the years at flea markets and auctions, looking for one particular thing. Mom and Bob were always going antiquing. Sometimes they would take me with them to antique shops and flea markets, but most of the time they would leave me behind and spend the day traveling the back roads of Wisconsin looking for treasure. I saw that Bob had emptied a box of my classic comic books into a puddle, and used the box to put some of his stuff into. The comics were ruined. I looked into the box and found what I was looking for. It was an antique thermometer I remembered him talking about at breakfast a few months before; how it was left in the drawer of some old end table he bought at a yard sale. I remembered him telling us modern thermometers used alcohol, but the old antique ones used mercury.

I walked back inside the house through the kitchen. Bob was in the bathroom taking a shower before work, and his morning coffee was sitting on the counter. I broke the thermometer in half, emptied the mercury into his coffee, and went back outside. I buried the glass under some tree roots in the backyard, and walked back in like nothing had happened.

Nothing did happen until the next day. I got home from the library and Mom was sitting on the couch. She said that she brought him to the emergency room shortly after I left because he was throwing up a lot. She said the doctor told him it was a bad case of the flu. Bob ended up spending several days in bed. I knew then that I didn't have it in me to kill someone, even someone as bad as Bob was. Besides, after two attempts, it was clear that I was terrible at it.

One day after school, Mom took me with her to the local IGA to do some grocery shopping. We picked up some simple items that were good for making multiple things; eggs, milk, flour, and a bag of dried egg noodles. When we got to the register, the cashier asked Mom if she wanted to pay with cash or check. Mom replied "food stamps" and proceeded to pull a little booklet out of her purse. I didn't know we even were on food stamps.

I looked up at her, and she gave me the best smile she could muster during what was obviously a really embarrassing experience for her. My eyes welled up, and hers did too. I wiped my tears away with my shirtsleeve.

Once we paid and left the store I said, "Things are bad, aren't they?" She said they were, but that we would be okay. Then we drove back home back to Bob, who was undoubtedly eating sardines, drinking Carlo and Rossi Chardonnay, and watching Cheers in the living room.

During fifth and sixth grade, Mom and Bob were drinking a lot more wine than usual. Bob always drank a lot, but Mom usually kept it to a few glasses. Wine seemed to make them argue less. Our money situation hadn't gotten better, which meant the added alcohol expenditure left even less room in the grocery budget for food than ever before. Some days, when Mom was out and Bob was in charge of making me dinner, he'd simply forget to do it. I didn't want to incur his wrath, so I found myself having to steal food to eat some days. Most kids my age were just discovering shoplifting, but they would pocket things like candy, baseball cards and the occasional issue of Penthouse from a magazine rack. I would regularly visit the University of Wisconsin convenience store that was a few blocks from our house and stuff a loaf of Wonder Bread under my sweatshirt. I'd bring it home and quickly shove a few slices into my mouth in order to kill my hunger pains. When I was done, I'd hide the loaf under my bed and pull it out any time dinner wasn't on the table. I wasn't particularly good at shoplifting, but the fact that the store was staffed by oblivious college students flirting with customers and swapping stories about professors they hated and crazy parties on campus, I was able to leave the store undetected.

Stealing made me feel awful. I didn't derive any joy from it, like most kids my age did, probably because I wasn't doing it for fun. I never told my Mom what I was doing, either. I knew it would break her heart to know our situation had devolved to the point that her son had to steal to eat some nights, so I kept it to myself.

By the time I finished sixth grade, Mom and Bob's relationship had deteriorated to an unending stream of screams and tears. Bob was drinking very heavily, and he would launch himself into episodes so animated and violent that I was sure he was going to hit her. I would sit at the top of the stairs and peek through the slats of the banister while he would dress Mom down in his booming, seething voice over any number of heated topics. He started getting into her face and insulting her about her financial difficulty, her awful children and even about her body. "YOU'RE GOING TO COMPLAIN ABOUT NOT HAVING FOOD IN THE HOUSE WITH THAT FAT ASS OF YOURS?!?" He would yell until his thick mustache was slick with spittle and the veins in his forehead would pop out. Mom would scream back in defense at first, but would eventually shrink away and take it until he was done, at which point he usually slammed the door and drove his little black Toyota pickup around until he cooled off. Then Mom would cry by herself on the couch in the living room, quietly as so I wouldn't hear her. When I was younger, I would sneak back up to my room after one of those episodes, but those days I always came downstairs and gave Mom a hug when Bob would leave.

I was in the driveway playing with a set of plastic WWF action figures during the summer vacation before seventh grade when Mom called me into the kitchen. She told me she phoned an old friend of hers from grad school that lived in Rye, New Hampshire and told her about our situation. Her friend told her we could stay in her unfinished attic until we were settled enough to rent a place of our own, and that I should pack up my things right away because we were moving home.

We filled the bed of Bob's pickup truck with boxes of books and trash bags filled with clothing while he was at work, and Mom drove us back to New Hampshire in only two days. At one point, we were pulled over by a state trooper who demanded we give him cash instead of us mailing in a check for the speeding ticket. Even I knew that wasn't right, but Mom calmly handed him money, and we continued on our way. I remember looking up at

Mom while we were on the highway heading home, and thinking she was the bravest person I'd ever met for taking off like that, and leaving so much behind in order to make our lives better. I never saw Bob again.

Teddy's Dream Girl

—⁓—

WHEN 1997 ROLLED AROUND, I was a sixteen-year-old and domestic Internet use was still a toddler. Back then it was all about 56k modems screaming the siren songs over phone lines, 3.5" disks were still the optimum portable storage solution because nobody could spend a grand on a zip drive and Yahoo! GeoCities were the be-all and end-all of modern communication. We didn't have a computer in our house, but my friend Teddy's parents had a sweet Gateway desktop with all the bells and whistles. They kept it in their sunroom, which was essentially the "go hang out in there because the adults can't stand you right now" room of the house.

When we weren't out terrorizing the lazy suburban streets of Portsmouth, New Hampshire on our skateboards and BMX bikes, we were at Teddy's house, raiding his fridge for sandwiches and ice cold cans of Coke, or on his computer messing with people in chat rooms. We'd log into single mother-themed rooms under the moniker "MommasGotQuestions" and ask the group how many times you could shake a baby to keep it quiet without giving it "Slow brain," or sexually deviant groups dedicated to hooking up in real life, where we'd pose as horny co-eds and get truckers to wait in a deserted Wal-Mart parking lots at 4:00 am for a quickie that just was never going to happen. We would all gather around the computer screen and scream out what to say next, while one of sat in front of it to hunt-and-peck it all out on the keyboard. People screamed at us, moderators banned us from room after room and we'd be rolling around on the carpet, laughing until we couldn't breathe. It wouldn't be until years later that we realized we were some of the world's first trolls.

What we did know was that screwing around with people on the Internet was incredibly fun. What we didn't know was that, when it got late and we all went to our respective houses for the night, Teddy was logging back in to chat with a girl. He was in the middle of a blooming Internet romance.

We finally found out about Teddy's secret affair when, in the middle of our regular chat room mayhem, Teddy checked his email and we saw a long string of messages from the same email address with headings like "hey baby" and "I'm online, where are you?" Teddy lasted through about five minutes of us questioning him before he broke down and told us everything. Her name was Tiffany, and apparently she was a sixteen-year-old model from the rural township of Milford, New Hampshire. Teddy met her in a chat room months before, and had been talking with her online and on the phone for hours every night. His inbox was full of her professional modeling pictures, which he proudly showed us.

At this point of the story, you're probably thinking to yourself, "Are you kidding me? How could Teddy possibly trust this person to be who she was?" I'd like to take this time to remind you that it was 1995, we were kids and the Internet was so new that stories of people falsifying their identities online had yet to appear on the NBC Nightly News. Plus she had pictures of herself. You can't fake that, right?

We were out building a wooden skateboard ramp with our friend Brendon on a cold January morning when Teddy broke the news to us that he was going to meet Tiffany for the first time, and that he wanted us to come with him for moral support. "I'm going to borrow my mom's car and we're going to drive up to her house in Milford this Friday night. She's bringing a friend with her, too. She's also a model. You guys will have to fight over her." Something about not just one but two impossibly hot professional models our age being single and living in Milford, which was a go-nowhere town carved out of the wooded wilderness of New Hampshire, was a little too good to be true, even for a gullible, impossibly horny teenager like me. Luckily for Teddy though, Brendon and I were just enough of that that special combination of loyal and stupid to agree to accompany him on his love quest.

That Friday night, Brendon and I piled into Teddy's mom's sensible Toyota sedan and followed a Yahoo! Maps printout all the way to Milford, New Hampshire. Once we were off the highway, the smoothly paved roads quickly turned into gnarled, windy dirt paths devoid of sidewalks, power lines and mailboxes.

"Dude, are you sure this is the right way?" I clicked the overhead light on, working hard to study the directions as the car jostled on the frost-heaved dirt pack. I'm honestly not quite sure why I was playing the role of navigator, as it was a well-known fact that I got lost very frequently, even in the town I grew up in.

Teddy rolled his window down, as if removing the glass between him and the winter air would somehow make things better. "I don't know. I mean, I guess so. We're on the right road. She said it was a white ranch style house at the top of a steep driveway. You see anything that looks like that?"

I didn't see anything that looked like that. I did see a dumpy looking trailer at the top of a steep dirt driveway with some kind of yellow artwork tacked on the left half of it. "What number did you say her house was again?"

"29" Teddy answered quickly and confidently. "Nothing on your side?"

"Go by that house again." Brendon pointed at the dumpy trailer that we were again approaching on the right. It happened to be the only house on the street with an actual mailbox, albeit a rusted, dented one mounted to an equally mangled piece of rebar jutting out of a dirty snow bank. As we got closer, a pair of peeling reflective stickers caught Teddy's headlights, and the number 29 was unmistakable.

"I guess we've arrived." I unbuckled my seatbelt as we crept into the driveway.

Teddy stared up at the dingy singlewide trailer at the top of the steep grade of dirt driveway. We made it about halfway up before we realized the entire driveway was encased in several inches of almost mirror polished ice. The tires on the car began peeling out, and shortly after that we were sliding back down to the bottom. Teddy let out a burst of curse words as we slid to a stop, his head-lights still pointing at the trailer.

"What that big yellow thing on the side of the house?" I squinted my eyes and tried to determine what it was. Now that we were closer to the house, you could see it was something cut out of plywood and then painted yellow. It was taller than it was wide, rounded around the edges and it took up the entire left side of the trailer.

Brendon got out of the car. Teddy followed, slamming his door behind him out of frustration and abandoning his car in the spot it slid to. "Fuck it, if I can't get to the top of that driveway, nobody else will either. I'll just leave it here."

I got out as well, and took note of the condition of the front yard, littered with rotting car parts, home appliances and plastic children's toys. Haphazardly placed laundry lines crisscrossed the property like climbing vines in an unkempt post-zombie apocalypse English garden, and sagged with the weight of clothing that froze in the brisk winter wind before they were able to dry. Plus-sized women's clothing.

"Tweety Bird." Brendon stared up at the trailer, and the grimace he made as Teddy slammed his door slowly morphed into a Cheshire Cat's grin. "Holy shit. That right there is a giant Tweety Bird head."

No sooner did those words leave Brendon's mouth that Teddy and I both finally recognized the top heavy, upside down pear shaped skull of Sylvester the Cat's mortal enemy and hero of America's uneducated, fashioned out of particle board, painted and fastened to the side of a trailer with a nail gun.

Brendon burst out laughing, and I followed suit. The white trash wonderland we'd unwittingly stepped into wasn't that funny in itself. Being from New Hampshire, all of our families had at least a twinge of hillbilly in them - a Golden Anniversary-swilling uncle on a three-wheeler here, a cigarette-smoking pregnant aunt there. It was that coupled with Teddy's "I was expecting Dynasty and got Married with Children" expression that was absolutely ridiculous. It couldn't have been a more perfect mix of surprise and disgust if he had just witnessed a mealworm crawling out of his mashed potatoes. That somehow made the scene throttle past funny and into a place where I was gasping for air. I managed to let out a "holy shit" before I doubled over in laughter, slipped on the driveway's ice and lay on my back, tears leaving cold streaks down the sides of my face.

Brendon eventually picked me up and we all skirted to the side of the driveway where patches of exposed dirt allowed us enough traction to make it to the rickety front steps of the trailer. Teddy took a deep breath, let it out and knocked on the door.

"COOOOOOOOME ONNNN IIIIIINNNNNNNN, THEENNNNN!!!" A booming female voice dripping with contempt greeted Teddy's knocks. "IT'S UNLOOOOOOOOOOOOCKED!!!" She half screamed, half sang this part, like a thirteen-year-old valley girl having a temper tantrum in front of a Dooney & Bourke outlet, but much raspier and huskier.

Teddy, Brendon and I shot each other the "here we go" look we used anytime we stupidly injected ourselves into a precarious situation, opened the door and stepped inside.

The sweltering air inside the trailer's interior was strangled with the intermingling fresh and stale smoke of a lifetime of cigarettes, creating a thin mist throughout. The trailer had no carpeting. Bare particleboard served as the floor. It was peppered with intentionally extinguished cigarette butts and food stains left to fuzz over in humidity created from the shower, kitchen and any combination of sweaty sex acts between out of shape, wheezing partners. Aside from one sticky, tar-coated wall acting as home to a linty black velvet painting of a tropical flower in a tarnished brass frame, the living room we were standing in was devoid of decoration. To our left was an expanse of empty room with a door leading into what I imagined was one of the bedrooms. Directly in front of us was a once red, now faded pink corduroy couch, pockmarked with circular cigarette scars that revealed the crumbling burnt sienna colored foam stuffing underneath. To our right was a peeling particleboard computer desk, on top of which rested a small, yellowing CRT computer monitor displaying an AOL chat room. Next to it was a yellow glass ashtray absolutely overflowing with stubbed out cigarette butts, one still smoldering on the top like a Phillip Morris volcano. Next to that, slumped over in a rolling computer chair entirely too small for her, was the three-hundred-and-fifty pound woman who ushered us into her home. She had closely cropped grey hair, and wore a blue housedress with pink flowers on it. Her bare legs roiled with varicose veins and fat rolls that glistened with perspiration at the creases.

"Hi, it's nice to meet you." Teddy was the only one of us who managed to squeeze out a pleasantry as we stood in front of the matron of the house. The woman's sausage fingers worked impossibly quickly on the discolored keyboard, never bringing her eyes away from the screen to meet ours even once.

"TIFFANNNNYYYYYYYYYY!!!" The words erupted from the flabby cannon of her throat, seemingly amplified by the smallness of the room. "YER FRIENDS R' HERE." Later on I would question why she bothered with this. I mean, we were in a trailer. Not only did she not have to yell, it's not like she didn't hear the door open and close. The process of us entering probably shook the rusty jack stands holding the place up.

"Coming, Mom!" A younger, more pleasant feminine voice echoed from the open door to our left. I don't claim to be psychic, but I swear I could feel apprehension drain from us the minute Tiffany spoke. If her mother had turned to us and said "It's nice to finally talk to you outside of a chat room," I'm positive Teddy would have had an aneurysm and died right there on the ashtray/floor.

Moments later, the international model and love of Teddy's young life walked through the door of her bedroom. And she was fat. Her face was a glistening battlefield on which acne and blackheads fought to the death, and was framed by short, greasy brown hair and a crow's nest of teased up, crispy bangs. She strolled into the living room wearing an oversized, dingy Dale Earnhardt "The Intimidator" t-shirt as a nightgown and had a slightly crooked 120 smoldering between two desperately unmoisturized fingers. She didn't just look a little different than the pictures she had been sending Teddy for months on end; it was as if someone looked at Tiffany's modeling pictures, and was then tasked with finding the human being on Earth that looked the least like her.

"Oh my gosh! Look at you, Teddy! It's so nice to meet-cha finally!"

I tried with all my might to keep from laughing. I looked at Brendon. He was frozen, staring ahead blankly. He took the scene in like a witness to a massacre involving a speeding Buick and a crowded playground. I looked at Teddy. Not knowing what else to do, he begrudgingly walked over to Tiffany and gave her a big hug.

"Oh...oh yeah. It's nice to meet you too, Tiff. Thanks for having us."

"It ain't nothin', Theodore. Are these your friends?"

"Um, yeah. Tiffany, this is Brendon."

"Hello there, Brendon." Tiffany outstretched her hand to meet Brendan's. He shook back, his eyes never losing their glossy sheen.

"...and this is my friend Mikey." Tiffany began to outstretch her hand, and as a preemptive strike, I quickly raised mine in a wave. She mimicked mine, and we both withdrew.

"Are those booyyyyys here?!" A different girl's voice emitted from the bedroom, jolting me into remembering that one of Tiffany's model friends was also slated to hang out with us. Before I could brace myself for what would happen next, a beanpole of a teenage girl tottered out of the bedroom, giggling like a mongoloid finger-painting with its own shit. She had short, oily black hair and a shotgun blast of freckles on the pale skin of her face and arms. Her goofy, immature grin showcased gleaming braces adorned with multicolored rubber bands that made her mouth look like the face of a clear plastic Swatch Watch. Falling in line with the Looney Tunes fascination this part of the state held, an oversized black t-shirt with none other than Sylvester the Cat on it covered the almost ghoulishly skinny upper portion of her body.

With a great "Whooooooooooooooo!" accompanying her actions, the newcomer jumped into the middle of the room, lifted up her shirt to reveal two mosquito bite sized breasts, and then ran back into the bedroom, cackling like a hyena. Tiffany also started laughing, but didn't look surprised at all, as if open-air teenage tits in front of mothers and total strangers were par for the course at Casa dePressing. Teddy, Brendon and I all shot gaping-mouthed looks at each other, all perfectly illustrating our shared sense of disbelief and disgust. Being sixteen-year-old boys, you would think an ex-posed pair of breasts (albeit virtually nonexistent and attached to a caffeine-addled special needs student) would be enough to shake the nauseating dread this trailer and the people in it were marinating us in, but instead it somehow amplified it. We were in a bad situation, but we didn't know exactly how to get ourselves out of it.

Tiffany plopped down on the pinkish couch and slapped one of the cushions in an invitation for Teddy to sit next to her, releasing a mushroom cloud of ancient human dander. He did so, and what proceeded was thirty minutes of the most painfully strained conversation between two people you can possibly imagine. Tiffany would begin some new topic pertaining to things her and Teddy regularly spoke about online. Teddy, still swimming in a sea of awkward realization and the inability to process what was going on, would answer her in short, staggered bursts. "Yeah. Yeah, that was...that was funny." Brendon sat Indian-style on the particleboard floor across from the couch and smoked his own cigarette, and being the nicest guy in the group, attempted making genuine conversation with Sylvester the Cat, who couldn't stop fidgeting or gnawing her nails with her almost mechanical looking teeth. I crouched down, refusing to actually let the bottom of my jeans touch the filthy floor of the place, and watched everyone in the room, intermittently nodding my head and grinning to feign interest and attention. *What the actual fuck is going on here? Why did this girl want to meet Teddy in real life after lying to him for so long? Did she not realize he'd figure it out? Is her mom just going to sit there the whole time? Was Teddy always talking to Tiffany, or did he sometimes talk to her mom? Why did I agree to come here? When are we going to leave?* My head reeled with a million unanswered questions.

After another ten minutes of mingling in the living room, Tiffany asked if we wanted to hang out in her bedroom, where there were more places to sit and a stereo to listen to. Teddy and I reluctantly agreed, both shooting each other a "We're not staying long" look, while the perpetually optimistic Brendon thought it was a great idea.

Tiffany's bedroom was surprisingly large, considering the size of the trailer it was in. It was lit with several black light machines from Spencer's Gifts and the uncarpeted, cigarette-burned particleboard theme of flooring continued in it. The intermingling smells of stale smoke and long-unwashed laundry created a cheesy, almost sweet musk that reminded me of the liquid left at the bottom of an unattended dumpster in high summer heat. The walls were covered with the typical teenage collages made from YM magazine cutouts and hunky boy posters, the whites of their eyes glowing in the room's black lights.

"Uh...hey. What's up?" Teddy spoke into what I thought was the empty room, but as I looked up, I discovered a pair of muzzy looking boys sitting on a dresser in Tiffany's bedroom. There was no door leading outside the trailer from that room, meaning those two boys had been quietly sitting in Tiffany's room for at least forty minutes while we were in the living room with the girls. I froze, movie stills of men being led to back alley muggings by double-crossing seductresses fluttered past my mind's eye. The boys, both around our age, were lanky and sported patchy teenage goatees. The one on the left wore a wife-beater that draped over his skeletal frame and a pair of baggy, dingy-looking Southpole jeans. His over-distanced eyes and thin upper lip reminded me of the chapter dedicated to Fetal Alcohol Syndrome we glazed over in health class. The one on the right had on a backwards black baseball cap and a black t-shirt with a menacing cartoon clown on it. It wasn't until later in life that we realized it was a logo for the yet to become popular band Insane Clown Posse, and that these two kids were in fact early versions of what we now refer to as Juggalos.

"Hey." Juggalo v1.0 muttered under his breath, eyes darting back and forth.

"Yeah. Hey." Juggalo v1.1 reiterated as he stuck his hands in his pockets and swung his dangling legs as he sat on the dresser, knocking it with the heels of his sneakers as he went.

"What are you guys doing in here?" Teddy wasn't even attempting to hide his unease at this point. All previous hopes of hooking up with a model already lay shattered in a thousand pieces on the floor. The need for tact had quickly followed suit. I nervously eyed the space between where I stood and the open door that led from

Tiffany's bedroom to the living room and the wheezing land manatee basking in the blue glow of her nicotine-yellowed Compaq.

"Rollin' up a jibbah, guy." Juggalo v.1.0 raised his head and smiled, revealing a set of teeth like the picket fence in front of a haunted house. Referring to people as "guy" and "bub", as depicted in countless Adam Sandler comedy cassette tapes, is a habit typically reserved for the upper crust of New Hampshire's blue-collar community. He procured a crooked looking pinner of a joint from the front pocket of his jeans. "You guys smoke?"

"No" I said out of reflex before my brain had a chance to process the thought. "I mean, I'm all set." I did smoke weed on occasion, but I sure as hell didn't want to with those people, or in that place. All I wanted was to get out of that trailer and into Teddy's car.

Teddy chimed in almost instantly after me. "Yeah, I'm all set, too. I think we're going to take off, actually. It's getting late, and my mom wants the car back home soon."

"Aw, seriously? You guys have barely been here an hour. Why don't we all hang out for a while and watch a movie or something?" Tiffany's tone was a chunky mixture of sugary country hospitality and petulant insistence.

Her friend with the Sylvester t-shirt chirped "If you stay I'll give one of you two a blowjob," referring to Brendon and I before covering her paper shredder teeth and hiding behind Tiffany's back in a classic socially awkward teenage girl recoil. Both she and Tiffany cackled loudly. The lack of humor or shock on the faces of the two Juggalos told me Tiffany's friend probably wasn't bluffing about the offer.

"Hey, would you guys possibly be interested in…selling me some of that weed?" Brendon, who I'd almost forgotten about because he had been quiet for the last five minutes, began fumbling through his pockets. "You know, like maybe an eighth?"

If there was ever a single life event that could sum my good friend Brendon up, it's this one. Regardless of whether a situation is going good or bad, it will not affect him or the course he allows the autopilot of his mind's ship to take whatsoever. If Teddy and I were Gregs, Brendon was the Dharma. Oblivious, carefree Brendon couldn't feel less awkward in a dimly lit room of a rotting trailer sixty miles from home surrounded by the extras from Gummo. In Brendon's eyes, people were just people and places were just places, no matter how weird they seemed or how uncomfortable anyone was around them or in them. Whether that's because Brendon is some kind of ultra-enlightened super being or just a goofy, over-trusting tree hugger is still under debate even now.

The minute Brendon requested to make a drug deal in Tiffany's bedroom, my heart sank. We were so close to getting out of there and going home. So close! Now our departure was going to be delayed even further because my friend couldn't leave Milford without a souvenir he could smoke.

Juggalo 1.1 reached into one of his cavernous JNCO jeans pockets, and pulled out a thin sandwich baggie filled with weed. "I can do an eighth. That'll be $20." After transferring what approximated an eighth into a separate sandwich baggie he happened to have on him, Juggalo v1.1 handed it to Brendon in exchange for a crumpled up wad of bills. Brendon's eyes grew large with excitement as he rolled the bag over in his fingers. "Cool beans. Thanks a lot, guys. I appreciate it."

"Yep." Juggalo v1.0 grunted in return, swinging back to face the swatch of floor in front of him, which was covered with several cigarette butts and a pair of boxers.

We all filed out of Tiffany's bedroom after that (everyone except the Juggalos, who stayed behind to spark up that crusty looking "jibbah, guy"), and Teddy went to grab his coat, which was draped over the arm of the living room couch. Tiffany's mom had since vacated the room. I heard a muffled grunt followed by a cough coming from an unseen place just past the kitchen, which led me to believe she was in the bathroom, undoubtedly evacuating a partially heated En-Cor Salisbury steak family meal that she believed was a single serving.

"Well, it was nice meeting you" Teddy said to Tiffany as he bent down to give her the kind of reluctant hug you see scared little kids give to their time gnarled great-grandparents. Tiffany hugged back with a manic tightness. She still clung to him after he had dropped his arms.

"Oh come on, you guys don't have to leave just yet. Let's just hang out and watch a movie on the couch. Your friends can hang out with Rachel. It'll be fun." With that, Tiffany shoved Teddy down on the couch, his mouth wide open in a frozen attempt to refuse. Her incessant demands for us to stay were starting to wear Teddy down. He turned from Tiffany to me, mouth still open, eyebrows raised and arms up in the universal *"What the fuck am I supposed to do?"* position.

Tiffany turned to Brendon and I. "You guys don't mind staying, right?" Her eyes were steeped in desperation. "Watch a movie with us and keep Rachel company?" Rachel gave her best innocently seductive grin from the other side of the room, only to flash her impossibly large braces that made her mouth look like a wheat thresher.

There we were; three young men in the prime of our lives, trapped in the web of a white trash black widow. Teddy looked at Brendon, on the verge of agreeing to stay. It was as if Teddy felt he *had* to get something out of this to pay for the months he devoted to electronic pillow talk, even if it was an awkward teenage handjob from the huskiest international model in New Hampshire. Brendon, who was just now realizing staying to watch the movie would mean he wouldn't get to smoke the weed he just bought, turned to me and motioned his head toward the door, slightly enough so Tiffany didn't notice. I looked at Brendon and then back to Teddy.

"I don't know. What do you think, guys? You want to hang out for a while?"

[If you are a man reading this, think back to when you were fifteen. Think back to that incredibly frustrating, sexually anxious period of your life, when you would get inappropriate erections in science class thinking about a bra model you saw in a J.C. Penny mail order catalog or an almost visible nipple you caught on scrambled Skinemax. Think back to when you would have sold your sweet little old grandmother to a Dutch human trafficking ring to date a girl from school long enough for her to let you slide her hand under her shirt. Shit, I'm thirty-three years old right now, and I'd still consider high-fiving the whirling blades of a running lawnmower or starting a fistfight at a Make-A-Wish fundraiser if it meant getting laid. I was a fifteen-year-old boy, a quivering lightning rod of newly discovered sexuality and I was essentially promised a hot, wet mouth for my trigger happy teenage erection, almost calloused from chronic sick day masturbation marathons, if I remained in that trailer for another hour or two…and I rejected it. That's how bad it was in there.]

"No, let's go, man." I looked at Teddy with a brow so furrowed I could have picked up a quarter with it. "Our parents will be pissed if we stay any longer." I turned to Tiffany. "Thanks for having us over, Tiffany. It was nice meeting you."

I opened the front door and breathed in the fresh winter air. After being trapped in that rusty, stinking lunch pail, it felt as good as one of those ridiculous 5 Gum commercials, where a guy in his boxers straps into some kind of gyroscopic contraption and rolls around a bowl full of industrial air conditioning units. Brendon barreled out the front door right after me following a series of warm smiles and handshakes with our hosts. Teddy was forced to give Tiffany one last uncomfortable hug before he was allowed to escape her insidious clutches.

In the end, Tiffany watched us from her doorway with her considerable arms folded across her considerable chest as we scurried underneath the crazily hung frozen clotheslines (I stole a yellow karate belt from one of them as a memento, which I proudly still have), and down the treacherously icy driveway and into Teddy's mom's car.

Brendon and I laughed at Teddy the entire ride home. Teddy stared straight ahead with his hands at ten-and-two, vowing to only date people he knew in real life and threatening to stuff our lifeless bodies in a drainage pipe if we ever told the other kids at school about the time we went on a road trip to Milford.

Two weeks later, I went over to Teddy's house and found him in the sunroom on AOL Instant Messenger. "Her name is Janessa. She's super nice."

Handicapped Parking

—ɯ—

ONE DAY BACK IN 1986, I was in the back seat of my mom's blue Toyota Corolla sedan as she ran errands. It was an overcast day, and I held one of my airplane Transformer toys up to the window and pretended it was flying.

Mom pulled into a bank, locking the doors and leaving me strapped in the back seat so she could run in, make a transaction and leave.

"I'll be just a couple minutes, Mike. OK?"

I dropped my toy on the seat. "But Mom—"

"And after that," she said cutting me off, "I'll drop you off at your friend's house to play."

"No Mom, you're in a handicapped spot!"

We both looked forward through the windshield, and sure enough, there was a reflective metal handicapped parking only sign attached to a concrete stanchion in front of the space.

"Eh, I'm already parked. Don't worry about it. I'll only be a minute or two." Before I could voice my disapproval of her plan, the driver's side door shut, the keys jingled outside the door and the locks bolted down in unison shortly after.

Gripped by anxiety, I watched her disappear through the bank's glass doors, and then the burden of our situation descended on me all at once. At some point before this incident took place, I deduced that handicapped spaces were for mentally challenge people, as if they were all out driving cars around town with us normal folks.

Oh man, this is bad. This is REAL bad. We're in a handicapped spot and we're not handicapped at all. We're really healthy and smart. What if a cop walks by and sees us here? This is against the law. We're criminals. He'll haul us both into jail for life. I can't let that happen. I have to take matters into my own hands here. I need to do it for both of us.

After much internal conflict, I finally decided the ONLY WAY to ensure our freedom from the American legal system would be for me to pretend I was retarded until Mom got back to the car.

As a six-year-old boy, I knew very little about people with special needs, so I combined several examples of special needs children who went to my elementary school and used them as inspiration to create an improvisational fruit salad of retarded. I rolled my eyes back in my head and attempted to bite my own ear off as I repeatedly slammed both of my fists into my chest, attempting the classic "reaping" motion. I made a conscious effort to conjure excessive saliva in my mouth, and let it cascade down my chin and dribble onto the front of my shirt.

A man in a blue and yellow striped polo shirt exited the bank and walked by my car, glancing at the entity in the back seat. Fearing he would contact the police and send my mother to some unforgiving Russian gulag, I turned my performance up a notch.

It's showtime, Mike.

I continued everything else, but added stomping my feet on the floor of the car and a rhythmic grunt that can only be described as a car with alternator problems trying to start or a pelican's mating call. "REHHHH. REHHHH.REHHHH."

The man quickly averted his gaze, picked up his pace and half ran/half walked to his car in the parking lot. I breathed a sigh of relief. *Good. That was good. You're getting the hang of --*

My thoughts broke off as a woman in a grey business suit with overly padded shoulders and her hair in a bun stepped through the doors of the bank and advanced toward our blue Corolla. My heart began to race. As she got closer, I panicked and over-amplified my acting. My tongue lolled out of my mouth like a panting collie as I smeared the saliva still dripping from my chin (you'd be surprised at how hard it is to will enough spit into your mouth to do this) all over the right-rear passenger window. "REHHHH.REHHHH. REHHHH?" was replaced with a garbled Gerber Baby cooing mixed with an inquisitive inflection, as if I were trying to ask the woman a question with a mouth full of Legos. "AHHHHH AHHHHHGGHHHHH?!AHHHHH AHHHHHGGHHHHH?!"

The business woman turned to the car, saw the saliva drenched whirlwind spinning out of control in the unsupervised interior of Mom's car, and instead of awkwardly fleeing like the last adult, decided to wave to me.

"Hello, little guy!" She smiled and looked me right in the eye, freezing my performance in its tracks. It was everything I feared the minute I realized where Mom parked. This woman was going to realize I wasn't actually retarded, and Mom and I would be in handcuffs going to prison ten minutes after that. *I can't let that happen. I can't let that happen. I can't --*

"AAAAAAAAAAAOOOOOOOGGGGGGGGG AAAAAAAAAAHHHHHHHHH!!!" Almost as if my body took over the control panels that ran my motor skills when my brain cut out, I bellowed my impression of an old-timey car horn and waved back, smearing more saliva on the window, and followed it up with a toothy, crooked smile.

Just as her smile widened and I realized I'd saved the day again, I heard the jingle of Mom's keys and the clump of the driver's door opening.

"MICHAEL ALBERT, WHAT THE HELL ARE YOU DOING?!" She had left her perfectly normal son in the back seat of her car for four minutes, and came back to a flailing, drool-saturated special needs child having some kind of heart-to-heart with a Good Samaritan from the back seat of her car.

"I HAD TO, MOM! YOU PARKED IN THE BAD SPOT! WE WOULD HAVE GONE TO JAIL IF I DIDN'T PRETEND I WAS HANDICAPPED!"

"NO WE WOULDN'T HAVE! I WOULD HAVE JUST GOTTEN A TICKET, THAT'S ALL! AND HANDICAPPED SPOTS ARE FOR PEOPLE WITH PHYSICAL DISABILITIES, NOT MENTAL ONES!"

"...oh."

Mom sighed, started the car and began backing out of the parking spot. The woman in the business suit, locked into position by conflicting feelings of confusion, anger and disbelief, stood there and watched us drive away.

And the Names of the Colossi were Lucifer and Bone Saw

—ɱ—

"The Hells Angels have sued the Laconia licensing board, which denied the group permits to set up booths to sell T-shirts, jackets and other items at the city's Motorcycle Week rally, starting on June 8. The board cited security concerns stemming from recent violence that involved the Angels and rival gangs. The club has sponsored booths at past Motorcycle Weeks." - The New York Times; May 29, 2002

"The City of Laconia has decided to abandon the concept of creating a "gun-free zone" in the Weirs Beach area during Bike Week." - The Union Leader; June 1, 2002

"According to a 1999 national truce, the Hells Angels must allow the rival Outlaws to establish a chapter in the state without retaliation. In establishing its New Hampshire chapter, the Outlaws is

converting members of the New Hampshire chapter of the Devils Disciples OMG into Outlaws. The rivalry that exists between the Hells Angels and the Outlaws has caused recent violent flare-ups throughout the state. This violence threatens to end the truce between the Hells Angels and the Outlaws, who often compete for control over lucrative drug markets." - National Drug Intelligence Center's New Hampshire Drug Threat Assessment; April 2001

—w—

My best friends Teddy and Timmy were stereotypical metal heads. Neither of them cared much for reading or writing. In fact, they didn't really care much for anything if it didn't involve boobs, fire, death metal or beer. I met them at a pretty early age and grew up with them in the local Portsmouth skateboarding and BMX spots.

One warm summer night, Teddy and I visited Timmy at his new place in Manchester. Manchester is the largest city in the Granite State; bigger even than Concord, our Capital, which is really more of a tumbleweed factory surrounded by pine trees than a legitimate city. Timmy moved there with his long-term girlfriend to work as a tattoo artist. Around the same time, Teddy moved to Portland, Maine for art school.

At the time, I was twenty-two and back in my hometown after being thrown out of college. Back then,

Portsmouth had more bars and restaurants per capita than any other city in the country, and all of them were within walking distance of each other in the downtown district, where I lived. I was knee deep in no-strings-attached pussy and icy Jagermeister; and I was content with using them both to hide from reality for the time being. This trip to Manchester was going to be both a reunion and a sort of escape from my escape.

Whizzing down the pine-lined Route 101 toward Manchester, Teddy spent the hour drive schooling me on all the new music he'd downloaded, mostly brutal death metal. "Dude, check this out, "he said at one point, "This band is called Cryptopsy, and they are going to hate rape your ears with awesome right now." I am regularly out of the loop when it comes to music (my car is usually littered with burned CD's full of 80's tunes and most of them don't play because they're too scratched), so I welcomed the tutelage and head banging with open arms and an open road soda.

Timmy's apartment was the antithesis of the Timmy I knew; perfectly matching IKEA furniture, kiwi-melon scented decorative candles, and framed prints of vintage French wine advertisements adorning earth-toned walls. I half expected to find him delicately manicuring a pastel topiary with Andrea Bocelli playing in the background. Contrary to that visual, we found Timmy doing shots of Jack Daniels by himself, while gut wrenching metal blared from Bose speakers shattering an otherwise pristine yuppie haven. The lady of the house had clearly left the building.

Me: "Whoa there, buddy! Should you really be blasting Cannibal Corpse and swilling booze? Doesn't that require a pair of nuts? How did you get them back from your girlfriend?"

Teddy: "Yeah dude. Shouldn't you be like, wearing a sweater vest or something?"

Timmy: "Fuck the both of you pussies. The wife piece is out dancing with her friends."

Me: "Are we going to bounce on your Pilates ball and scrap book our memories like the last time we came up here, or are you going to force us to have fun this time?"

Timmy: "Shut your fuck. Drink this." Timmy handed me the bottle of Jack with no shot glass.

The night was officially underway. The three of us put together in one room always meant one of us was going to end up burnt or bleeding, and something expensive and irreplaceable was going to end up in pieces. The details of the middle part of that evening escape me now; partly because this happened a long time ago, and partly because thirty cans of beer and a sampling of the loudest, angriest music ever put to disc are enough to scramble anyone's circuits. I do remember that we decided to finish off the night at a bar in downtown Manchester with two-dozen PBR tall boys, a smattering of Wild Turkey shooters, and a rousing round of "let's make up hilarious names for heavy metal songs."

Timmy: "Jeweled Gauntlets of Evisceration!"

Teddy: "The Unveiling of the Gutted!"

Me: "Nursing Home Sledgehammer Orgy!"
Teddy: "Tusk Armor Created by Lightning!"
Me: "ChainsawDomy!"

Last call brought our fun to a screeching halt, and we piled into Timmy's cramped Toyota Echo, steaming drunk for the short ride back to his place and the ritual handful of nightcap beers, drunken food preparation, and the couch-surfing booze coma that would surely follow.

As we rolled up to Timmy's place, however, we noticed something peculiar; two grown, grizzled looking men were passed out face-up on his front lawn with empty beer cans strewn around them. Being 2:00 a.m. in one of the few places you can feasibly call a city in the vastly-unnoticed-yet-most-drinkingest state in the country, this wasn't an entirely foreign event.

Both men woke up from their late night picnic nap when we pulled into the driveway blaring our music and Teddy fell out of the car when he opened the door. They two men struggled to their feet and much to my surprise, the vagrant lawn jockeys began walking toward us as we waited for Timmy to unlock the door to his apartment.

I immediately expected the worst, and reached into my pocket for a box cutter. I always carried something with me whenever I visited Timmy in Manchester. Muggings and drunken, late night ambushes were regular occurrences in that neck of the woods. As I prepared to unleash my 9/11 instrument of death, the two men became visible under the naked bulb illuminating his back door, and Timmy and Teddy's jaws both dropped.

Teddy: "Whoa, this dude is wearing an Emperor t-shirt. That fucking rules! These guys fucking rule!"

Standing across from Timmy and Teddy, both men sported stained, ripped t-shirts featuring brutal artwork and the band names "Emperor" and "King Diamond." I pulled my hand out of my pocket sans box-cutter, and started laughing. It was like Timmy and Teddy were looking at themselves twenty years into the future; aging, retarded metal heads. *Tim and Ted's Excellent Adventure.* It was uncanny. The only way these two could have looked any more stereotypically metal would have been for them to crawl out of a panel van with a medieval dragon airbrushed on the side.

"What's goin' on, brothers? You guys into metal, huh?" The one wearing the Emperor shirt spoke up first in a deep, gravely smoker's voice.

"Fucking A right we are, dude." Timmy was ecstatic. "What the shit are you guys doing passed out on my lawn?"

The man in the Emperor shirt pulled a fish-hooked Marlboro Red out of a well-worn soft pack and sparked it. He had long, greasy black hair down to his shoulders, and a thick 5 o'clock shadow. He was a behemoth; much bigger than all of us. I could totally picture him lugging amps for WASP on the Last Command Tour. "Oh yeah, that. We were drinkin' in some apartment in this here building, when my friend and his old lady got into a huge brawl. We just took their beers and started pounding 'em on the front lawn, hopin' that they'd calm down. I guess we took us a power nap by accident."

Timmy: "That's awesome. We just got back from the bars ourselves. You guys want to come in for a couple beers and listen to some metal?"

I couldn't believe what I was hearing. I wanted to tell Timmy I thought it was a bad idea to invite two sketchy old men into his apartment to drink our beer after finding them unconscious on his landscaping, but he was drunk and there was no stopping Timmy's decision-making processes when he was drunk out of his skull. It doesn't matter if he's trying to shit out of a third story bay window at five in the morning or running out into a blizzard in his boxers to head-butt parked cars. Teddy didn't give a fuck because it wasn't his apartment, and he was even more enamored with the strangers than Timmy was. Besides, he only lived a couple of hours away and had a getaway car at his disposal.

I didn't share my friends' optimism. The prospect of hosting a late night after party with a pair of anonymous alley dwellers in a house full of valuables was starting to read like the first act of a horror movie. It definitely wasn't going to make the short list for 2002's Drunken Decision of the Year.

"Sure thing. Oh yeah, my name's Lucifer, and my friend over here's Bone Saw."

Lucifer extended his bear paw of a hand to shake all of ours as Bone Saw stood silently in the background and waved. Bone Saw was short and stocky with a red ponytail. He looked like Mario Batali's Down's Syndrome-slighted son if God took a day off from protecting the world, and allowed Mario to slip some of his vermicelli past the colander. My internal creep alarms were screaming.

Within thirty seconds of getting inside, Lucifer and Bone Saw were piercing PBR tall boys in the living room. Timmy furiously rifled through Teddy's overflowing CD case.

"Oh man, you guys are going to fucking love this band. They are so fucking metal. Oh man, you are going to shit your intestines out. THIS IS SO METAL!!!"

I leaned on the kitchen counter, sipping my beer and struggling with my options. I could break down and accept the fact that those two guys were going to be part of the brat pack for a few hours, or I could convince Timmy and Teddy that our new friends needed to catch the first train to GoTheFuckHomeVille. Luckily, Lucifer and Bone Saw would help me make my decision right then and there.

Teddy: "Did you hear about the Hell's Angels fucking some Outlaw dude up at a bar here a few weeks ago?"

Timmy: "Yeah, the fucking HA's are some pretty tough dudes. They're awesome."

Lucifer: "Oh yeah? You know something about bike clubs, huh? Tell me a little something about bike clubs, brother."

Teddy and I looked at each other, immediately sensing that something was drastically wrong from the tone of Lucifer's voice. Timmy, as usual, continued to blindly trample right through a minefield of his own design.

Timmy: "All I know is that the Hell's Angels are where it's at, dude. You can't fuck with an outfit like that!"

Lucifer's demeanor quickly shifted when Timmy was finished with that sentence. Veins popped out of his neck, and he clenched his jaw as he spoke.

"So yeah, me and Bone Saw here are Outlaws. You know who the fuck they are, right?"

The Outlaws, if you aren't familiar, are one of the largest motorcycle clubs in the country. They have a perpetual beef with a little group of vigilante justice enthusiasts you might be familiar with, the Hell's Angels. The tension between the two organizations is all too well known in New Hampshire. It comes to a head every year at nearby Laconia's infamous Bike Week. I was well aware of the potential damage that two large, drunken members of a notoriously tough membership could wreak on a trio of unarmed pussies like ourselves at 2:00 a.m.

Lucifer glared at Timmy as he waited for some response, any response that would justify beating my friend to death with a wrecking ball cable.

Timmy: "Whoa, you guys are Outlaws? That's fucking BADASS! I just tattooed one of you guys up at my shop. What's his name? 'Undead', I think."

I breathed heavily and massaged my temples to ease the beginnings of a tension headache.

Lucifer: "Aw yeah, Undead's a good buddy of mine. That ink you gave him was the cat's ass!"

The term "One Percenter" was derived from an old statement made by the American Motorcycle Association that said only one percent of all motorcyclists were criminals. Today, bikers use it as a term of endearment. Undead wasn't the first One Percenter Timmy tattooed. I don't remember the guy's name, but he is responsible for the worst story I've ever heard. As Timmy pushed ink into his skin he explained, in detail, his initiation to his group: he had to earn his grey wings. What are "grey wings"? Boy, am I not glad you asked. You may or may not know, the term "earning your red wings" refers to having oral sex with a woman on her period. Well there are any number of different kinds of wings you can get for accomplishing various sexual feats. Grey wings are the worst. To earn them you have to go down on a dead chick. The guy talked almost fondly about the woman's genitals going from warm to very cold as he performed oral sex on her.

When I heard that I did an immediate double take -- *she was alive when it all started?!*

As I stood by myself, unnoticed, in the kitchen, I thought about how much that story freaked me out; how it forever ripped away the sense of security and insulation that living in New Hampshire gave me. I wish I never knew about it. I don't want to know people like that exist, let alone live in my state or the city I'm visiting. I thought about how many bikers actually claim New Hampshire as their state of residence and how it's impossible to spend your life here without running into a One Percenter like Lucifer or Bone Saw or, God forbid, Undead.

Fortunately, Timmy's words diffused the situation as quickly as they created it. Lucifer and Bone Saw took a seat on the living room couch, as Timmy and Teddy crafted a death metal buffet for them while they got drunk, again. My friends seemed oblivious to everything about the situation. Nobody even noticed that I wasn't hanging out. Not that it mattered, because no amount of alcohol was going to drown my insecurities. I barely spoke a word unless Lucifer and Bone Saw left the room, and even then it was just to badger Timmy and Teddy to rifle our new friends out of the apartment and on their way. Timmy and Teddy presented a united front.

Timmy: "No fucking way!"

Teddy: "Stop being a pussy, Mike."

The scene in front of me was an exercise in contrast: two young, drunk metal heads and two weathered members of a biker gang, pounding brews and flailing their long hair to death metal that bounced off the walls of an apartment that could very well have been plucked from the cover of a Pier 1 catalog. I started to doubt myself.

Am I really being a pussy? Should I just relax? I mean, these guys said that they were Outlaws, but they might not be. Maybe they're just saying that so we'll think they're cool. Besides, they seem nice enough. Timmy and Teddy enjoy banging their heads and sharing their beers with Lucifer and Bone Saw. I should calm down.

Lucifer: "Aw shit, we're outta beer. You guys wanna go to our friend's place on the other side' a town and do some shots?"

I checked my watch. 4:00 a.m.

Timmy: "Fuck yeah! Let's do it!"

I shouldn't calm down.

Visions of multiple stab wounds and corpse-identifying trait removal danced in my head as Timmy started shutting off all the lights in his apartment. My insecurity emerged from its booze cocoon as a panic butterfly. I literally began sweating from the anxiety. I begged him not to go. I pleaded with him that four in the morning was no time to stumble into a stranger's house. My words were landing on deaf ears.

I stopped voicing my opinion quietly and began shouting. Teddy was already out the door, conversing with Bone Saw about Death's "Live in L.A." DVD (he'd just picked it up), so he couldn't hear me. Instead, I told Timmy I was going to crash on his couch, and that he and Teddy could go march to their deaths if they were so inclined. As soon as I shouted those words, Timmy spun around, grabbed me sternly by the shoulders, and addressed me in a hushed tone.

Timmy: "Mike, what the fuck is wrong with you?! Seriously, I've never seen you act like such a pussy in my entire life. Don't worry. We're just following Lucifer and Bone Saw to their friend's place. She's a chick. It'll just be the six of us doing some shots and hanging out. Sack the fuck up; you're coming with us."

Me: "What the fuck is wrong with me? What the fuck is wrong with YOU?! THEY ARE GANG MEMBERS, TIMMY. THEY ARE MEMBERS OF A FUCKING BIKER GANG; A VIOLENT GROUP OF PEOPLE INVOLVED IN ORGANIZED FUCKING CRIME. That's not awesome. It's not awesome, it's not 'metal' and it's not cool at all. We don't even know their real names! It's bad enough that you let these people into your fucking home to probably case the joint for a future robbery, you want to follow them to an unfamiliar place across the city at four in the morning and you want to make your friends come with you?! Are you just drunk or are you legitimately fucking retarded?!?"

I looked in Timmy's eyes and saw the conviction and frustration pouring out of them. At that moment, I felt like I was the one that was fucking retarded. *Was Timmy right? Was it worth it to roll the dice in order to find out if he was right?* I was doubting myself all over again.

There was no stopping Timmy and Teddy from getting into a car and leaving, that much was certain. If I was wrong and those guys ended up being legitimately good people, then I wasn't risking anything by coming along for the ride. If I was right, and Lucifer and Bone Saw turned out to be homicidal, drug addled ass rapists, then I would never be able to forgive myself for not being there to help fight them off of my two best friends if anything went down. I was far too loyal a friend to leave Timmy and Teddy to the Fates. The guilt would tear me apart, I just knew it.

I fumbled through my front pocket for my box cutter. Still there. I fumbled through the other pocket for my cell phone. There was one bar of juice left; just enough to make a frantic 911 call. I shut the phone off to save the battery, and took a deep breath. "OK, let's go."

Timmy, Teddy and I piled into the cramped Toyota Echo. Timmy insisted on driving. "I don't care how drunk I am, I live in this city. I know where the fuck I'm going. I'm driving."

Me: "Timmy, we're following Lucifer and Bone Saw. Whoever's driving doesn't need to know where the fuck they are go -- never mind."

I shut my mouth. Logic and reason were not going to penetrate my friend's decision-making process. Arguing over who was more sober to drive us to our impending doom was like arguing over the brand of knife with which somebody was going to stab a puppy. I plopped back into the back seat and stared with defeated eyes at the street-lights trailing by. I felt numb. Timmy and Teddy sparked cigarettes and cracked their windows in the front.

We followed Lucifer and Bone Saw on windy back roads for ten minutes or so before Timmy turned the music down and threw his smoke out.

Timmy: "Oh. Whoa. I didn't know we were going to the West side of Manchester."

Me: "What do you mean? What does that mean?" I didn't feel so dumb anymore. I leaned forward and surveyed our surroundings. We were in what looked like the industrial sector of the city. Rusted warehouses and long-abandoned mill buildings lined a trash littered street that looked like it hadn't been paved in 30 years.

Timmy: "Um, yeah. This isn't exactly the best part of the city to be in at any time of the day, let alone now."

I felt more anxiety pain, this time around my left pectoral as I fumbled through a pocket for my cigarettes and lighter.

Me: "What? WHAT?! Are you fucking serious, Timmy?"

Teddy chimed in. "I don't think it would be the worst idea for each of us to be holding on to some kind of weapon when we go into this place, guys. I know Jihad-Fu Mike has his stupid box cutter." He began rummaging through the door jams for anything sharp or heavy. "Timmy, you put this screwdriver in your pocket. I guess I'll take this roll of quarters."

Timmy: "Dude, relax. I'm just saying that we're driving through a rough part of town. It's going to be fine. It's just...I hope you have your fighting shoes on, Mike."

Me: "ARE YOU FUCKING KIDDING ME, DUDE?! TURN THIS FUCKING CAR ARO –"

I was intentionally cut off by a rapidly turned up stereo. Timmy wanted no part of my assessment. Teddy looked back at me and laughed. I slumped back into the seat and took heavy drags off my Marlboro Red, anxiety ravaging my chest. We now had both the characters and the setting for a horror movie. All we had to do was stumble across a plot and we were on the fast track to the back of a carton of Hood 2%. I thought again about whether or not I was making the right choice in sticking by my friends while they threw caution to the wind.

There might not be a huge chance that we'll actually die tonight, but there is definitely a better chance that we'll get kidnapped and a great chance that we'll just be robbed, car jacked, and thrown out of this place on our asses. The best chance is that these guys will turn out to be OK. We'll do a few shots with them and leave when we see the sun starting to come up in a couple hours. Just stay alert, and watch for anything sketchy.

Lucifer and Bone Saw's car slowed to a stop in front of a navy blue, ranch style house. The dirt-matted paint was cracked and peeling. The browning, patchy front yard was littered with rusty car parts, bags of trash, and empty cans of Golden Anniversary. I remembered thinking about my grandfather and how Golden Anniversary was his beer of choice. I also remembered that it was consistently one of the cheapest six-packs in the grocery store whenever my dad picked some up for him.

The condition of the house led me to believe that the squalor spread out before me was not simply the aftermath of a party. It was much more likely that the people responsible for it lived inside the house and were not exactly contributing members of society. They probably gave the landlord--who was obviously more of a slumlord if he left one of his rentals maintained so poorly--false personal information for the lease. Fuck, they'll probably leave a stack of bodies in the basement, rolled up in shrink-wrap to hide the stink, and disappear without a trail for authorities to follow.

As we pulled up behind their car, Lucifer and Bone Saw walked to the side door at the end of the driveway without saying a word. Bone Saw looked toward us standing outside of Timmy's car, and motioned for us to come in. We walked in a line up to and through the door, Timmy in front, Teddy behind him, and me trailing far behind. I stood at the threshold for a split second. I thought about the weapons we brought with us and how we might as well have been armed with foam pool noodles. I nervously gulped and entered the house, shutting the door behind me.

The first thing I noticed was a foot-sized hole in the inside of the door. Very comforting. Lucifer and Bone Saw were visibly shitfaced and tapping into a depleted liquor stash on the kitchen counter. Amid a dozen empty bottles, they found a bottle of sour apple Pucker's and a handle of Jose Cuervo. I immediately sensed doom. I cannot drink tequila straight up. Mixed in a drink? I'm fine. In a shot? I'm ralphing instantly. I can't even handle the smell. I've gagged just watching people do shots of the smoothest Patron. This left me in a predicament: I was going to be offered shots by Lucifer and Bone Saw, that was a given. It was also given that I wasn't going to be able to refuse them without looking rude and having my teeth pried out of my lifeless head. My options were to either do a shot of Cuervo and barf, or do three shots of sour apple Pucker...and barf syrupy green sludge.

"Here you go, brother. Down the hatch." Lucifer handed me a shot brimming with Jose Cuervo. It almost slipped out of my sweaty hands when I grabbed it. *Fuck. Take it like a champ, Mike. Fuck.* I slugged it back and set it down on the kitchen counter, immediately sensing the vile taupe liquid trying to force its way back up my esophagus and onto Lucifer's beard. My mouth started watering, and my hands involuntarily balled up into tight fists. Knowing that I literally had seconds before the inevitable happened, I punched my own leg as hard as I could to distract myself from the nausea. Everybody in the kitchen was too busy doing their own shots to notice me. *Thank God.*

Lucifer and Bone Saw led the three of us into the living room. Timmy, Teddy and I sat down on a blue corduroy couch peppered with cigarette burns, and what I hoped to hell were stains from a yogurt spill. I wiped my sweaty palms on the knees of my jeans and looked around the room. A poster of an airbrushed wolf howling at the moon hung on the opposite wall. To my left, a Brookstone water fountain complete with water vapor fog effects babbled on the end table next to me. To my right, a Wiccan altar adorned with a bejeweled pewter dagger, a stone goblet half full of red wine, a worn leatherback copy of some weird tome, and rune stones scattered all about. The only normal thing in the room was the coffee table directly in front of us, and it had a Slayer logo crudely carved into it. We sat there together without a word for a few moments. The silence was palpable.

Timmy: "So Lucifer, have you like, killed anybody before?"

The air escaped from my lungs. I had vastly underestimated the stupidity of my best friend, and with one idiotic sentence, he managed to put us collectively on the endangered species list. Bone Saw looked down at his feet and said nothing. Lucifer looked into Timmy's eyes for what felt like a minute, not saying anything. Finally, he leaned forward in his chair, reached back and pulled an unsheathed bowie knife out of the back of his jeans. Before any of us knew what to think, Lucifer made a movement that seemed far too quick given his gargantuan stature, and plunged the blade into the center of the coffee table with a hollow thud.

Lucifer: "You sure that's the kind a question you really want an answer to, brother?"

Timmy laughed, which prompted Lucifer and Bone Saw to laugh as well. Teddy and I shifted in our seats, unable to comprehend what just happened. Silence fell on the room again until our host came strolling down the stairs to join us.

Her name was Lexus, and she was definitely a witch. She was pale and skinny to the point of malnourishment, with scraggly brown hair strewn over her sunken, pockmarked face. She was probably in her late thirties, but she looked older from the years of self-inflicted wear and tear. She wore a grey tank top that wasn't quite long enough to cover her grinning C-section scar. Her L.E.I. Jeans were torn at the knees, and had a strange black smear on the left thigh.

Lexus sat down on the stained carpet and said hello to us. Lucifer and Bone Saw almost immediately went into the kitchen to bring out more shots. Lexus followed behind shortly after. That was my first opportunity to ask Timmy how long he wanted to stay.

Timmy: "Dude, I don't know. Whatever. We'll stay as long as we want to, and when I say 'we,' I mean 'me and Teddy.' You are uncontrollably lame."

I whispered as loudly as I could without our hosts hearing me. "I'm sorry, am I the only person that is noticing the MASSIVE CROCODILE DUNDEE KNIFE STICKING OUT OF THE FUCKING TABLE?!? DOES BEING WEIRDED OUT BY THAT MAKE ME UNCONTROLLABLY LAME?!?"

Teddy: "Yeah dude, that's kinda freaking me out, too. I can't stop looking at it. I mean...Lucifer just stuck a knife in the fucking coffee table. He had a fucking gigantic blade tucked into his ass crack!" Teddy started showing the beginnings of sobering up a bit.

Timmy sighed disappointedly and went to go fuck with Lexus' stereo. "I'm going to put some fucking metal in. Hopefully it'll toughen you two Nancy's up a little."

We sat on the couch and listened to Timmy's new Vehemence album for a while, before we realized that Lucifer, Bone Saw and Lexus had been gone for a long while. Timmy got up and brought some more shots in. He set a sour apple Pucker's shooter down in front of me, obviously an attempt to calm me down. "Uh, yeah, they're all in the bathroom together."

Me: "Great. That's great. We're in fucking Gangland, sitting in an all-but-abandoned house with two One Percenters who we only met because they passed out on your lawn, some creepy witch that looks like the

Cryptkeeper, and a fucking broadsword driven into the table in front of us...and all three of our hosts are in that tiny bathroom together doing God knows what kind of drugs. Oh yeah, AND LUCIFER MIGHT HAVE KILLED PEOPLE BEFORE!!! Timmy, let's leave. Let's just leave now." I took my emerald Sweet Valley High shot and grimaced.

No sooner did I say than when Lucifer, Bone Saw and Lexus saunter back into the living room. Lucifer and Bone Saw plopped down on individual recliners, and Lexus made sure we all had shots of Cuervo to do together. Great, more tequila. I wasn't sure my leg is going to be able to take this kind of punishment if I was going to keep having to punch it. Lucifer and Bone Saw looked like they had just come out of an anesthetic fog; drifting in and out of consciousness and staring at the ceiling with glazed over, watery eyes. I stared at them for a while, silently going over a list of drugs they might have done.

Ecstasy? No, that would take way longer to kick in, even if they snorted it. Special K? Who the fuck does K anymore? Heroin? Were they just doing fucking heroin? Yeah, they must have. Jesus Christ. The only real question is whether they were snorting it or cooking it. Jesus fucking Christ, I'm in a fucking smack shack with a pair of Outlaws.

I downed my shot and punched my leg immediately, hoping that the pain would once again numb the watery-mouthed nausea that tequila delivered.

No such luck.

I bolted up, ran to the bathroom, and slammed the door shut. I could hear everybody in the living room laugh in between heaves. I allowed myself to get a good ten seconds of vomiting in before I stood up, struggling to stop the stomach contractions. I looked in the mirror. I was sweating bullets, and my chin was glistening with fresh bile. *It's no wonder the ladies can't keep their hands off you, Mikey my boy.*

As I rinsed my mouth out and patted my face down, I noticed something lying underneath the cabinets below the sink. I bent down and picked it up, thinking I happened to knock something over in my haste.

It was a spoon with brownish black char on its concave side, bluish pink flame discoloration on the other. I put the spoon back down where I found it. My stomach dropped and I puked again, this time out of panic. My main concern was no longer holding my tequila.

A wave of laughter and applause greeted me as I walked back into the living room. I noticed that the sun was just starting to come up, bathing everything in light blue and highlighting just how filthy the Berber carpet was.

I reclaimed my seat on the couch and, sure enough, another shot of Cuervo was sitting in front of me on the coffee table. Everybody laughed when I noticed it. I cracked a smile, but couldn't muster a laugh. I was beyond sketched out. My stomach was in knots and I was perspiring heavily; partly from retching, partly from sheer terror. It was clear we were in a house with three heroin addicts, two of them genuine threats to our well-being (all of them if you count AIDS and Hepatitis C). *Was their plan to lure us somewhere unfamiliar and rob us?* Heroin addicts don't typically work with an unlimited budget. Lucifer and Bone Saw certainly weren't big time Hollywood actors throwing a tragically hip needle feast; they were old, rough and tumble bikers living in Manchester, New Hampshire, who invited three young strangers to their place on the wrong side of the tracks and booted dope right in front of them.

I knew I had to get us out of that house as soon as humanly possible, but our exit had to look natural. Who knew what those guys would do if they snapped out of their opiate daze as we stumbled our way out. In the middle of my scheming, Lucifer, Bone Saw and Lexus got up and shuffled through the kitchen together to fix another spike full of Major Tom.

Me: "Guys, listen to me. When I was in the bathroom a while ago, I saw a burned up spoon on the floor. These guys are slamming dope. We need to get the fuck out of here right now, either while they're in the bathroom now or casually when they come out. This is no longer a fucking joke; we can't be around this."

Teddy's eyes lit up like a pinball machine and his mouth gaped. "What?! Dude, are you fucking serious?! Yeah dude, it's time to split. Let's finish these shots and bounce."

Timmy: "Teddy, Mike is probably just making this shit up so that we'll finally leave and he can scrub the fish stink out of his cunt. Don't even listen to him."

I would be lying if I said I didn't see Timmy's response coming from a mile away. His trademark "booze horse blinders" were up, and they weren't coming down for something better—too cliche. I had actually planned on him being unable to take my word for it, especially because making something up like that would be an underhanded ploy I might have tried to pull off in a different scenario. He knew me well, and I knew then that he was going to have to see the spoon to believe me. That meant we were going to stick around until the three junkies fell out of the bathroom. By then it could have been too late.

Me: "Timmy, when they get out of the bathroom, I want you to go in there and look for yourself. If you see a burnt spoon, can we get the fuck out of here?"

Timmy grabbed the shot of tequila that was sitting in front of me. "Sure thing, Joe Isuzu. I'll be sure to let you know if I find any burned spoons, unicorns or Excalibur." He downed the shot as the trio returned from the bathroom. Lucifer and Bone Saw looked like the living dead, ghastly pale and sweaty with dark circles under their eyes.

I looked at Teddy. The dangerous reality of the situation was starting to register with him. Timmy walked into the bathroom right after and mentioned aloud about something smelling like burning plastic. Lexus nervously exclaimed she had burned incense in the bathroom. Teddy and I looked at each other, thinking the same thought. I heard the toilet flush, and out came Timmy. Cold, hard reality had slapped him in his face.

Timmy: "Yeah, it's getting light out. We should probably jet."

Timmy went to shake hands with Lucifer and Bone Saw, only to find they were both passed out in their respective recliners. We said our goodbyes to Lexus, who demanded that we stay and take one more shot of tequila with her. I declined, and was just about to open the side door when I heard Timmy say something so foul that it still makes me queasy just typing it out.

Timmy: "Mikey, you should totally do a body shot off of Lexus before we leave."

"Yeah Timmy, that's hilarious. I'll pass. It was nice meeting you, Lexus." I laughed it off, but Timmy's passing recommendation managed to send shivers up my spine. Lexus looked like she had an agitated case of tuberculosis; not exactly the most elegant specimen from which to drink.

Lexus looked at me with longing, seductive cougar eyes. "Oh come on, you party pooper. I promise I won't bite." My mouth watered from nausea again. With her biker buddies passed out, she was definitely looking to get fucked by one or more of us.

"Fuck yeah. DIY, baby. Take that shot, brother." Lucifer had managed to mouth his approval before slipping back into his golden brown coma.

I looked at Teddy, the only person in the house other than me with some semblance of self-control and understanding of the gravity of the situation. I wanted him to interject on my behalf and get us the fuck out of there.

Teddy: "Just do it, Mike. You have to."

Fuck. Fuck, fuck, fuck. Fucking shit. I fucking hate my friends. Fuck. "Okay, I'll do it."

Lexus laid back and poured a shot of tequila into her cavernous navel. Timmy tossed her a salt shaker from the kitchen. She grabbed it, licked her hand, smeared it on her neck, and then sprinkled salt all over the moistened portion of her neck. I held back a dry heave as I watched her try to make it all look sexy.

Lexus: "Sorry, tiger. We ran out of limes earlier."

Sorry, you crusty, scabby cum slut. I'd rather chase this with a fucking Lysol wipe after putting my tongue on your beanbag mom stomach.

I got on my knees, moved up to her neck, and coated my tongue with salt as she groaned and gyrated. I took a deep breath, leaned in and slurped the Mexican bathtub grog out of her lint trap, as her C-section scar smiled back at me like The Joker. I choked and gagged. The nausea hit me from all angles. I stood up, leaving Lexus on the floor, and stumbled outside without saying a word. Timmy and Teddy chuckled as they followed behind.

We piled into the Echo, and headed back to Timmy's apartment. The clock on the dash read 6:30 a.m. Timmy and Teddy laughed until they cried, as they went through a drunken postmortem of the previous five hours. Silently, I stared at my feet with my arms crossed. My eyes stung from lack of sleep. Teddy turned to me in the back seat, soaked in my pure disgust for him, and pointed and laughed at me.

That's when I threw up all over the back of Timmy's car. Timmy screamed bloody murder. Victory was mine.

Requiem for a Pepperoni Pizza

—◁Π▷—

"MIKE, YOUR MOM JUST CALLED. Your father's just had a stroke. He's in really bad condition. I'm so sorry."

It was the day before Thanksgiving during my sophomore year of high school. I had just walked in the door at Seth's house after a long evening of skateboarding by streetlight when Seth's mom gave me the news. My flannel shirt still smelled like the smoky, New England fall air that I had been exerting myself in for the last few hours. I dropped my skateboard and Seth's mom ran over to give me a hug. Seth just stood there, not really knowing what to say or do. I don't think he had ever had to deal with any kind of family crisis before. About a minute passed before I released myself from her hug. I stuttered out some broken response about needing to go home and I walked out to my '87 Buick Regal in the pitch-black driveway, trying to wrap my head around what I'd just heard.

I gripped the steering wheel firmly at ten-and-two as I wound my way through dimly lit back roads on a dead silent ride home. My father, to whom my mother had been married for fourteen years and divorced for ten, was an alcoholic, as well as a bookie and chronic gambler. To get back at my mother for divorcing him, he refused to pay child support, and spent most of that money drinking, smoking, and eating himself into critical condition. He made a large portion of my childhood nearly unbearable. As I drove, I went from numb to furious.

How dare you try to check out on us? Not until I've had a chance to finally tell you how I feel about you. After that, you can go ahead and die if you want, but not yet. You aren't going to die yet. Don't die, Dad. Don't die.

My eyes welled up as I pulled into my parking space.

Mom was standing in the kitchen when I walked in. She wasn't crying. In fact, she was very composed. I didn't really understand it, but I figured a decade of separation was probably enough time for love to turn into indifference. Seeing the redness of my eyes, she walked over and gave me a hug to comfort me. She explained to me what happened.

Dad had been taking care of Pop Pop up in Vermont. Louie, the shifty, hairy, lecherous Albanian manager my grandfather hired to take care of Pop Pop's Inn discovered Dad stumbling around in circles in the kitchen. He called the paramedics, and they flew my father by helicopter to Mass General Hospital in Boston, because his condition was far too serious for any facility in Vermont.

Mom told me they had to crack his skull open to release the pressure on his brain from the aneurysm. The doctors didn't know how much brain damage the pressure had caused yet. Mom said we were going to the hospital right away, and that a lot of the family was already en route.

The ride down to the hospital was almost completely silent. My mom just stared ahead and drove, while I sat in the passenger seat and stared out the window. I tried to picture what life would be like if Dad died. I thought about how much I hated my mother growing up because we had no money, and how much I loved Dad, because when I visited him, he lavished me with toys, candy, spending money, and all sorts of fun day trips to the dog track in Hinsdale. I thought about getting older, and realizing he was not paying my mom any child support in order to make us love him more. I thought about how much I resented him for making me build him up to be some kind of super hero, while my mom struggled to pay rent and feed us. I thought about how I was his favorite kid growing up, and all the times that friends and family told me how much Dad loved me. I started thinking about the duality of people (out of the mouths of babes, right?), and how nobody was thoroughly an angel or a demon. I didn't even think it was possible to be half angel and half demon; that idea was too black and white for me.

During that ride, I decided all people had both good and bad sides to them. The sides weren't equal, though. They were distributed in people more like toppings on delivery pizzas. You might order a half pepperoni and half mushroom, but it's never truly split evenly; there's always a little more pepperoni than mushroom, or vice versa. All of the sudden I felt sick to my stomach, disgusted with myself for thinking the way I did on the drive home from Seth's earlier that night. Dad wasn't a bad person; he was just more mushroom than he was pepperoni.

A couple of my older half-brothers were waiting outside the main hospital doors when we arrived. They said Dad's condition had stabilized, but they had to wait until he woke up in order to understand just how much brain damage he'd suffered. But there was a chance Dad would never wake up, they told me. I walked in the main entrance with everyone, and a sense of fear immediately washed over me. Something about the contrast of the soft, waiting room Muzak and the white, sterile environment of the hospital with the knowledge of the sickness and agony people were suffering through inside of it terrified me. I imagined that if there was a hell, it probably looked a lot like a hospital.

We rounded the corner and entered Dad's room. He was lying on a bed unconscious, with a bunch of tubes and needles sticking out of him. He had lots of electrodes taped to his bald head and chest. From the cranial surgery, his head reminded me of the stitching on a baseball. His whole body was grayish, save for that big red wound with staples holding it together. I asked my brother if he could hear me. He said he didn't know, but he had been talking to him anyway. My brother Martin tried to lighten the mood by telling jokes. He said that when Dad got out, he could be the new mascot for the Red Sox. "They'll call him Baseball Head!" I laughed. I was so glad that my brothers were there. They were always good in tough situations.

I walked over to the side of the bed and held Dad's hand. It was cold. I tried to warm it up by rubbing it, but it didn't work and he didn't squeeze back. I tried to be tough, but my eyes started to fill up with tears. I told everyone that I was going outside for some fresh air. I didn't know if Dad could hear me or not, but if he could hear, I didn't want him to hear me cry.

I walked outside the hospital doors and headed over to a spot where the overhead light wasn't illuminated so I could dry my eyes and light up a cigarette without anyone seeing me. Nobody in my family knew I'd started smoking. Emmett, one of my brothers, came out a few minutes later and managed to find me almost immediately. He didn't even ask me about the cigarette, he just asked me about how school was going and what was new in my life. I think he knew that I needed to talk about something other than Dad for a minute or two so I could compose myself. Inevitably, the conversation looped back around, and Emmett asked me if I knew everything about what happened to Dad. I told him that I knew he had a stroke in Vermont and had to be flown to Boston in a helicopter. Then my brother filled me in on what really took place.

"Apparently, Louie was eating dinner in the kitchen with the old man when it happened. He dragged Dad into his bedroom and shut the door, leaving him to fucking die. Only when Pop Pop asked what Dad was up to did Louie admit what happened and called the paramedics." Emmett's body and voice were calm, but his eyes were wild and dilated, a telltale sign that he had reached the end of his legendary short fuse. I listened on while taking amateur drags off of my stale Marlboro Red.

"If they had found Dad in time he would have been fine, but since he was left like that for so long, there's no telling what he's going to be like when he wakes up. If he wakes up."

"Why would Louie do something like that?" My mind was a swirling tempest of anger, curiosity and confusion when I came to grips with what actually happened. The cause of Dad's condition had gone from a freak accident to attempted murder.

"I don't know why," Emmett continued, "but I do know that Louie is nuts and he's always hated our family. You've heard about his migraines, right?"

I silently shook my head "no."

"Louie always gets these intense migraines during a full moon, like brutally painful migraines. He actually howls out in pain all night when he gets them, scaring the guests at the Inn, like a wolfman or some shit. He's fucking nuts. I can't believe Pop Pop hired such a scumbag lunatic. Don't worry, me and Martin are going to drive up to the Inn tomorrow morning and we are going to take care of Louie." The intensity in his eyes penetrated the darkened nook that we were talking in. He asked me for a cigarette and we sat there in the dark smoking together. I balled up my sweaty little fists and thought about what Louie's pizza would look like; all mushroom with maybe one shriveled, burnt pepperoni slice dangling from the crust.

On the car ride home, my mom explained the different kinds of things that can happen to stroke victims, and how one half of the body or the other is usually affected. She said Dad might have paralysis in half of his body, but chances were that he would be able to regain most of his motor function through physical therapy. I didn't really say much on the ride back to New Hampshire. I couldn't stop thinking about what Dad used to tell my sister and me on long rides in his old Caprice Classic station wagon as we gorged ourselves on convenience store snacks and he sucked back nip after nip of Fleischmann's whiskey.

If I ever end up in a hospital bed and I can't take care of myself, I want one of you to pull the plug. If there's no plug to pull, just get a gun and shoot me. I could never live like that.

We always thought Dad was just being ridiculous and, as kids, we never thought he would end up like that anyway. He was invincible to us; the hero who let us have candy and soda for dinner and stay up late to watch scary movies. He was the hero who gave me my first Nintendo after it "fell off of the delivery truck." Dads don't get sick; Dads are the toughest people on the planet. I nervously flipped through the cigarettes in my pocket the whole ride back to our house as I thought about Dad, Louie, my brothers, and what my life was going to be like from that point forward.

A week later, the doctors told Mom that Dad was awake, and the left side of his body was paralyzed. They were going to move him into an inpatient physical therapy clinic because they believed he would regain control over most of what wasn't working if he devoted himself to rehabilitation. They let me talk to him on the phone a few minutes later.

"Hey, Mickey MacDoogle.Whatchappening?" He sounded funny, which my mom explained to me was because he could only talk out of one side of his mouth.

"DAD! How the hell are you?"

"I'll tell you, I've got a schplitting headache."

We both laughed.

"I'm arive, and thatch pretty good iv you ashk me. I'm gonna be in here fer a whire doing de rehab monkey dance, but I won't be in fer long. I've rearry got to schtraighten out and put my nose to the grindstone show I can get back on my feet."

"Awesome, Dad. I'm so psyched to hear your voice. You sound pretty good, actually. So do you think that you are going to be doing the rehab thing for a while?"

"Hopefully not, the food here ish terrible."

I laughed again. Leave it to my father to be cracking jokes immediately after he suffered major bodily trauma.

"But scheriously, this was a wakeup call for me, Mikey. Dere's a lot about my life thatch got to change, and I'm going to do it. I'm going to pull through."

I remember hanging up the phone feeling upset that my dad, once again, had managed to put a spark of hope into the wet kindling that was my relationship with him as a young adult.

A few hours later, I got a call from Emmett.

"Hey, Mr. Mike, what's happening? I heard you talked to Dadoo."

"Yeah, he sounded kind of weird, but he seems like he's in good spirits."

"He sounds like he's chewing on a tree branch, doesn't he?"

I laughed. "So did you end up going to Vermont with Martin?"

"Yeah, we went up the next morning. We threw all of Louie's belongings into the street, and shortly after we threw Louie into the street after them. He didn't put up a fight or anything. Marty and I told him we didn't want to see him around the Inn ever again. His brother came to pick him up a couple hours later, and he was gone."

To this day, nobody knows Louie's whereabouts. Some people say he went back to Albania; some people say he actually died. I like to imagine that Louie actually turned into a werewolf, and a bunch of fearful peasants hunted him down with pitchforks and torches through the hilly woodlands of his homeland. That always makes me laugh.

The first few months of Dad's recovery went great. He ate well (or as well as the nurses would let him eat), made daily progress in physical therapy, and he read voraciously. His friends and family couldn't send him books fast enough. He took special comfort in flipping through the Bible.

Dad was always a Christian, but in his own way. I remember one day when I was young, and he asked me, "Mikey, you know Jesus loves you, right?" I didn't know what to say. I mean, I knew who Jesus was, but I didn't understand how my mother's decision to return the BMX bike Dad got me for my birthday so we could buy food could be construed as the warm touch of Jesus' love. Nor did I understand how drinking, gambling and gluttony could be part of a sentient Christian's lifestyle. He might have been kind of a hypocrite, but I was glad that Dad was enjoying his religion. Nobody needed a crutch, literally or spiritually, more than he did at that point. I was proud of him.

We talked regularly on the phone. He would tell me about his progress on the parallel bars and how he wooed the staff into submission with his legendary storytelling abilities. He was overcoming the odds, and doing it in style. It was amazing. For the first time in a long time, Dad was my hero again.

During my senior year in high school, I was so busy trying to finish school with good grades, making preparations for college, working as a mattress delivery boy and enjoying the last months of carefree high school living that my phone calls with Dad had become a bit staggered. Dad always told me college was for losers. "Screw college, Mikey. You don't need it. You're smart, you'll do fine. I went to college, and you don't see me using my degree at all, do you?"

Before the stroke, on top of being a bookie, Dad sold bulk depilatory wax of a questionable origin to low quality salons for a friend of his. At one point, Dad was a legitimate businessman. He and my uncle through marriage started and built a small skin care salon business into a rather large franchise around the New England area. When it came time to sell the business off for a big profit, Dad was left out of the deal entirely, the details of which are still unclear. Since then, he held down dozens of strange jobs for varying periods of time and, despite a degree in mathematics, never rejoined the world of legitimate business.

It was a few days before Christmas when I got a phone call from Dad.

"Hey there, Mickey MacDoogle. How are ya?"

"I'm good, Dad. I'm really good. Getting ready for Christmas break."

"You coming to see your old man?"

"Of course, Dad! Do I get to do snow donuts with you in the wheelchair?"

"Go ahead and bash my legs into the wall for all I care. I can't feel them anyway. Listen, I've got something very important to ask you, and I want to know that you can come through for me."

"Um, sure. What do you need, Dad?"

"Look, Mikey. I'm not getting any better. I'm not going to be able to walk ever again, and I'm starting to get gangrene in my leg. The doctors are going to have to start hacking pieces off of me. I can't live like this, Mikey. I just can't."

It was at that moment I realized I was being kept in the dark about Dad's true condition. I was always the last person to hear bad news about anything. Being the youngest in the family, I only had Mom or Dad to rely on for information about what was going on, and bad news was something that I would get last, if at all. There were times I would hear about family members dying weeks, sometimes months after they actually passed. It was just Mom's way of protecting me from the harshness of reality, I suppose. As for why Dad never mentioned anything before that point; he never complained. Not about anything. I remember one time, when my sister and I were staying at Dad's dingy apartment in a very bad neighborhood in West Springfield, Massachusetts, he had a bad tooth and decided to pull it out himself rather than go to the dentist. Dad never wanted anyone to feel bad for him, and that was why I was so nervous about what he was saying to me.

"What about physical therapy? You're doing so well. Don't get down on yourself. You can totally do this, Dad." I started thinking about those long trips in the Caprice Classic and what Dad would tell my sister and I about how he wanted to go out. Waves of anxiety beat against the inside of my chest.

"I can't, my boy. I've hit a wall with the therapy, there's not much more they can do with me. They want to move me into a nursing home, Mikey. A nursing home. I can't do it." Dad's voice started to sound more muffled than usual.

"Dad, I...I don't..." I didn't know what to say. Everyone was telling me that Dad was doing just fine, and he wasn't. Dad wasn't fine at all.

"I want you to go to your Uncle John's house and get a gun, and I want you to bring that gun here. I need you to help me end this, Mikey."

Thirty seconds into the conversation, my father had asked me to euthanize him. My stomach hit the floor and my eyes welled up. I felt a lump in my throat and I could barely breathe. I was clawing at the air for something to say; anything to say. I knew how hard it was for him to live like he had been living, but I had no idea that he was in so much despair that he needed it all to end, and now Dad wasn't just telling me that he wanted to die, but he wanted me to facilitate his death. I knew Uncle John didn't have a gun, and even if he did, he wouldn't give it to me for any reason, let alone to stop my Dad from existing.

"Dad, I...I can't...I can't do that, Dad. You don't really mean this." The words struggled out of my mouth.

Dad's voice started to rise. "Michael, I really mean this. I need to know that I can count on you."

"No, Dad. You can't. I won't do this, and I can't believe that you want to do this; that you would want me to do this. Why would you ask me to do this?!" I slowly started going from scared to angry as the conversation continued.

How dare he make me believe in him when he was just going to give up and check out like that? How dare he ask me to fucking kill my own father? Does he have any God damn regard for my well-being?! Doesn't he fucking care about how irreversibly fucked, legally and psychologically, that I would be if I ever went through with something like that? Fuck him.

Tears streamed down my face and stained my shirt.

"I know this is a big thing for me to ask you, Mikey, and I know that you are the only person that I can ask to do this."

"Dad, no. Just...no. I can't do this, and I can't talk about this with you anymore. You are tearing me apart. I can't do this. I have to go, Dad. I just have to go right now."

"Wait, Mikey..."

I hung up the phone, ran upstairs, stripped out of all of my clothes, and jumped into the shower so I could cry without Mom hearing me. I didn't know whether or not I should tell someone about what Dad said to me. I didn't want him to be in pain, but I figured if he really wanted to do it, he would do it no matter what anybody said or did to stop him. I lay in the fetal position in the shower for some time, until the hot water cascading over me made me overheat and feel sick.

I spent the next month waiting for something to happen. I never told anyone about the conversation Dad and I had, partly because I didn't want the family to worry about him any more than they already were, but mostly because I was scared that he would hate me for making people pity him. Dad never ended up going through with it, though. I'm not sure if it was because he wasn't strong enough to pull the trigger or if he ended up feeling like life might have been worth living for a little longer, but whatever it was kept him from killing himself, it kept me in suspense to the point that I started to develop health problems. I began suffering bouts of insomnia and crippling headaches, and I suffered knifing pains in my chest and gut which would later be diagnosed as stomach and esophageal ulcers. The guilt and anxiety were literally eating me alive.

As it turned out, all of Dad's predictions from that fateful phone call came true. The staff told him that he couldn't stay if he wasn't going to concentrate on physical therapy. A month later, Dad was moved to a seedy assisted living apartment building in Chicopee, Massachusetts. Nurses came in to wash him and take his vitals from time to time. I never visited. I stopped calling Dad after that phone call a month prior. He called and left messages for me at home all the time, but I refused to answer any of them. Part of me was furious at him for giving up on life, and part of me was ashamed of myself for giving up on him. I just couldn't focus on Dad and myself at the same time.

Luckily for Dad, he had an unending supply of old friends who visited him on a daily basis. Also luckily for Dad, his apartment was situated directly above a disgustingly unkempt Polish Vet's bar into which those same friends would wheel him and get him drunk on a daily basis.

My Uncle John set Dad up with his very first computer and a dial up connection in that dingy apartment so he could keep in touch with the world. Dad set himself up with an email address and an AIM screen name, and, with a little snooping, found out all of my information. I started getting random emails and instant messages from him all the time, and I responded to none of them.

I couldn't imagine how long it took Dad to type everything out with one hand. He had regular contact with the rest of my family through the Internet, and he would spend his days cooped up in his little handicapped dungeon hunting, pecking and forwarding around pictures of his grandchildren.

Nobody else had a problem with Dad except for me. The way my brothers and sisters saw it, Dad's choice to stop trying was his own, and we just had to accept him for who he was. The way I saw it, Dad stopped trying not when he was in physical therapy, but when he was married to Mom. He refused to put the bottle down to save his marriage. He had a lifetime to get his shit together before he got to that point, but he said fuck marriage, fuck responsibility, and he gave up right then and there. Dad had let me down from Jump Street, and forgiving or forgetting just weren't in my bloodstream at that age.

A couple years later, I left school and started working at a financial brokerage in my hometown of Portsmouth, New Hampshire as a temporary coffee and bagel boy for the big money energy traders in the back of the building. My half-sister Chrissie was the branch manager at the time, and she managed to squeak me into a little role there in the hopes that I would prove myself and move up the ladder. I did pretty well; going from a useless joke of a position to operations manager in the span of a couple years. Working in a crazy, fast-paced atmosphere turned out to be really good for me. I could focus all of my energy on the job, which helped me block out my issues with Dad and kept me out of trouble. I worked seventy hours a week, sometimes coming in at midnight and not leaving until the sun went down the next day. I studied and crammed and busted my ass until I literally felt ill by the time I came home every night. I worked like that job was my only chance to make it; to not become my father. I was determined to be nothing like him.

One day when I was on a conference call with one of our more important institutional clients and a floor broker from the heating oil pit on the NYMEX, my sister walked into our office and slid a note onto my desk in front of me. I picked it up.

[Mike, your Dad just died. Meet me in the foyer.]

I walked out of the office and into the foyer, where my sister was waiting for me with puffy, red eyes and tears sending makeup down the sides of her face. We didn't share a father, but she spent a lot of time with Dad growing up and she always liked him a lot. My sister told me that Dad died in his sleep, and it was a very peaceful way to go. She gave me a hug, told me to go home immediately and wait for a call from the mom we did share. I grabbed my coat and headed out the door. As soon as I crossed the street, the reality of the news caved my soul in like an ethereal sledgehammer. I crumbled to my knees on the sidewalk, unable to breathe or speak;

the guilt was already tearing me into shreds. The tears started to come, and I beat the frozen sidewalk with all of my strength until my palms bled.

It's been over a decade, and I have never fully forgiven myself for not making things better with my Dad before he died. The guilt I feel when I think about how foolish I was for not making the most of what little time I had left with him turned me into what many people would call a crude and awful person, and I lived like that for a long time. I lashed out at others for no reason. I refused to let myself succeed at anything because subconsciously I didn't believe I really deserved it. The bulk of my family wouldn't speak to me anymore, and a large chunk of what was left I all but abandoned. I couldn't hold a job down to save my life, there was rarely a day that I left the house giving a shit about what I looked like, and I let many, many great people in my life slip through the cracks because when I was at my very worst, I could not stand the broken, withered husk of a human being I became.

I do get better as time goes on, and the only way I am able to repair myself is to remember Dad not for the wasteful, irresponsible things he did during his life, but to remember him as he is pictured here; a jolly, silly, friendly, goofy, loving, fatherly pepperoni pizza.

Mike Discovers Organic Smooth Move Tea

—⁊⁊⁊—

I WAS AT ENJOYING A pint at the Coat of Arms when I ran into Alex, a friend of mine that I hadn't seen in years. I gave her a hug, ordered a beer, and sat down at a table with her to catch up on things. She looked amazing. Not that she was fat before, but she had definitely lost a lot of weight since the last time I saw her. She genuinely looked like a different person. I didn't hesitate to tell her how great she looked, or to ask her what she did to shed those pounds.

"You look...you look...awesome. I mean, really! It's not that I ever thought you were a chunker or anything, but... no, fuck you. Stop making me give you compliments! If the rest of these people hear me, they'll all expect me to be nice to them too."

"Oh Mikey, I don't think anyone is in danger of falsely thinking you're a nice person."

"Good call, but seriously - how did you do this?"

I was in the middle of suffering through an imprisoning New England winter on top of being five days into quitting the cancer sticks. My spare tire was inflating rapidly, regardless of how many miles I was clacking out on the treadmill. I needed some pointers.

"So, what did you do?"

"Well, the first thing I did was go vegan. That helped a lot."

"That's dumb. Meat is awesome, and I only plan on having gray skin when I'm on a mortician's slab. What else did you do?"

"Well, there's this thing I do called the 'Master Cleanse'. No solid food is ingested for ten days. Instead, you consume a mixture of lemon juice, maple syrup, water and cayenne pepper."

"Add vodka and I've probably made that drink at an after party before."

"I wouldn't doubt it. Since this is considered a cleanse, the second half includes guzzling a sea salt solution as a top-down enema, and something called 'laxative tea'."

"They make tea that makes you poop?! So basically, you eat nothing for ten days but force yourself to shit like a Pembroke Welsh Corgi after an ice cream smorgasbord in order to rid your digestive system of...what?"

"Toxins and congestion that are supposedly the root cause of a laundry list of illnesses. When the ten days are up, you can either break the fast slowly by reintroducing your body to fruit juice first, followed by soups, fruits and nuts, or you can continue on for longer."

"Wait, isn't this that shit that Beyoncé did a while back?"

"Yeah. She lost like fifteen pounds or something. It was on the news, I think."

"So how much weight did you lose doing this?"

"A little less than fifteen pounds. It's not as much for weight loss as it is for cleansing yourself from the inside out, but you do lose weight."

"Fifteen pounds in ten days?! Fuck."

We talked about all sorts of stuff before I left, but the back burners of my brain were still fired up over that Lemonade Diet. *Could it work? It probably does, but it would probably be the worst ten days of my life. You like food too much. Besides, you just quit smoking. How are you going to quit eating right now?*

"So you're living in Portland now? That's awesome. I love Portland." *Shit, I didn't even think about my ulcers. Nothing but lemon juice and cayenne pepper for a week and a half? Yeah, that won't have me shitting blood at all. My boxers would look like Curt Shilling's socks.*

"How's your boyfriend these days? When's the wedding? Oh, I'm just pulling your chain." *You know what does make sense? The part about pooping a bunch. I can't see myself not eating for ten days, but I can see the value of eating really well and forcing your intestines to rid themselves of Orcs and dragons. Think about it; if I skipped the*

Mexican lemonade, ate really, really healthfully and did the natural laxative tea stuff, it would probably help me 'evacuate Thetans' and maintain my weight until my metabolism corrects itself. Fuck maintaining my weight, this could actually help me shed a few pounds in the process. I think I'm going to try this.

"Hey Alex, what's the name of that ca-ca tea that you drink so you can pee out of your butt?"

The following day, I found myself wandering through the aisles of the Portsmouth Health Food Store on a mission for two weeks' worth of organic vittles and a box of Smooth Move herbal laxative tea to attempt my own makeshift version of the Master Cleanse. I had never been in the Portsmouth Health Food Store before. In fact, I had never been in a health food store anywhere before that day. I noticed that I was getting bad looks because I didn't bring my own burlap potato sack to carry groceries home with. I also noticed that people don't move out of your way in a health food store, even if you ask politely. They just stand there, blocking the lanes with some kind of sprawling yoga position while they read the back of every single food item on the fucking shelves. This is fine and dandy if you have nothing to do with your day besides float through life like a granola bar meandering down a babbling river of ignorance, but I didn't have Nature's Valley tattooed across my chest, and I was itching to get home.

A few well-placed shoulder checks coupled with my ability to make almost anything look like an accident, and I was unloading my items at the register, steeping in the panicked embarrassment that only comes from buying laxatives from a silently judging cashier girl.

I threw a pot of water on the stove, and began reading online testimonials from other people that used shitty shit tea as soon as I got home. One woman mentioned you shouldn't plan on going anywhere an hour after drinking a cup. Another mentioned one to two hours before liftoff. None of my roommates were home, which guaranteed me all the throne time I could ever need. I cracked the box, pulled out a tea bag, and poured myself a cup of sweet release.

After two hours, I noticed I still hadn't spackled shit all over my bedroom walls. Thinking I might need an extra poop boost because I have the tolerance of a well-fed lumberjack, I decided to make myself another cup. An hour later - nothing. I picked up the back of the box and read. Organic Smooth Move will generally produce bowel movements in six to twelve hours. SIX TO TWELVE HOURS? What the fuck were those two women talking about? I would have shit naturally within six to twelve hours anyway. Christ, I could have been drinking Elmer's glue and I still would've taken a dump after that amount of time. All of the sudden I was jealous of those trust fund hippies in the health food store; studying those boxes, understanding the products they were buying.

I finished my second disappointing cup and left to meet some friends at the bar. A few hours later, I came home and had yet another cup of tea before I went to bed, effectively taking three times the recommended amount of senna leaf stimulant laxative in a twenty-four hour period. That health food store snake oil was going to make me crap if it killed me.

Fortunately, it didn't kill me. It just robbed me of my innocence.

Luckily, I wouldn't have the time to drink another cup of tea because I spent the next five days suffering from uncontrollable, explosive diarrhea. I confined myself to my room, where I would pass the time by rocking back and forth in the fetal position until I had to run to the bathroom again. I would eat the solid food from the health food store, but nothing resembling solid poop was coming out of me. The toilet water looked like chicken broth. I was wiping so much that I actually started spotting the toilet paper with blood.

I literally sat on the throne anywhere between fifteen and thirty times a day. By the afternoon of day four, I began icing my asshole down with a tray of cubes from the freezer. I couldn't go to the gym. I couldn't go to the supermarket. I couldn't go to Blockbuster. I couldn't leave my apartment, because there was a very real chance I would end up shitting myself in public. I debated going to the emergency room, but a quick scan of my last e-room bill made me decide I couldn't afford it. I was walking like I spent a week riding a horse with no saddle. I couldn't string two hours of sleep together without being shaken awake to offer what little water was left in my body as sacrifice to the plumbing gods. By the fifth day, I was a dehydrated husk of a human being; broken both physically and emotionally in ways that would have made Josef Mengele skittish. My eyes showed no joy. I was defeated.

The night of day five rolled around and I was starting to feel much better. I was in the bathroom washing up after one of the last bouts of soul expulsion I would have to suffer through, when I noticed a dusty scale on the floor. *I wonder.* I dragged it out, calibrated it and stepped on. Sure enough, I ended up losing eight pounds in five days. I knew most of that had to have been water weight and I would gain it back when I fully regained my continence, but it was enough for me to realize the effectiveness of the Master Cleanse if done properly. It was also enough for me to realize I wasn't nearly vain enough to endure that inquisition for five more days, especially sans food and plus an Olde English 800 bottle's worth of salt water steadily fucking my colon to shreds. I didn't understand why anyone would use that as a means to lose weight when they could just work out. Did working out really sound that terrible to some people? I actually enjoyed exercise. Why would anyone do this to themselves on purpose?

I thought about all of the Hollywood types I met out in Los Angeles who would do anything to stay skinny.

Diet pills, meth, coke, laxatives...anything; just as long as it didn't call for any kind of physical exertion. I thought I could cheat the system, albeit on a smaller scale. I thought about every one of those wannabe debutante girls I met and spoke with and hung out with and fucked, and how they probably spent their days shitting their brains out before getting in the car to meet me for drinks. A whole different kind of nausea washed over me; the kind that harsh self-realization brings. I didn't have a destructive sense of vanity, but I was essentially wringing out my intestines in the efforts of losing a few pounds. I didn't share the mentality of Lindsay Lohan or Demi Lovato, but our physical actions were similar. *I have something in common with those whores? Those terrible whores?! Put me in a frilly pink tunic and oversized sunglasses, and I'm ready for my OK! Magazine cover shoot.* There wasn't enough soap in the world to clean the look of perfect disgust off of my face.

I went into my kitchen, pulled out the box of Organic Smooth Move laxative tea, opened it, poured water all over the bags as to destroy them, and tossed the whole thing in the trash. The last thing I needed was homeless person poop spackling my walkway.

Blind

—◆—

SHORTLY AFTER I FAILED OUT of the University of New Hampshire, I moved into my half-sister Chrissie's house in Portsmouth and landed a job working as a delivery boy for the Portsmouth Pizza Factory, a little pizza joint tucked into an old strip mall about a block away.

I loved delivering pizza. The money wasn't great, but the job itself was awesome. I'd hang out in the restaurant and fold pizza boxes until an order came up, snatch it up before the other bored delivery drivers could start fighting over it, toss it on the front seat of my car, and speed around town, smoking cigarettes and blasting music until I found the house my greasy cardboard box and/or greasy brown paper bag belonged to. You'd get stiffed on a tip every now and again, but you'd meet all sorts of people along the way, and it gave you an opportunity to see new parts of town and learn a little more about where you lived.

I was terrible with directions and still am, but the Pizza Factory didn't have any kind of "30 minutes or less" policy, so I was safe to roam the streets without having to invest in a GPS system or frantically unfold road maps while swerving over the double yellow line. Police ate at the Pizza Factory for free, so I left an insulated delivery bag in the back seat of my Jetta at all times, which made me immune to speeding tickets.

Half of my income from the Pizza Factory went to my sister for rent, and the other half went to food, booze, and entertainment. I had no health insurance or savings account to speak of, but I was able to pay the small amount of bills I had and live a rather care-free life of my own design, which is all I was really capable of doing after my disastrous attempt to appease my mother through higher education.

On Friday June 14th, 2002, I met up with my then girlfriend Leslie, my friend Zach and few others in Portsmouth for late night beers after a night of slinging pies. After slugging several back and getting ready to call it a night, we got a call from our mutual friend Emily around 1:00 in the morning. She was at a raging house party in Rollinsford, which is only a few minutes away from the University of New Hampshire campus I had recently been rifled from.

Being twenty years old and having no real responsibilities to consider, we decided we'd drive over and see what it was like. I threw a couple cases of Heineken into the back of Zach's Subaru wagon and we headed to Rollinsford; me, Zach, Leslie, a girl from our old high school named

Britt, and Mark-Tard. This wasn't his real name, of course. Mark was from across the bridge in Kittery, Maine and looked like a clean-shaven Geico caveman, on a good day. This coupled with the fact that he was always running his mouth and getting into trouble because of it earned him the moniker "Mark-Tard" in high school. I was never really friends with Mark, but I felt bad when someone would call him out on his bullshit in public. He'd shrink back from it like a scolded toddler and make any onlookers believe he genuinely didn't know how big of an idiot he was being. On this particular night, he happened to be just likable enough for us to invite him along.

We arrived at the white two-story house on Portland Avenue in Rollinsford around 1:18 am, and not only was our mutual friend Emily no longer at the house by the time we go there, all the other party guests were either leaving or going to bed. Several people in the backyard were still drinking and playing beer pong, so we decided to stay and play one round before heading back to Portsmouth and calling it a night. The trip would have felt like a total waste if we just went home, especially on a weekend night.

Just as we were entering the backyard, one of the guests spotted us and told us the party was over and that we should go home. Shrugging our shoulders and sighing, we complied and began piling back into the car. Before we were able to turn the motor on, a different guest ran to our car.

"Oh guys, no big deal. A few of us are still hanging out, at least for a little longer. Come on back and play a couple games of beer pong."

Shrugging for the second, we again piled out of the car and walked into the backyard, where we met several friendly faces who accepted us into the fold, and before you knew it, we were knee-deep in a great game of beer pong. When the strangers ran out of beer to fill their cups with, we offered our thirty-pack to them. We laughed, we talked shit during the more intense parts, and we drank copiously. At some point during the game, one of the guests mentioned that most of the Spaulding High School wrestling team was at the party but were inside the house.

Just as Zach was about to sink one of their three remaining cups after we made them re-rack, the game was frozen by the angry chanting of dozens of people pouring out of the bulkhead basement doors of the house. The stream was seemingly endless. Several dozen boys walked toward us with fists balled up and fire in their throats. In a fleeting moment of clarity, I understood what was happening all at once:

This was a trap. None of these people were actually nice. We are about to get jumped. There was no time to be scared or angry or to conjure up a crude exit strategy. We were about to get our asses handed to us. I still don't understand why, but I knew it was coming, and I knew it immediately.

One of them walked up to Mark-Tard and accused him of stealing beer from the party. Mark, who was sitting on one of the thirty packs we brought with us, was able to get three words into explaining just that before he was punched right in the mouth, toppling him like a sack of Idaho's Best.

Before I even had a chance to blink, another walked up beside me and threw a sucker punch at my temple. Later in life, I would be told by a doctor about how fortunate I was to have turned my head before his hand connected, because it would have instantly killed me if I hadn't. I turned toward the fist at just the right time, and noticed a metallic twinkle before I was punched in the face with a set of brass knuckles.

I flew backwards in the air like a stunt double in a bad Jean Claude action movie, and landed on the sheet of particleboard that made the beer pong table, folding it in half and sending the folding stands holding it up crashing to the ground.

I was knocked unconscious, and when I came to, it was to a cacophony of Lord of the Flies-esque roars, shrieks and laughter, all in unified approval of the beating I just took. To this day, that backless, emotionally dead and perfectly human chorus echoes through my waking life and has pulled me into several perspiration drenched spirals of post-traumatic stress disorder while out in public, just trying to enjoy myself. When I die, that will be the soundtrack to my Hell.

Several seconds later, I pulled myself to my feet, and my vision was clouded with bright, swirling stars. Like in most firsthand reports of traumatic injuries, I was immediately enveloped in the déjà vu of a childhood injury I couldn't quite remember at the time, but later recognized from the time I split my skull open when I was five-years-old. The sparkles in my eyes, the pressurized feeling in my sinuses, it all seemed very familiar.

It's funny how you can't remember pain. You can remember that you experienced the pain, but something in your brain keeps you from remembering the real details of how it felt until you suffer a similar injury down the road. Only then do you have a clear understanding of past pain, and even then it's fleeting.

As I struggled to my feet and began to shake the wooziness of a clinical concussion off, it registered to me that the same kid who hit me with the brass knuckles was fly tackling Zach to the ground. Zach, having been fortunate enough to skip the bulk of the teenage fistfights that give most adults a basic concept of self-defense, hit the lawn with an earthy thud, his assailant on top of him. He quickly got back up and started backpedaling across the lawn.

Not knowing if the people I came with were still around, I blindly screamed for them to get back in the car while I ran to Zach.

Zach was surrounded by the party guests. He held his hands up in the air, and confirmed over and over again how everything was cool and that we were leaving. One of the kids grabbed a handful of Zach's shirt and started chanting "YOU COME CORRECT OR DON'T COME AT ALL!!!" Someone stuck their foot out while Zach was backpedaling, and the two of them tumbled to the ground.

Zach took a punch in the face before I was able to use my velocity to shove the guy on top of him, and send him rolling across the lawn. I picked Zach up and ran with him down the sloping side yard toward his parked car. Leslie and Britt were already piling into it.

About a hundred feet from the car, the guy that hit me - *is this guy made out of Teflon?* - tackled Zach again from behind and smashed him in the head with what was, for certain now in the glare of the street light, clearly a pair of brass knuckles. He clung to Zach's legs, and started trying to climb up them like some kind of unrelenting demon for another shot at his face. I kicked him in the head several times, and he finally let go.

I picked up Zach again and made it to the car. I climbed in the back seat, and Zach got in the driver's seat and slammed the door shut. As soon as he slid his key in the ignition, the guy smashed one of the rear windows out, spraying glass all over us and repeating the other attacker's "YOU COME CORRECT OR DON'T COME AT ALL!!!" chant as he did it. The girls in the car screamed. I did too.

Zach started the car, and we all jolted when the death metal we had been listening to on the way up to Rollinsford started blaring out of his speakers. We peeled out, and drove down the otherwise sleepy suburban street. Brass Knuckles stood in the wash of the street lamp as we went, screaming at us until he disappeared from view through the rear windshield. Zach eventually turned the radio off, and the car was silent, save for the whistling of wind through the broken window and our collective heavy breathing. We were all in shock.

Once we were a safe distance away, we pulled off the next available exit, which happened to be the parking lot of Red's Shoe Barn in Dover, where we piled out of the car, assessed each other's injuries, and called an ambulance. While we waited for them, Leslie noticed that Mark-Tard, instead of helping Zach and I while we were getting our heads bashed in, grabbed one of the cases of beer we brought with us and threw it back in the car before we escaped. If any part of this story helps to illustrate just how much of a self-serving, alcoholic ronin Mark-Tard was, this is it. Despite his pleas, we threw the remaining beers in a dumpster on the property so the girls, just months away from being able to drink legally, wouldn't get in trouble, just as the ambulance arrived with its sirens blazing.

Police from Rollinsford followed the ambulance and took an initial statement from us, while the EMTs quickly gave us a once-over in the parking lot. When they were done, the police made their way to the scene of the incident, and we drove the rest of the way to Portsmouth Hospital in silence.

Leslie and Britt sat in the waiting room, while the three boys were attended to by emergency room physicians. Mark-Tard needed stitches in his upper lip, Zach needed nine stiches above his right eye, and I – the luckiest of the three – looked like I had been hit by an eighteen-wheeler and was bleeding all over the place.

Storm clouds had been gathering while we were being seen to in the parking lot, and a steady downpour blew in just as two members of the Rollinsford Police Department arrived at the house on Portland Avenue and knocked on the door. All the lights had been turned out, but the place looked like an open-air frat house and the police were familiar with Ryan, the child of the couple who owned the house. Nobody answered the knocks at the door, despite the twenty-something parked cars strewn about the street, driveway and front yard, so the two policemen walked around the perimeter of the house and took pictures with a digital camera. A thousand empty beer cans and red Solo cups, an empty case of Heineken, shattered automobile glass and blood... all being cleansed of precious DNA evidence in the deluge. They also found a roll of paper towels soaked in blood, which was picked up and bagged as evidence.

—ʍ—

We left Portsmouth Hospital just as the rainy night became a rainy day, vowing to reconnect later that day and file an official statement at the Rollinsford Police Department, and went back to our respective homes to get some rest. Not wanting to worry Chrissie, I snuck back into the house, swallowed a couple Percocet given to me by the emergency physician, and quickly fell into an exhausted, dreamless sleep.

I woke up around noon and discovered that my broken nose continued to hemorrhage blood in my sleep, effectively gluing my head to the pillow. I sat up and peeled the crusty pillowcase away, sensing that my face felt tight and hot. My lids of my left eye felt like they were sealed shut with eye sleepies – the way they do when I suffer from allergies or a bad cold – but when I pried them open with my fingers, they immediately snapped shut again. *Swollen shut*, I thought.

Chrissie is going to lose her shit. Famous for her low threshold for anything pain or blood related, there was a good chance Chrissie was going to see my face and faint. I could hear her, her grumpy boyfriend and her son mulling about downstairs and knew I couldn't get out of the house without them noticing me, so I begrudgingly threw on some clothes and walked down the stairs. Chrissie's jaw dropped open the minute she laid eyes on my face, and sobbed as I told her the story of what happened. Her boyfriend mumbled something about "That's what you get for going to parties", and continued watching an old black and white movie playing in the living room.

With those formalities out of the way, I walked into the bathroom to finally get a look at my face. Instead of Mike's face, the mirror above the sink showcased the swollen, oozing, purplish-black face of a man beaten to death with a chain link steering wheel and left to rot in a sun baked salt marsh. My left eye was indeed swollen shut and discolored, and the entire left side of my face had expanded so much that it was honestly hard to recognize my own reflection. My right eye began to swell, and there were several lacerations on my face, all of which had since clotted over. My nose was a twisted mass of floating cartilage held together by taught skin, and it was STILL gushing just as badly as it was five minutes after I'd been laid out. The condition of my face was obviously concerning, but the fact that the bleeding wasn't slowing down really terrified me. *Can you really die of a bloody nose?*

"I'm calling Mom", Chrissie proclaimed from the kitchen.

An hour later, I met with everyone in front of the Rollinsford Police Department. Mark-Tard tried making several excuses as to why he couldn't make it, but was eventually roused from bed and dragged to the station late. Everybody looked at my face and shuddered, and Leslie started crying.

Halfway through filing a police report with the officer on duty, my face started swelling up badly again and I felt faint, so I excused myself early and drove directly to the hospital. My right eye started to swell even more, prompting me to put the pedal to the metal before it shut completely and left me going ninety miles-per-hour on the highway completely blind. The flow of blood from my nose became much heavier on the drive, and the stray t-shirt I found in the back seat that I was using to blot my face was completely saturated by the time I made it to the emergency room doors.

I checked in at the registry window, and bled in the waiting room for a little over an hour before I was taken into an examination room. By that time, the front of my grey hooded sweatshirt looked like the scene of a gristly road kill, and sharp pulses of bright pain zigzagged in my face and behind my eyes. I was immediately given a much stronger pain medication and a CAT Scan, so the doctor could get a better handle on my condition.

Aside from the mild concussion, we discovered I suffered from a fractured face, broken nose, deviated septum, multiple lacerations and collapsed sinuses.

"Wow, this guy really gave you a wallop, huh" the young doctor told me when he came back to the examination room with images from the scan. Dizzy and groggy from the medication, I stared at the floor and nodded in the affirmative.

Mom showed up shortly after, and started crying the second she got a look at my face. "I can't even recognize you. You don't even look like you. My God."

"You're lucky he hit you square in the face with those brass knuckles." The doctor interrupted. "If you hadn't turned into the punch in time, he would have struck you in the temple with the same amount of force, and that most likely would have killed you."

My injuries were so severe that my nose would probably continue to bleed for a couple weeks. To help keep me from looking like Carrie at the prom for half a month, the doctor inserted nasal tampons – close cousins to the vaginal model, each roughly two inches in length – in my nostrils and all the way up to what felt like the bottom of my eyeballs. My mind immediately drifted to that Always commercial from the '80s, but altering it so *I had to leave the party with a jacket tied around my **face***. Once in place, the doctor took the tampon strings and taped them to the bridge of my shattered nose so they wouldn't be dangling in front of my mouth.

As the doctor wrote out several pages of prescriptions for pain pills and several other medications I can't remember (blood coagulants and antibiotics?), he recommended a face and nose specialist to follow up with, and that I should apply a cold compress to my face as much as I could stand to help with the swelling.

Once I was discharged, Mom said Chrissie didn't want me in the house because she didn't want her or my young nephew to be freaked out by how I looked. She said I could stay on her couch until I was well enough to go back to work, and looked well enough to not give Chrissie panic attacks, or my nephew nightmares.

Mom insisted on driving me back to her house, which I welcomed because operating a vehicle with one eye half open didn't sound like a fun time, even though I was positively swimming in opiates. I called a friend and asked them to pick my car up from the hospital, and slid into the passenger seat of Mom's car. Just as we were about to pull out of the parking space, she realized she had some questions to ask the doctor about my medications, and left the car running while she jogged back through the automatic doors of the emergency room.

Thirty seconds later, my nose began to tingle, and I sneezed. The pressurized left nasal tampon shot out and splatted against the dashboard. The right nasal tampon fired out of its respective nostril like a potato cannon, but was held back by the string taped to the bridge of my nose, nunchucking the sanitary napkin in a downward arc, exploding against my mouth and chin with a meaty slap, and sending bloody mucus cascading down my neck and chest. I looked up and the entire windshield looked like I had just been shot in the head from behind. Dammed up blood dripped from seemingly every square inch of the vehicle's interior and my own person.

I slowly got out of the car, shuffled back through the emergency room doors and had the doctor reinsert a couple of fresh snot box Tampax.

After quickly checking to make sure Chrissie's house was empty before stopping in to pack a small bag of clothes, we arrived at Mom's house; a tiny little three room bungalow several miles away. That night, I slept on the couch with a bag of frozen peas draped over my face.

A week after the incident on Portland Avenue, there was no progress in the case, and things started looking bleak for us. Between the lack of progress made by the police department coupled with the rain ruining what little physical evidence was left behind, we were starting to think they'd gotten away with it.

Zach's mom, knowing that members of the Spaulding High School wrestling team were at the party, had a flash of brilliance and went to the high school's main office under the guise of a parent with children who were "interested in joining the wrestling team," and was sold a yearbook right on the spot. After bringing it to the station, we were asked to come to the Rollinsford Police Department and look at the yearbook in an attempt to point out people that were at the party. We each did this with a police officer present in one of the examinations rooms, and despite how nervous we all were about being able to recall brief flickers of faces from the poorly illuminated yard and the fast-paced flipbook of insanity that unfolded there, we were collectively able to identify several party goers, as well as both of the assailants; Zachariah Thone and Terrence McDonnell.

When I woke up the following morning, I was unable to open my right eye, just like the left one. I bolted upright in a panic, and tried prying it open with my thumb and forefinger like I had with the left one, but it was like looking through a window smeared in Vaseline. I yelled for Mom and got no answer. *She's at work. I'm here all alone.*

I stood up and frantically fumbled around for the portable phone I remembered seeing in its charging cradle on a table by the television before I fell asleep. I found it, picked it up, and was about to dial Mom's cell phone number when I realized I couldn't see the buttons on the phone, nor could I see the digital display to make sure I was even hitting the right buttons. After a dozen attempts, all resulting in those notorious three notes followed by "I'm sorry, your call can't be completed as dialed." I felt my way back to the couch and sat down. I sat there, starving, needing to go to the bathroom, and utterly incapable of helping myself or even knowing what time it was, until Mom came home later that evening.

Mom helped me find the bathroom door, and let me do my thing while she whipped up a quick meal for us to eat, and then drove me back to the emergency room to figure out what in God's name was happening to me.

"Oh yeah, that was bound to happen," my doctor calmly explained to me as he was yanking saturated tampons out of my nose and replacing them with new ones. "You sustained severe facial trauma. The swelling is due to the increased fluids and white blood cells rushing to the parts of your face that were damaged, so it's actually a good thing to see some swelling. The downside here, obviously, is that you've been rendered temporarily blind by it. Just keep taking your pills, use ice as much as you can without being too uncomfortable, and make sure you're not doing anything too physical. Seriously, additional stress can make your swelling much worse and cause complications, so just chill out."

I started laughing at this, but it killed me to smile, so I ended up delivering this stone-faced, humorless chortle that would have scared the shit out of me, had I been able to watch it in a mirror.

"Are you trying to tell me I have to drop out of the Lumberjack World Championships this year? I can't see, dude. I can't even walk five feet without smashing my shin on something, let alone go for a friggin' jog."

We both laughed at that. He told me it would probably only last a couple days and then I'd regain some sight in at least one of my eyes, which would make life a lot easier while the swelling went down naturally.

READER EXERCISE: To better understand my feelings of panic and frustration, put this book down, close your eyes, and count to thirty. No cheating. I'm watching you and I'll know if you fake it. After thirty seconds, get up and try to do something simple while keeping your eyes closed, like turn on your home stereo, get a can of soda from the fridge, or find a pair of sneakers to put on. When you start to experience the first pangs of anxiety, open your eyes again and relax. I felt the same exact way, only I didn't have the option of opening my eyes, so the tension built and built and built. OK, now you can continue reading.

Mom left for work early the following morning. I woke up shortly after, and when I was done feeling my way to the bathroom, splashing water in my face and hoping to Christ I didn't accidentally brush my teeth with a tube of Neosporin, I decided I better learn how to be self-reliant if I was going to live without sight for what I thought was only going to be a couple days.

I couldn't dial out on the phone, but I did learn how to feel for the slightly larger "Talk" button on both the landline and my cell phone, so accepting incoming calls became an option. Mom would call to check on me a couple times a day, but the bulk of the calls that came in were from telemarketers, and I couldn't screen those calls because I couldn't see that the number showed up as "unknown" or was originating from a state in which I didn't know anybody. Once I realized it was a cold call solicitation, I'd try to hang up, only I couldn't find the red "end" button nearly as easily, so I'd select random buttons and hear "Hello? *beeeeeep* Sir? *beep beeeeeeeepboop* Hello?" for an excruciating thirty seconds or so before I was able to end the call.

The television presented a number of challenges. I obviously couldn't watch TV with my eyeballs hidden behind an inch of puss and swollen flesh, but I thought listening to it would keep me entertained through the day. I couldn't read or write, so listening was really my only option. I couldn't find the remote control, and wouldn't be able to use it even if I had, so I got off the couch, felt my way over to the television and fumbled around until I found the power button. E! Entertainment was playing the True Hollywood Story: Fabio. I cringed until further exploration led me to a button that changed the channel, only every time I pressed it, I was offered nothing but the crackling of snow. It then dawned on me that the TV must have been on channel three, and that I'd have to both find it again and figure out how to change channels on the cable box, which was devoid of buttons and relied on a separate remote control I couldn't find. After several minutes of hunting, I sat back down on the couch and listened to dramatic music accompanying a theatrical reenactment of the infamous "rollercoaster/bird/face" incident.

Shortly after, my stomach started to grumble. I got up and attempted to feel my way over to the refrigerator. After smashing my bare toes into the legs of a coffee table at full stride, I felt the handle of the fridge and opened it. I stood there for a moment, mulling over a brand new basket full of blind people problems. To start, I had no idea what was in the fridge. Secondly, I didn't know what I was grabbing in there. I could tell I was touching a plastic half-gallon jug, but I couldn't tell you if it was filled with pulpy orange juice or expired milk. Worse still, my broken, dammed up nose couldn't smell, which meant I couldn't even taste the difference between the two. Was the Tupperware container I was drunkenly pawing through with my bare hands in an opiate haze filled with last night's goulash, or the silica gel packets you find in new shoes? Every trip to the refrigerator before Mom came home from work became a game of Russian roulette. After mistaking a dish full of coffee beans for M&M's, I broke down and asked Mom to prepare simple sandwiches, and place them on a certain shelf in the fridge before leaving for the day.

Like most people, I visited the bathroom several times a day. Unlike most people, the steady regimen of antibiotics and pain medication rendered me constipated, and the normal feeling you get when you're ready to make a bowel movement was replaced by the less frequent but a thousand times more intense need to pinch your cheeks and speed-waddle to the toilet. Aside from not knowing how much to wipe (ouch), number twos were a breeze.

Urination was a much different, much messier story. The first few days of total blindness were spent attempting to pee standing up. I'd feel for the toilet lid, lift it up and was initially confident that the stream would make it into the bowl. When I was greeted by the sound of liquid splashing on linoleum instead of into a vessel filled with water, I'd panic and try to correct my aim, resulting in soaking the walls, sink, toilet cistern and bath mat. For those of you who are unaware of the baffling biological fact that men can't stop going once they've started without experiencing considerable pain, it can be a terrifying thing. I'd furiously wave my penis around the room like a runaway fire hose until I could hear it hitting the toilet water, after which I'd feel around for the flusher and laugh at the futility of flushing four drops of urine. After experiencing this twice, I decided Mom would probably be happier if I peed sitting down like a newly dominated prison bitch. *My name's Mike – I mean Darla. I wear a mop head like a wig. You want a backrub, Inmate #28347421?*

After not hearing from them in a few days, Mom called the Rollinsford Police Department to get an update on the status of the investigation. There were no breaks in the case to convey. Mom hung up, and it suddenly dawned on me that this case could potentially go unsolved. Rollinsford is a small town of roughly two-thousand residents, and above fishing, hunting and potluck dinners at the local church, rural America saw high school sports as the height of recreation. Entire families flock to watch a high school football game on a Friday night, even if they don't have a kid on the team. Grown men wore letter jackets and festooned the bumpers of pickup trucks with bumper stickers reading "GO CLIPPERS" and "RED REBELS – [insert current year] STATE CHAMPIONS." If the people that shattered my face were found to be on that wrestling team, also part of the Division I athletic program of a small town high school, there was a chance all of this could get swept under the rug by an overly-enthusiastic fan that spent his days as a coach, town councilor, selectman or police officer. *Whoops, the evidence was tainted by a spilled cup of coffee. I took statements from Zachariah Thone and Terrence McDonnell, and they seem pretty darn bulletproof. Shucky darn, it looks like we might never find these guys. GO RED REBELS!* The thought of these people getting away clean was so horrifyingly rational that it made my stomach turn.

As if things on the justice front weren't looking bad enough, Mark-Tard made things even worse for the investigation with his patented lethargic apathy. He was chronically late for every meeting we scheduled with the Chief of Police. Sometimes we'd be standing in front of the station, each of us taking turns calling Mark-Tard until he'd answer groggily "I don't have a ride, so you'll need to come and get me." We'd drive Mark-Tard to and from line-ups and statement interviews, even though it was useless because he was only capable of giving garbled half-answers and petulant snark.

At one point Mark-Tard told an officer that one of the attackers took $60 out of his pocket, which was entered into his official statement. I had no idea whether or not that actually happened until he approached Zach and I with a goofy grin, saying he was going to tell the police it was actually $100 that was ripped out of his pocket. It took a few seconds for us to process the fact that this soggy brained opportunist was willing to submarine our entire case over $100; risking us seeing the guys that almost killed me being brought to justice and my massive uninsured medical bills being taken care of, for what you can make in an honest day's work as a grunt on a construction site.

Zach and I tore him a new asshole, making him swear on his life that he wouldn't, even though we both know that kind of a promise coming from him was about as sincere as a hoarder's promise to pull the mummified cats out from under their couch. Luckily enough, the Rollinsford Police Department realized Mark-Tard wasn't worth the trouble, and stopped calling him for information and scheduling him for meetings.

Mom eventually drove me to Dr. Yeganeh, a face and nose specialist in Portsmouth. He and his assistants pored over my medical records, and took several x-rays of my head. On top of discovering that the left side of my face had sustained severe nerve damage and that much of it would be permanent, the doctor concluded that I'd need two separate surgeries – one an open reduction of displaced nasal septal fracture, or "correcting a deviated septum" in layman's terms, and another called a bilateral turbinate reduction, which was essentially reconstructive plastic surgery – to the tune of roughly $15,000. Being an uninsured pizza delivery guy with a checking account balance of ($47.80), I was obviously unable to have the procedures done. Because of that, the injuries I sustained to my face all those years ago turn a common head cold into an incredibly painful week-long ordeal, and there are still patches of the left side of my face that are completely numb to the touch.

When the swelling didn't go down and I still couldn't open my eyes two weeks after the incident, I found myself in the emergency room for the third time. The doctor examining me explained that everything looked as good as it could be and that it might take a little while longer for the fluid to drain from my face. Nobody in that room knew that by the time it was all said and done, I'd be totally blind for just shy of three whole weeks.

I got a call from a concerned best friend one afternoon, whom we'll name Ricky for the sake of potential legalities. At first the conversation was dominated by inquiry. "How are you holding up? Is there anything I can do? How is the case coming along?" to which the answers were: "Terribly," "Mom pretty much has me covered," and

"Maddeningly slow." Once that was out of the way, the real meat of the phone call surfaced.

"We want to get the guy who hit you."

"What?"

"Dude, a bunch of us got together the other night and talked about it, and we've decided that we're going to take a few cars up to Rollinsford in the middle of the night, find this kid and fuck him up. Tie him to a tree deep in the woods and break his fucking face with a hammer. Do to him what he did to you. Nobody fucks with our boy."

As gutturally violent as the subject was, the sentiment behind it was enough to get my eyes painfully welling up with appreciation. My friends hadn't forgotten about me and left me to wallow in misery alone; they were literally organizing black ops missions to avenge their fallen comrade.

I'd be lying to you if I said I never once entertained the idea of giving his proposal the green light during that phone call. Picturing my mugger being dragged into a dark corner of forested New England by a large group of masked men, cinched to an old pine tree, and having his face shattered to match mine sounded pretty good at the time. The thought of the good time he was having while dodging the law being torn away from him as savagely as my good time in life was torn away from me was downright exciting. I wanted him to feel how I felt. I mean, that was fair, right? The Rollinsford

Police's investigation was moving at a slug's trot, and just like on the cop shows on TV, hope for bringing him to justice dwindled with every passing moment. There was a chance they would never catch the guy, and wouldn't that be enough to drive me insane? Maybe vigilante justice was the right move. Maybe I should tell Ricky to go through with it.

Of course, that was only the logic denying rage fantasy of a wronged man talking, and I ultimately thought better of it. What if my mugger died on that tree before people found him? None of us were hardened criminals. The guys would inevitably get caught and our lives would be destroyed because of it. Hell, my life would have been destroyed by it as an accomplice, even though I was lying on a couch fourteen miles away with a bag of frozen tater tots draped over my unrecognizable face.

Like most victims of violent crimes, I loathed how slowly the process was moving, but I resigned myself to allowing the American justice system to get the job done. As a young man living in a rural area, I'd experienced enough wantonly cruel policemen throwing kids skateboards into the Piscataqua River instead of just telling us to move on, and bizarrely puritanical judges doling out unnecessarily heavy-handed sentences to people my age, people with futures ahead of them. The way I saw it, most of those infractions were crimes of convenience. *Who's going to stop me? I'm in Podunk New Hampshire, and nobody's watching the watchmen here.* My view of "The System" was jaded, and now that I was officially someone the system was supposed to protect, I needed to see them come through for me. It was a pivotal moment in my life where I was either going to despise authority forever or have firsthand knowledge of the thing keeping America from devolving into a riotous rape and murder machine actually working. What I ended up with was going to be up to them.

I told Ricky not to bother, explaining that the mugger's wounds would eventually heal, but a felony conviction would haunt him until his dying day. I hung up with Ricky, and then I waited.

The next several days were spent in solitary contemplation. I couldn't watch television, I couldn't drive, I couldn't read, I couldn't write, I couldn't masturbate because the pain pills made it impossible to climax, I couldn't smoke cigarettes or go for a walk because I couldn't find my way outside, I couldn't take pleasure in food because I couldn't taste anything, and Mom wasn't allowing friends to visit until I started showing signs of healing. I couldn't see, and losing that one sense us sighted folk take for granted every waking moment of our lives turned me into a flailing, hopeless invalid. All I could do when I wasn't sleeping was lie still in an empty house with two of my senses temporarily disrupted, and think. So I resigned myself to thinking as hard as I possibly could. I guess some people call that meditating.

At first the thoughts were just vague, superficial blips. *The sun hitting my face is turning everything orange. These pain pills are making me itchy. I wonder what time it is.* I basically just rattled off individual facts and things I was feeling at that very moment as a way to pass time.

As the days progressed and I started running out of base observations to catalog, my mind naturally drifted toward the anger and frustration I felt by being put in my situation. *They better catch this guy. They better throw this motherfucker in jail. Why me? Of all people, why am I the one that's lying on a couch at his mother's house on a weekday, blind as a bat, unable to afford surgery and wondering what my face is going to look like once this swelling goes down? IF the swelling goes down?!* The welling, idiot fury, which had been as dammed up as my nostrils for days thanks to my emotion-dulling pain pill regimen now flowed through me freely and easily. *Why am I here, and THIS WHITE TRASH HIGH-SCHOOL AGED MOTHERFUCKER is probably out having a grand old time bragging about how he made a couple out-of-town assholes "come correct."* I grinded my teeth and oozed hatred as the sun shined and the birds chirped just outside the walls of my mother's house; outside the prison of my broken body.

As it turned out, I was right about the bragging. After hearing reports of him being arrested the next town over for beating somebody else up just weeks later, witness interviews in a physical copy of the police report I requested six months later revealed that Terrence was in fact bragging about how he beat up a bunch of people at the party, including a girl that came with them "because she was running her mouth." Of course he never struck Leslie or Britt during the altercation (thank God), but to illustrate what kind of a person this guy was, he was apparently bragging about how he had.

Before long, the incident in Rollinsford started playing in the back of my head, boiling it down to its core elements with every pass while the front burners of my brain steadily simmered pots of rage, like a little boy will put an animated movie on repeat to enjoy in the background as he sits on the floor and plays war with his action figures.

The call from Emily. The drive to Rollinsford. Playing beer pong with people who were just pretending to be nice. The door to the house bursting open. The people pouring out with their fists balled up and eyes glimmering with violent intent. Mark-Tard getting punched in the mouth. Turning my head and seeing something shiny greet my face out of the darkness of night, then everything going white. The laughter. The cruel, haunting laughter of hollow people. Struggling to my feet and seeing someone trying to hurt Zach. Not knowing if I can help him. The feeling of helplessness.

rewind

Emily. Rollinsford. Beer pong. Door bursting. Balled fists and violent intent. Mark-Tard getting punched.

Something shiny. Whiteness. Laughter. Someone's hurting Zach. Helplessness.

rewind

Helplessness.

rewind

Help.

Angry, frustrated tears would come, even though it hurt my face and stung my eyes like lemon juice to cry. I cried because the false security blanket of rugged toughness most men drape over their shoulders before leaving the house for the day - the thing that forces fleeting "What the fuck are you looking at?" moments held silently between young men masking their insecurities in bar rooms was lost next to the broken glass and pools of blood in Rollinsford. I cried because regardless of how healthy, wealthy and wise we become during our lives, we're all just one step away from being physically and emotionally disabled. The horror of the human condition is that it is steeped in chaos, and nothing can protect you from it. Even the strongest, meanest guy in the most subdued rural area is only a set of brass knuckles, a car accident or a doctor's diagnosis away from becoming a blubbering invalid, suffering alone in a dark room. Or dead.

Finally, after all that weak Nietzian bullshit ran its course, I would come to the real crux of the issue and the end of the thought train – *my ego*. I had been emasculated by a total stranger; worse, a high school kid, and the fact that I was bested by someone bothered me far more than the chronic throbs of pain in my face and the laughably perfect inconvenience of temporary blindness. I'd pause on that for a minute, allowing myself time to draw lines between how I grew up being bullied and feeling helpless to stop it, and how I'd transformed myself into a callous, combative person so potentially dangerous people would steer clear of me and I wouldn't have to suffer through that feeling of helplessness anymore. When I finally figured out how to keep helplessness from paralyzing my sense of self-worth, I vowed to myself that I would never again be a victim to it. Ten years later, all that hard work spent as the architect of the person I portrayed to the world was toppled to the ground with a pair of brass knuckles, and that old, familiar helplessness crept back into me.

And then, back to thinking about minutia like "I wonder what kind of bird is chirping outside" and "These pain pills are making me super constipated" to keep the nervous breakdowns that typically come with negative personal realizations at bay. I spent a solid week locked in that awful, cyclical train of thought. I probably would have entertained the thought of suicide if I wasn't positive I'd just end up in the bathtub, sawing at my wrists with a soggy banana I mistook for a bread knife.

Mark-Tard, Zach and I were asked to go to Wentworth Douglass Hospital in Dover to have our blood drawn so it could be used as DNA evidence when crossed with traces of blood found at the scene of the crime. Warrants were issued for Zachariah Thone and Terrence McDonnell, who were escorted by police to the hospital for the same process. It was later determined through DNA testing that Terrence's blood was on the paper towel and the shattered automobile glass found at the scene. That coupled with a series of witness interviews, which all pointed toward them as the aggressors, resulted in Terrence McDonnell and Zachariah Thone arrested and charged. The Chief of the Rollinsford Police Department called us to let us know that afternoon, and it wasn't until then that I realized how much the sickening weight of their freedom had been impacting me.

They caught you, you fucking fucks. In reality, my swollen face wouldn't allow me to smile, so I just opened my mouth a little and chuckled until I needed to take a Vicodin. In my mind's eye I grinned savagely, and found strength in knowing the legal repercussions of their actions would soon haunt them as much as my physical wounds haunted me then and my emotional wounds would haunt me for long after.

One day after I'd spent a considerable amount of time mashing my shins and toes into every piece of sharp-legged antique furniture Mom owned, I came up with an idea. When she came home, I told her about a scene in Minority Report, a movie that arrived in theaters a few days before everything in my life went to shit, where the guy who did Tom Cruise's eyeball transplant tied ropes to the handle of the fridge and doorknob to the bathroom, so he could pick them up and follow them to their respective destinations while he was healing. Mom grabbed a spool of old twine she used for various gardening projects and did the same. It worked, and I was thrilled to put another check in the "win" column. Of course, I figured this system out at the tail end of my blind period, and was only able to get a few days of use out of is before blessed sunlight began to creep through the slit of my left eye.

I'd be able to see out of one eye for roughly forty-five minutes every morning before the swelling would kick back up with my increasing heart rate or the heat from the shower, and then I'd be blind for the rest of the day again. The sight was still milky and fuzzy, but I could make out shapes, the layout of the house and differentiate between foods in the fridge. I'd rush over to the freezer and lay a bag of frozen peas over my eyes for as long as I could possibly stand it in order to stretch my "sight time." It worked, and before long, I was enjoying two to three hours of vision a day, with better clarity every day that followed. I was still unrecognizable with my face swollen and discolored and my nose was STILL leaking blood two weeks after being struck (although it had slowed down to a trickle by that point), but by God, I was regaining my eyesight.

The words needed to describe how good it felt to see again; to regain even the smallest sliver of control over my life after weeks of infantile uselessness, just don't exist in this language.

Leslie came over to my mom's place to visit right around the three-week mark. We occasionally talked on the phone while I was staying there, but like the rest of my friends, Mom had also barred Leslie from seeing me until I was on the mend. It didn't bother me much, because I didn't want her seeing me in that emasculated state anyway. Most couples would have probably balked at those rules and found ways to meet, but Leslie and I were already in the process of drifting apart before the incident, like young couples tend to do when the magic of new fucking inevitably dissipates, and you come to terms with the notion that you really aren't meant for each other.

When she came in and sat down on the couch, I knew guilt was making her feel like she was stuck with me until I was healthy enough to break up with. I let her go on feeling that way, because I was a man in my early twenties, and the concept of love for that demographic is usually interchangeable with juvenile possessiveness and other assorted symptoms of underdeveloped emotional attachment.

After about an hour, Leslie insisted it would be good for me to get out of the house. She gave me a pair of oversized women's sunglasses to stretch over the hellscape of my pulpy, discolored face, pulled my nasal tampons out and threw me in the passenger seat of her car.

"We're going downtown to get a cup of coffee." I protested at first, thinking people I knew would stop and ask me all sorts of awkward questions about my condition that I didn't feel like answering.

"You look like shit; like a completely different person. Nobody is going to recognize you."

We parked, walked to a busy cafe in Portsmouth's Market Square, ordered a couple of iced coffees, sat on a bench and people watched for a while. Other than Zach coming by to meet us, not one person realized who I was. I watched good friends of mine, locals I regularly shared beers with and talked about local politics with walk right past me like I was a tourist. There was something exhilarating about going unnoticed in a place where you are surrounded by people who know you very well, but there was also something terrifying about it. It made me think of the story about the boy who kept making faces and his mother warned him that his face would stay that way if the wind changed.

We talked until my nose started bleeding again, and we all decided it was time for me to go home and get some rest. Leslie dropped me off, and we broke up a few weeks after that.

Zachariah Thone was sentenced on January 21ˢᵗ, 2003. He was fined $750 and received a six month suspended sentence in the New Hampshire House of Corrections. Terrence McDonnell was sentenced on January 22nd, roughly eight months after a handful of good-natured twenty-somethings piled into a car and drove to a house party in Rollinsford, laughing and singing along to the CD player.

All five of us went to the courthouse, even Mark-Tard, and watched. It was the first time we came into contact with our attackers since that hellish night, and even though it was a large courtroom and we were sitting in the very back, I struggled with a knot of anxiety in my chest. Despite the fact that my face was mostly healed and I was finally able to breathe through my right nostril again, I was suffering from panic attacks and a lot of seemingly tame situations now made me jittery. It would be years before I would agree to attend a party whose host I hadn't known most of my life, and even then I would have to keep my jacket on so guests didn't notice the dark sweat stains under my armpits.

The presiding judge asked if we wanted to say anything just before he was about to deliver the sentencing. I didn't, but Zach stood up and delivered a heart-wrenching statement to the room in which he revealed to Terrence his own emotional distresses stemming from the incident that he still couldn't get past; social anxiety and general paranoia that would take a lot of time to dilute. Terrence stared at us from the front of the courtroom while Zach spoke. Zach stared right back at him, but I stared at my feet. I couldn't look Terrence in the eye. I truly believed my eye contact would spark a murderous fire in him that would smolder all through his time in prison, and fuel a merciless Cape Fearesque revenge killing when he was released. I had already been through enough senseless violence, and the doting mommy in my brain demanded that I shut up, let the sentencing happen, and move on with my life as quickly as possible. Zach sat down when he was done, and the judge followed by saying the defendant didn't want to address the people in the court, but that "he has expressed remorse for his actions". Terrence McDonnell was ultimately sentenced to a year in New Hampshire State Prison.

I experienced a mixed bag of emotions walking out of that courtroom; relief that it was finally over, satisfaction in knowing the justice system actually worked, great shame for not having the courage to address my attacker when given the opportunity, and a sudden, desperate drive to better myself. The guy who nearly killed me was going to spend a year locked up, and decades after living with a felony record in order to pay for his misdeeds. It only felt right to view moving forward as a second lease on life, and it would be criminal to spend it like I had before the gears of misery were put into motion.

Shortly after the sentencing, I quit my pizza delivery job, took a position as an assistant in a local brokerage, and moved into my very first apartment, with Zach as my roommate.

Eventually, the physical pain and emotional turmoil from this part of my life eventually faded away, thanks to the brain's handy-dandy safety switch, as did my new-found appreciation for sight, health, and life in general. For me, inspiration has always been a finite fuel that I can choose to burn slowly over a long period of time or quickly for passionate bursts of productivity, but the end result is always complete depletion. Over time I became just as lazy, complacent and apathetic as I was before Rollinsford, which I guess can be seen as evidence of a full emotional recovery, or at least a return to version of life I was comfortably familiar with. Regardless of how messy you left it, home never feels better than after spending time away.

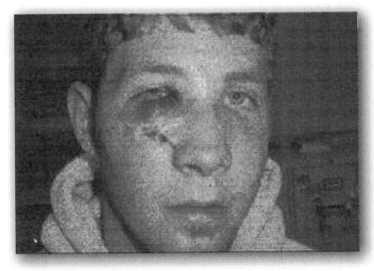

Bobby, Ravager of Dreams

—◦◦◦—

MY SENIOR YEAR OF HIGH school was a mad dash to the finish line. I'd transferred to my third and final high school halfway through my junior year, only to discover that many of the previously accrued credits from my first two schools, one of which was a private Christian academy, weren't transferrable. In order to graduate with my class, I had to fill all of my senior year free periods with the classes I was missing, which meant being the only senior in junior and sophomore classrooms and having underclassmen thinking I was some kind of mental deficient. Conversely, it also meant I had to take an English literature class at an adult education center several nights a week, in which I was the youngest person by decades. I had to drop my martial arts classes and virtually everything else that didn't immediately pertain to academics. It was a hectic, isolating year that left me scrambling to complete assignments and cramming for exams while the rest of my friends were taking off for the beach during their free blocks.

The craziness of my senior year also left me with a great excuse for why I wasn't dating anyone, other than being honest and saying "my social anxiety outperforms my teenage libido" or "I genuinely don't know what I'm supposed to tell a girl in order to receive a blowjob." There was the occasional make-out session at the occasional underage house party I was invited to, but the two semesters before graduation were largely spent writing papers, lugging a fifty-pound Jansport backpack filled with textbooks, and masturbating myself to sleep at the end of every miserable day.

My scholastic misery was relieved, albeit briefly, by one of my high school's more unusual amenities. Dubbed "the smoking trail" by its regulars, the first twenty feet of the entrance to a wooded cross-country running path was reserved for smokers. Anybody who could prove they were over the age of eighteen to the security guard could walk out to the smoking trail and light up between classes. If this seems appalling to you, you have to understand this was 1998/1999 "Live Free or Die" New Hampshire, and smoking wasn't even banned from bars and restaurants until 2007. Smoking was just barely starting to become uncool to young people, but people basically smoked everywhere. I wasn't a heavy smoker at that age, but it balanced on the border of being a casual indulgence to something I was genuinely depending on, and the stress brought on by coursework was enough to tip me into addiction country.

My best friend Timmy and I would regularly meet on the smoking trail when the bell rang, and then run back in so we weren't late for our next class. While it was obviously unhealthy, it offered a brief respite from the anxiety of teenage responsibility, and I took respite where I could find it. Of course, no respite from responsibility comes without a cost, and that cost for me came in the form of a special needs student named Bobby.

Bobby was afflicted with Smith-Magenis syndrome, which left him with moderate mental retardation, delayed speech and behavioral problems. Despite his setbacks, Bobby regularly overcame adversity, was very active in school activities, and well loved by students and faculty alike. For all intents and purposes, Bobby was crowned the unofficial mascot of our high school.

Everybody loved Bobby and Bobby loved everybody in return, but for reasons I've yet to understand even fifteen years later, Bobby did not love me. In fact, Bobby had it in for me.

"GET OUT OF MY WAY!" he would bellow at me in the hallways, even though I couldn't have been less than ten yards from his person. He would shoulder check me every chance he got, and once he even took a slice of pizza out of my hands and touchdown spiked it on the foyer floor, confidently strutting away from the scene like a special needs John Travolta in Saturday Night Fever. Bobby was a beacon of positive energy to everybody else he came in contact with, but decided I was a worthy target of his venomous Bobby rage, and was deceptively good at keeping his transgressions against me from the public.

One of the ways Bobby would fuck with me on a daily basis was by locking the swinging steel double doors on me as I was heading back inside from the smoking trail. I'd be several feet from the door, see his face through the glass, hear a metallic clicking sound and then watch him openly guffaw at his evil genius when I tried to open the doors to no avail. I'd knock on the door and beg Bobby to open it for me, but he never did. Sometimes he'd pretend he unlocked it, only to double down on laughter when I'd try the door again and found it still locked. This led to the inevitable walk around the perimeter of the entire school to the front doors, which never failed to make me late for my next class.

What could I say? Could I explain to the teacher that everybody's favorite Bobby was purposefully making me late for class? Could I really tell anybody about Bobby's vendetta against me without coming across as an insensitive asshole? Torches and pitchforks couldn't come far behind painting a special needs student as a part-time villain, even if it was warranted. I had enough problems trying to get through my senior year without adding school-wide alienation to my plate, so I did the only rational thing I could think of; take the lateness lectures from my teachers, and tried to acknowledge Bobby's existence as little as possible, hoping he would lose interest in me and find another hapless victim to torment until June.

The school year progressed and I trudged down my personal warpath to graduation with enough success to keep me reasonably motivated. Papers were passed in, final projects were graded and exams were taken at a frenzied pace that was becoming rapidly familiar. Scrabbling for ways to stack up credits with what little resources I possessed, I was approved to do a special extra credit project to make up the difference, in which I suited up in my uniform and gave an entire gym class a martial arts demonstration. Timmy was my assistant, and my audience oohed and aahed as I flipped him onto gym mats and pretended to kick the ever-loving shit out of him.

I was on the fast track to graduating on time, and it felt good to see my hard work and social sacrifices paying modest dividends. It was on my way back to the locker room to change into regular clothes when I first noticed Natalie.

A year below me, Natalie was walking through the gymnasium to some unknown destination wearing bright green jeans and a tank top. She had short brown hair that just grazed her shoulders, and somehow seemed to accentuate her bi-racially softened Asian features. She was effortlessly pretty in her awkward, artsy way, but my dry spell during what should have been sexual monsoon season made her seem supermodel radiant.

My spineless attempts to get Natalie's attention began almost immediately. When I saw her in the hallway, I'd pay attention to whom she chatted with, hoping we had a friend in common I could leverage into an initial meeting. When those prospects ran dry, I put my feelers out and asked friends of friends if they knew anything about her: did she have a boyfriend? Was she open to dating at the moment? I did anything and everything but the easiest thing, which would have been just walking up to her and asking her out on a date. Nothing yielded any concrete answers. To an outsider, watching me pine over Natalie must have looked like watching an apprehensive little boy in water wings walk laps a swimming pool, dipping his toes in periodically and saying "Too cold" despite how overheated he was.

Standing on the smoking trail with Timmy a month before graduation, I'd decided enough was enough, and that I was going to march straight up to Natalie and ask her if she wanted to go out for ice cream. I was finally able to mitigate my fear of rejection by knowing even if she openly laughed at my advances and told everybody about the stuttering guy with the nervous sweats who had the hots for her, I'd only have to see her for a few more weeks before grabbing my diploma and sprinting away forever.

I was newly empowered by a "now or never" mantra which looped in my head over and over again as I crushed my cigarette butt out and walked toward the rear doors of the school. *I'm going to ask her out. I'm going to ask her out. I'm going to –*

Like the reemergence of a ghost previously thought to be exorcised from a haunted house, Bobby's toothy, malevolent grin appeared behind the glass of the metal security doors. It had been several weeks since Bobby's last attempt to lock me out of the school, which I'd falsely attributed to my ignore/evade strategy. The fact that he happened to rear his head just as I was beginning to build up my courage and act like a man in front of a woman for the first time in my life made it almost feel like God was using Bobby to convey a message, that message being "Nope, you're going to be a pussy forever."

Unfortunately for God and several other people, including myself, that message came too late. I wasn't going to get locked out. I wasn't going to allow myself to be emasculated by Bobby and be forced to walk around the school. I was going through those security doors like a man and I was asking Natalie out on a date, like a man.

"No you fucking don't, Bobby."

My walk turned into a gallop, arms outstretched to bear the brunt of the impact with the steel doors. My backpack, heavy textbooks and notepads, jostled left and right as I ran.

Bobby, finally registering the fact that I was vaulting toward the doors at high speed, rushed to find the lock on the handle, his smile fading. Seeing this, I brought

my arms in and angled my shoulder toward the door at
the last minute, hoping Bobby would know to step away
from the other side of it, or else be caught in front of the
human locomotive barreling toward him. What I didn't
take into consideration was the fact that Bobby, while
devious and vindictive, was still a special needs student,
and wasn't as capable of that kind of split-second decision making.

The resulting metallic clang echoed through the
hallway as it blasted inward, connecting with Bobby's
face and body with a meaty thwap. My feet caught the
threshold of the door, sending me sprawling to the floor
face first, my backpack sliding up my spine and connecting with the back of my head. Bobby was thrown backwards as if he'd been fired out of a circus cannon, his
legs in the air and arms akimbo, flailing for purchase.
He skidded several feet, and his fleshy arms squealing on
the well-polished tiles of the hallway floor until he came
to a full stop.

For roughly a second, the hallway was silent. All traffic
and conversation halted, and every neck craned to find
the source of the commotion near the doors. Mortified
beyond repair with the result of my actions, I began to
pick myself up and assess the situation. The crowd looked
at me, and then looked down at Bobby on the floor, and
then looked at me again, their eyes and faces filled with
shock, disgust and righteous fury. The situation couldn't
have appeared any worse to an onlooker unfamiliar with

my quiet rivalry with Bobby, which, because of my inability to describe the events before this happened, was everybody in the school. As far as they were concerned, I'd just beaten up a developmentally challenged person.

Just as I opened my mouth to protest what I knew everybody was thinking and salvage what was left of my good name, Bobby began to cry.

"A A A U U U U G G H H H H H H ! ! ! AUUUGGGHHHHH!!! WHYYYY?!?!"

His peals for help echoed through the hallway, cutting off any chance I might have had for explanation or redemption. Several students came to Bobby's rescue, lifting him off the ground and checking his body for wounds. When he was deemed unharmed, all eyes veered to the assailant, whose hands were raised in the air as if the police had drawn guns on him.

"I can't believe you just did that" Came from one student.

"You are a fucking scumbag, dude" Came from another.

"You think you're tough or something? I should kick the shit out of you right here" Came from a football player who could have easily folded me like an accordion and played a song of my agonized screams through the halls.

Defeated, embarrassed, guilt ridden and afraid for my well-being, I side-stepped members of the mob hoping I could escape to the sanctuary of my next class when I saw Natalie standing at the scene of the crime.

My heart thrummed with teenage excitement when I registered that it was the first time I'd made eye contact with Natalie since I first noticed her in the gym that day. She looked beautiful, as she always did, and despite reeling with the anxiety that comes from earning the title of your school's newest pariah, the sight of her restarted the motor of my courage. I was going to ask her out, right then and there.

Then I noticed she was standing with her arms folded across her chest, shaking her head disapprovingly and scowling at me as if I'd just assaulted a special needs student, which apparently I had. My newly revving courage motor started backfiring and sputtering as she turned and walked away, and completely stalled out when I heard her tell a fellow student "That kid is such a piece of shit."

My dream of dating Natalie died right there on the floor, right next to the scratch-and-sniff pencils that had fallen out of Bobby's pockets.

The Pee Pee Haircut

—⚶—

THE SUMMER OF MY SEVENTEENTH year, we were fully stocked up with booze, Penthouse magazines and illegal fireworks, all courtesy of Pete's mom. The plan was to have as casual of a get together as teenagers could possibly have when given unlimited resources and a virtual guarantee that you wouldn't have to call your mother from jail.

As the sun was going down, I was sitting on the trunk of my car with a beer, waiting for Pete to come home. The first time I met Pete's grandmother, she asked me to pull my rusted '87 Buick Regal up to the garage on the left, hidden by the shrubs so "The police wouldn't think she was being robbed by drug-addled rapists." Instead of incurring the wrath of the Ring Wraith if she decided to come home early, I parked in that shaded, secluded corner of the drive every time.

About an hour later, Pete's Dodge Caravan slid into the gravel driveway with Biggie's "Hypnotize" bumping on a pair of blown speakers. Pete stepped out with two of the sluttiest girls I had ever seen, slathered in makeup and clothing that I could only imagine came off of a rack on the back lot of Pretty Woman. They introduced themselves, and walked right into the house to grab drinks. Pete and I stayed in the driveway smoking cigarettes, and I asked him who the strange girls were.

"Dude, I saw them at the beach. I talked to them for about three minutes, told them that I had a mansion on the beach, and they said that if they were invited that they would fuck everyone at the party!"

"Awesome...wait, what? What are you talking about?"

"I'm telling you Mikey, they mean it. Trust me."

Shocked but completely fascinated, I walked into the house where the girls were already mingling with Brendon and Timmy, sipping on some hastily mixed Mr. Boston's Cape Cods in red Solo cups. Pete was notorious for inflating the value of things like the "perfect skate spot nobody knows about" and throwing gold spray painted Mercedes hubcaps on his minivan, so I laughed his promise of sexual party favors off and forgot all about them. Before you knew it, drinking games had begun, music started to play, people filled up the driveway with cars; we had a decent little shindig on our hands.

Once the word got out, a whole bunch of girls from surrounding towns arrived, which as a horny teenager I was thrilled about, but I could not stop watching the two girls Pete had brought to the house, staring intently to see what they were going to do. I still didn't believe Pete.

I just could not rationalize in my head that there were girls my age that did shit like that, aside from my teenage masturbatory fantasies, of course.

A few of us and the two girls, who I will now refer to as Cindy and Mary, headed to an upstairs bathroom to smoke some weed. Upon Pete shutting the door, one of the ladies spoke up.

Cindy: "Tee hee, so when do we get this shit started fellas?"

I rummaged through my pockets. "I have a lighter."

"No, not that." Cindy dismissed me for Pete. "Are you guys ready to party or what?!"

Pete threw his hands up like he was waiting to catch a beach ball at a concert. "Hell yeah!! This is going to be awesome!"

"I'm ready to get wild with you boys right now. So how much are you going to pay us?"

Cindy put her thumbs through Pete's belt loops and began gyrating against his body.

I stopped fumbling though my pockets and stared at my shoes, because I honestly didn't know what else to do. I was wrong about everything. Pete had not only found the skankiest girls on York Beach, he had found the skankiest seventeen-year-old prostitutes. I had no idea that there were girls my age that actually accepted money for sex, let alone in New England. That was big city shit, as far as I knew. Big city shit for adult women. I might have been a horny little devil who would rub his dick raw to a paused recording of

Kiana's Flex Appeal, but their willingness to fuck for money threw my undeveloped little sensibilities for a loop.

The fact that they were so ready to do the things we only dreamed about and saw in the magazines Pete's mom bought us was entirely fascinating to me. Unfortunately, Cindy had an amazing ass, but no tits and a killer set of peach fuzz mutton chop sideburns. Mary was a redhead with an entirely average face and body, but looked like she would suck an antelope dry for bus fare. If I've discovered anything about myself in my lifetime, it's that I'm an expert in gift horse dentistry.

The question of payment remained unanswered, and nobody wanted to give these girls any money. None of us had any money anyway. Pete lived in the east coast equivalent of the Playboy Mansion, but it wasn't like his grandmother was shelling out an allowance. There was a long, awkward pause.

Out of nowhere, a huge, generally feared Senior from my high school who actually beat me up a year prior because I once made out with his girlfriend before he even met her popped into the bathroom unannounced, checkbook in tow.

Bully: "Here you go, here's a check for $30,000. Split it between the two of you. My only stipulation is that you both have to get naked and walk around the party completely naked for the rest of the night. Deal?"

He handed the check over without even cracking a smile.

Cindy was elated. "Fuck yeah! You got it! For this kind of money we'll stay all weekend!!"

What kind of knuckle-dragging mouth breathers would accept a check for $30,000 from an eighteen-year-old boy, you might ask? These two, that's who.

My jaw dropped wide open. Mary quickly snatched up the check, and before you knew it they both started getting naked in front of us while we smoked weed and watched. I felt like I was an extra in the movie Kids. I turned to the bully, who just one year ago had spit in my face and slapped the shit out of me. He just smiled and winked, motioning with his head for me to watch the show.

Once completely naked, the amateur hookers each grabbed one of my friends. Cindy grabbed the bully and headed to the bathroom while Mary and Timmy started making out and fondling each other right in front of the rest of us.

I couldn't hold it in anymore; I started laughing so hard that I actually had to stifle a few puke burps. This was the funniest thing I had ever seen unravel in front of my eyes. I decided not to hang around and possibly catch a glance of one of my buddies' erections, so I made my way downstairs to drink more.

Once downstairs, I managed to tell a handful of people what had happened before I got dragged into a whiskey shot competition with a mix of public and private school kids. Eight shots and some toilet time later,

I rinsed my mouth out and headed outside to smoke a cigarette. Once there, I ran into Brendon and immediately told him about the goings on in Pete's room.

"So they're just fucking everybody, for no reason."

"I think that's the gist of it."

"And the senior who beat you up because you defiled his freshman girlfriend used a check to pay for it."

"Yep. That's the long and short of it."

"You know he was bragging about how he found a checkbook on the side of the road the minute he walked in here, right?"

"Well it wasn't like I thought a senior at our high school who drives a '92 Volkswagen Golf could toss $30,000 around like a Koosh ball."

That's when the un-oiled gears of teenage ingenuity screeched to a halt. He had just committed check fraud paying for seventeen-year-old whores. For some reason that felt worse to me than paying for seventeen-year-old whores with cash. I immediately felt pangs of disgust and resentment about the whole situation, but I couldn't say anything. Had I spilled the beans to Lolita 1 and Lolita 2, I would have reduced myself to social pariah status among my peers. Was the burden of this lie supposed to rest on me? All I wanted to do was drink with my friends, and all of a sudden I had been unwittingly dragged into a brothel rife with financial deviants.

I was an awkward teenager, unable to control or understand the emotions and ideas that come with being drunk. Maybe the whole situation made me uncomfortable, but I didn't want to leave either; I was drunk at a party with my best friends - one of the greatest feelings a teenager can have. It's freedom. Liberation. You're socializing. You are doing something that you are not supposed to be doing with your peers. More specifically, you are being seen doing something that you are not supposed to be doing by your peers, which in turn solidifies your social standing. It is truly a defining part of growing up.

Nevertheless, I felt dirty, and the only solution my drunk seventeen-year-old brain could pump out to rectify the situation was to act out against it.

"We need to fuck with those girls somehow, Brendon."

"Duuuuude, just let them get passed around the party, maaaan." By the end of his cigarette, Brendon's eyes were at half-mast. He was wasted.

"Dude, no way. I am going to fuck with them. Are you going to help me?"

One thing about Brendon is that he buckles under peer pressure like the floorboards under a Lane Bryant fitting room.

"...I guess. Ok."

Brendon and I walked back inside, and sure enough, Mary was in the kitchen pounding Red Label out of the bottle and groping stranger's crotches. This would be our target.

We watched her saunter out the kitchen door and into the backyard like a crippled kid who lost her polio crutches, only to plop down on the grass, totally annihilated, half naked and giggling. Brendon and I snuck up behind her like a pair of drunken ninjas.

When you've known someone for a long time, you don't have to necessarily say something to say something. A look, a hand gesture, even a certain exhale of breath can convey a message. Brendon and I looked at each other, and our teenage boy brains knew exactly what we were thinking without saying a word.

We were going to pee on her.

We both unzipped our pants and got ready. One... two...three...

I saw Brendon let loose a stream of urine splashing directly onto her back, soaking a good portion of her hair.

"Ughhhh...what's warm?" Mary sluggishly acknowledged the rank yellow fluid splashing all over the back of her head and neck.

I started laughing, which propelled the piss out of my dick even faster. It hit her right arm only for a moment before she started getting up. For some reason, my reflexes made me feel like it was important to not get caught urinating on a teenage hooker, so I turned around and pretended that I was pissing in a bush the whole time.

"What was that? It's all warm and stinky..." Mary asked while her drunken eyes fluttered like moth wings in a drizzle.

Brendon was immediate in his response. "Oh don't worry, that was just a Super Soaker. You should probably go back inside and grab a drink."

I don't know how that worked, but it did. By some miracle, Mary found her footing and Franken-walked back into the party to troll for more cock.

After laughing about having urinated on a living human being for roughly twenty minutes, Brendon and I headed back in as well. We didn't tell anyone about what we had just done in the hopes that someone else would fool around with a girl that was unintentionally marinating in our collective piss. Nobody in the kitchen was talking about a sloppy girl who reeked of pee stumbling by them so we assumed that the coast was clear.

Timmy spotted Cindy, who was standing in the kitchen naked as a jaybird, looked over at me, smiled and walked her outside. It had been about two hours since the girls had arrived, and as a team they must have fucked at least six or seven guys. Mary, who we had just relieved ourselves on, was nowhere in sight.

The topic of conversation in the room had shifted to whether or not I could pound an entire 40 oz. bottle at once. Being Captain I'm-Seventeen-and-I-Can-Do-Anything, I accepted the challenge.

On the way to the bathroom to forcibly empty the contents of my innards, I noticed Mary, slumped over against the wall, still conscious...but barely. I don't remember seeing her drink, but I imagined that if I was a hooker I would rather be drunk than sober if I had to have public sex with [a roughly estimated] ten anonymous men. I closed the bathroom door and spewed forth an angry foam hurricane into the toilet.

The next thing I remember is being outside and alone on the porch, holding on to the railing and emptying the last ounce of bile from my body. When I finished, I had a seat, relished in my newfound spark of energy and lit a cigarette, only to begin to hear faint moaning coming from the rocks on the private beach that extended a bit past the backyard. I walked down a little way to investigate, and sure enough, it was Cindy on top of Timmy. Squinting to make the spins stop, I saw him put his clothes on and walk back towards the house. Cindy was still gloriously naked.

"You're next, right? I hope so, you're a cutie..."

My dick wanted me to say yes, but by brain overrode those instructions. "Uhhh...you make me uncomfortable."

"I'm getting mad dick here. I love it." She brought her hands to her pussy as she said this, and a waft of her musky femininity reached my nose.

"It's official - I am never having a daughter. Ever."

I questioned Timmy about what happened at the water. "You better have used a condom, man. Please tell me you used a condom."

Timmy was elated. "Fuck yeah man, of course I used a condom. She was on top the whole time 'cause I was lazy, but she was so dry that the condom broke. I got right up and told her to find me when she got wet again. She wasn't happy, dude."

Around 2:00 a.m., I had somehow gotten my ninth wind, and was drinking scotch in the mahogany-paneled library with a few of the rich, private school guys who were all pretending to be civilized adults. This was the awe inspiring moment in my life when I realized getting fucked up was the great equalizer between races, colors and creeds. Rich private school kids drank drams of spendy scotch, smoked weed and blew coke, and poor people drank dollar drafts, smoked weed and blew coke. I was having an absolute blast with people, who when sober, would have been entirely outside of my strata. What I learned in that room was that regardless of your place in life, you can identify and connect with another human being through a couple of drinks, and quite honestly, that's fucking amazing. I NEVER would have been able to have a conversation with those people otherwise, and God bless it. If you're an AA aficionado who's upset with this paragraph, I don't know what to tell you. I've never inked a business deal over milk and cookies.

My glorious spin on a utopian hyper reality was immediately dissolved when a couple of girls from the party walked into the library. One of them was very angry.

"Who the fuck is the girl in the sleeping bag upstairs? She's sitting up against the wall mumbling about who is going to fuck her next."

"Mary, probably." I spoke to my feet.

I was forced to explain to these newcomers what had transpired between the other partygoers and the teenage whores. As it turned out, these girls already knew care free, fuck-for-a-dollar Mary. Apparently, all of the guys these new girls had crushes on in school had fucked Mary at one point. One thing led to another, and the new girls convinced me to mess with Mary again, and probably because they were all the subject of more than one of my discombobulated teenage fantasies, so naturally I went with it.

We debated on what would be worse than peeing on Mary for some time. Someone thought of peeing on her again. Another thought of drawing on her with a permanent marker...and then someone came up with giving her a haircut.

Yes, that was much, much worse. Upstairs I went.

The small group of conspirators from the library and I had come up with an ingenious plan:

* Step 1) They would turn off the lights.
* Step 2) I would sneak over and cut Mary's hair.
* Step 3) Run away.
* Step 4) ???
* Step 5) Profit.

I forgot to grab scissors before I headed upstairs, so I ran back down into the kitchen to find a pair. Three minutes later, I had found nothing that remotely resembled scissors; However, I did find a rather dull, serrated steak knife. I was wasting time...this would have to do.

I ran back up the stairs and scanned the room quickly. Mary was still leaning against the wall, oblivious to the world around her. I noticed that her hair came down to the middle of her back. Everyone else had gathered around the light switch, awaiting me to acknowledge that I was ready. I look over to them, and the lights went off almost immediately.

I tiptoed over to Mary, and without hesitation despite my ingrained disgust in what I was doing, I squatted down, grabbed a handful of hair, and began sawing at it with the steak knife. It was barely cutting; the knife was just sliding back and forth over it. I had to bear down with a considerable amount of force to begin tearing through it. I kept sawing for about forty-five seconds, hastily cutting through half a handful.

"Whaaa...??! Who is that? What are you doing?" Mary was coming to. She began to squirm. I shot up like a lightning bolt, dropped the knife, and ran like hell towards the staircase, down the stairs, and into the kitchen where the majority of the party was hanging around, nervously laughing the entire way to mask my Kramer-esque entrance. I looked in my hand, and there was a clump of light-brown hair, about four inches in length.

The people in the kitchen listened to me tell them what I had just done upstairs while I was hunched over, holding my knees and panting after sprinting for what seemed like forever. Once I finished my story, the entire kitchen roared with laughter and applause. I was a hero. I had just peed on a prostitute that had been compensated with a bad check, given her a haircut with a steak knife...and I was a hero in the eyes of my peers.

I wanted to laugh with everyone, but I couldn't. I didn't know what to think of myself. I just kind of stood there, getting patted on the back, holding the lock of hair, replaying the night in my head over and over. My stomach got queasier every time I got to the part with the steak knife. Everyone kept laughing. I was mad at myself for what I did; I was genuinely upset, something that I wasn't used to feeling, but I was discovering that I was even more upset with the crowd for approving of it. I mean, how could they? What I did was disgusting. I wanted to project my self-loathing on the people around me, but I knew that wasn't possible - I was the only bad guy in the room. I felt like I was about to have an anxiety attack.

I left the kitchen, went back upstairs, drank what was left in a bottle of cheap vodka and passed out, alone with my demons in one of the mansion's empty bathtubs.

I woke up around noon with a staggering headache. Crawling out of the bathtub and into the living room,

I saw unconscious bodies scattered everywhere; some clothed, some not. My first thoughts were of the whore twins from the night before. After briefly scanning the room I saw no sign of the pair, and I wasn't about to take the chance of being spotted by one of them by lounging around.

Seeing a chance to escape, I ducked outside and raced home as fast as my jalopy would take me. I hugged my mom hello, cleaned my room without her asking me to, and nervously filled out college applications for the rest of the weekend. I wasn't accepted to any of the colleges I applied to that day, and as strange as it sounds, that string of crushing failures made me feel like I had somehow made good on a cosmic debt I incurred that night.

The Jamaican
Clambake Debacle

—⟶⟶—

I SMOKED MY FIRST JOINT with my father. I was thirteen years old, and had accidentally walked in on him as he was firing one up in Pop Pop's workshop several minutes before dinner was slated to be ready. At first he attempted to hide it behind his back, but after realizing how futile it would be considering how small the workshop was and how little the smoke smelled like his cigarettes, he handed it to me and said "Shut up about this and I'll give you a hit." Better parenting through botany, I suppose. I took the skinny, smoldering joint from his fingers, brought it to my lips, inhaled and promptly began coughing like a tuberculosis patient for the next sixty seconds. He chuckled and slapped me on the back, shortly after stubbing the joint out and walking us both out of the workshop and toward the kitchen. I remember feeling elated after having performed what I regarded as a ritual of passage into adulthood. Most kids my age were trading baseball cards and getting their choice of flavored fluoride at the dentist's office. I was getting high with grown-ups.

Before Dad shared a joint with me that day, he had shared one with my sister after discovering her rummaging through his ashtray for roaches. Instead of getting mad at her, he rolled up a fresh joint and shared it with her, so she wouldn't have to reduce herself to pawing through stale cigarette butts for smokeable treasures like an extra in *Salaam Bombay*.

My first experience actually smoking wasn't my first experience with pot, however. Growing up, the bulk of my father's side of the family all smoked it recreationally and didn't see it as a thing to be ashamed of. I'm sure it's how I developed the bulk of my tolerant views on marijuana in American culture as an adult. I personally think the lives destroyed and the money wasted on the war against cannabis have made it one of the greatest American tragedies, and is something our great, great, great grandchildren will be ashamed of when they come across that chapter in their history books.

When it came to my father's side of the family, smoking a joint was as casual and acceptable as drinking a can of beer. Once when I was ten and visiting the house my brothers shared in Hyannis, they decided to have me play a prank on their then employer, who was known to secretly enjoy a toke here and there but never made it a public thing. They had him over for a few beers one night, and at the predetermined point of the evening, my brothers yelled "BONG BOY! PLEASE OFFER OUR GUEST REFRESHMENTS!" at which point I strolled out with a two foot glass bong which was packed and ready to go, along with a lighter, and handed it to their boss.

Imagine the look on his face; a ten year old boy handing a loaded bong to an adult out of nowhere. After a few seconds, my brothers couldn't stifle their laugher any longer, and everybody had a good laugh about it. I spent the next handful of years as "Bong Boy" for my brothers' parties, and would walk around with a fanny pack full of weed, packing bongs and bowls for tips.

When high school came around and my classmates were just beginning to delve into getting high, I already had a lifetime of experience with it. While freshmen were struggling with the basics of joint rolling, I was constructing honey dipped Garcia y Vega blunts and growing a couple plants in the loft of our garage using kitty litter and a roll of tinfoil, which I read about in a copy of The Anarchist's Cookbook I'd borrowed from a friend at school. While kids were out buying their first Cypress Hill albums and smoking bowls in the graveyard after dark, I was helping my brother to make pot infused pound cake, which made our ailing Pop Pop feel better in his last years (he may not have known exactly what was in it, but that didn't stop him from asking for "Magic cake" when his appetite wasn't good or his pain levels were high). I smoked socially with my friends my age, but I smoked more like an adult than like a kid, because it was already old hat to me. I was never compelled to finish a bowl "just because" or to light up in places that were rather conspicuous for the hell of it. I didn't get high every day or by myself. I was responsible with weed because I grew up learning how to be.

One afternoon when I was twenty, I got a call from my friend Micah asking me to come over to his apartment because he was having people over for a little mid-winter get together. "We're going to attempt a Jamaican clam-bake." I knew a "clambake" was just sitting in a closed up car or a room and smoking in it until it was totally cloudy with smoke, but I'd never heard of a Jamaican clam-bake before. I didn't want to let on as if I was clueless, so I just agreed to come over in a few hours. I was the guy that knew everything about weed, right? God forbid I wasn't the expert on something for five minutes.

I arrived at Micah's that evening, and there were about eight of our other friends already hanging out drinking. The shower was running, but Micah was hanging out with the guests. Still trying to figure out the whole Jamaican clambake mystery event without actually admitting I didn't know what it was, I cracked a beer and said hello.

Twenty minutes passed. The shower was still running, and steam started misting through the tiny space between the door and the carpet. Micah went into his room and emerged with a three- foot glass bong, a glass bowl, and a giant gorilla-finger sized blunt behind each ear. He then opened up the bathroom door, and told everyone to get in. All eight of us filed into the tiny bathroom, seven guys and one girl, and closed the door behind us, leaving us less room than a clown car. You couldn't see a damn thing in front of you because of the steam that had been collecting for roughly forty-five minutes.

Micah then told everyone to be quiet so he could address the group.

"Alrighty folks, this is it. The Triple-B Olympics. The events: Blunt, Bowl, Bong. You are not allowed to open the door for any reason. The hot steam from the shower will open up the capillaries in your lungs, allowing more THC to enter your bloodstream, getting you higher than normal. If you open the door, you are out of the bathroom for good. Last man standing wins. Let the games begin!"

I was intimidated by this immediately. Being half French Canadian, I don't take extreme heat and humidity well. I already had beads of sweat forming on my forehead from the sweltering rainforest-like atmosphere and I was having a hard time breathing. I liked to smoke, but not like that. Never like that. This was not my event, but it was too late to back out.

The first blunt was lit. I took my first pull, exhaled, and passed it to my left. I was surprised at how smooth it was going down; the steam really did make the smoke easier on my lungs than normal. The air quickly became heavily laden with the acrid, earthy smell of smoldering cannabis, adhering to the water molecules in the air, making every breath a hit in itself. The blunt came to me again. This time I took a bigger pull, expecting it to be as easy as the last. Sure enough, it was smooth and satisfying. After that one I was visibly high, and giggling at anything that came out of anyone's mouth. *How the hell am I going to finish this?* I was slightly worried, but that feeling dissipated shortly after the second blunt was finished.

The bowl: This glass instrument of torture had room for an exorbitant amount of the sticky-icky. While Micah packed it, I surveyed the situation: Everyone else was extremely high as well, which made me feel better about my own state of being. I was truly fucked up and I wanted out, but my legs had abandoned me and wouldn't listen to my brain. The only way I could stay focused on conversation was by staring at the tiled floor. Most of us had sweaters or hooded sweatshirts on when we first walked in, but by this point they were discarded on the bath mat.

I was sweating my ass off and in dire need of a glass of water - or better yet, a beer. My mouth was incredibly dry at that point, and I'm sure a cold beer would have tasted better than after having mowed the lawn on a hot summer day. The girl that was in the bathroom took the first pull off of the bowl, coughed bronchially, and passed it. After my turn I felt nauseous and overheated, with sweat beading on my upper lip, soaking the armpits of my t-shirt and turning the crotch of my boxers into an uncomfortable, bunched up wad of wet cloth. As soon as I was done, the girl, who was sitting at the edge of the bathtub, fell backwards into the running water, completely dehydrated and incoherent. Two of the guys picked her up and shoved her outside, quickly shutting the door afterwards. The cold, fresh air from the other room hit my face briefly, making the sticky, smoky air of the bathroom seem even thicker and more toxic.

At that point I could only look on. I was unable to move and my vision was starting to become nauseatingly staggered, like when you go to bed drunk and somebody flips the light switch on after only five minutes. I was beyond your garden-variety stereotypical paranoid high, and I had entered a state of "under-medicated schizophrenic high", if that is even possible.

The bowl was consumed by flame three times before the bong was brought out. Only four of us, including Micah, were left at that point. I could hear relieved laughter and the hiss of cold beers being opened in the living room. I was only wearing a wife-beater and boxers, and was glistening with thick, merciless sweat. It beaded up on my forehead, rolled into my eyes, slid down the bridge of my nose and dripped onto the crotch of my already sopping wet boxers. The hopes of making out people's faces and conjugating complete sentences had been abandoned entirely. I was retarded in every sense of the word.

I looked around again. Everyone else was down to their boxers. Four sweaty half-naked men sitting altogether way too close. This wasn't a Jamaican clambake; this was a Turkish bath house. The bong was passed to me. I filled the tube as thickly as humanly possible before releasing the carb.

I was done.

I started seeing quick flashes of light, and knew I was about to lose consciousness. I hadn't had a breath of fresh air in what seemed like a lifetime, and that was all I wanted at that point. The game was a stupid idea and I wanted out. I stood up, staggered towards the door, opened it, and was hit with what felt like a blast of the purest artic air imaginable. My knees gave out, and the side of my face hit the beige carpeting, rattling my teeth and sending up bright fireworks behind my eyes.

Unconsciousness covered me like a flight attendant on the red-eye.

I came to sitting on the couch upright with a plate of Chinese food on my lap. I squinted (well, not squinted - my eyes were as Chinese as the food in front of me) at who was sitting around me as I began piecing things together. Everyone was still there, staring blankly at an infomercial on the television and shoveling food into their mouths. Somebody was throwing up in the bathroom, but I didn't know who.

"Whaaaaat the faaaaaack happennnnned?!Who won?!" I rubbed my bleary, bloodshot eyes and spoke without moving my head from the television screen.

Micah, typically one of the more reserved out of our group, responded with a mouthful of boneless spare ribs. "Duuuuuuuude, you passed out mannnn. What a fucking Nancy boy lightweight."

"Who got the Chinese?! How did this get on my lap? Wait, I just asked you who won...who won?!" Not seeing any silverware, I picked up a fistful of pork fried rice and shoveled it into my mouth.

"Oh, we all gave up after you passed out on the floor. It was a three-way tie."

You have got to be fucking kidding me.

My stomach knotted up and churned violently. I tried to ignore the burning pain in my gut and join the other stoners falling in love with Ron Popeil, but the more I tried to stay focused, the more the pain in my stomach amplified. When a considerable amount of pressure hit my sphincter and tested my ability to hold it in, I set my plate aside and shot into the bathroom.

I dropped my pants and still soaking wet boxers down to my ankles, and straddled the cold toilet seat, hoping that getting it all out would make me feel better. I had my elbows on my knees hunched over on the toilet, so I could study the tiles on the bathroom floor as my bowels let loose a violent torrent of muddy soup with the force of a fire hydrant that had been struck by a drunk driver. I started to relax, taking deep breaths and collecting my-self. *Ugh, starting to feel normal again. Good. I just want to go home.*

That's when the tiles started moving. Not due to a trick of the eye or that staggered, drunk vision; they were moving themselves around like one of those sliding square puzzle games you can buy in souvenir shops. Up and down, side to side. I gnashed my teeth as my eyes fol-lowed the moving tiles. Faster and faster they went.

Holy shit. I'm tripping.

Sometime before this incident, I was flipping through an issue of High Times magazine at a local bookstore. I read that smoking pot could make you trip, as marijuana was actually classified as a hallucinogen, but you either had to be a very inexperienced smoker, or be an experi-enced smoker who just smoked a bale of the dankest weed by himself to make it happen. I was no stranger to getting high, but not in that quantity, and I was certainly not used to smoking that much of the potent strain Micah was loading us up with in his bathroom.

I glanced towards the towel on the wall; it was waving like a windsock on a yacht. I closed my eyes, hoping that when I reopened them I would be sober and happy again. I reopened them, and a wave of nausea slammed into the center of my chest. I had to throw up right then and there, but murky water was still pulsing out of my asshole like a severed artery.

Thinking fast, I switched my seating so I was on the toilet side-saddle while throwing up in the sink, evacuating my insides from both ends. I was always good at multitasking.

And with that, darkness took over once again.

—ᨈ—

Bang bang bang

"Mikey, did you die in there?!"

bangbangbangbangbangbang

"Hey, we're going to the Tiki Bar, come on, let's go!"

B A N G B A N G B A N G B A N G B A N G BANGBANGBANG

I came to once again, in the same position with my head resting on the refreshingly cool porcelain sink. The faucet was still running. Globs of partially digested fried rice floated mingling with phlegm spun on the surface of the collecting water. The air in the bathroom smelled like a campfire somebody put out by taking a shit on it.

I pulled my pants up and staggered back into the living room. I was scared. My heart was beating a mile a minute, I couldn't breathe regularly, and nobody could notice the panicked look in my eyes because they were too stoned to get their winter jackets on, let alone judge someone else's state of being. I was in a room full of people, but I was all alone. Tripping my face off.

We arrived in downtown Portsmouth. Micah and everyone we were with filed into the Tiki Bar except for me... the door guy wouldn't let me in because I was several months away from my twenty-first birthday. I yelled for my friends, but they were too high, and the bar was too loud for them to hear me.

Fuck.

It was February in New Hampshire, the temperature was in the low teens, I had no car or any way to get home (at that point I lived about ten miles away), I had no money on me whatsoever, my cell phone was dead, and I was high. Not just high, tripping, staggering around in my own little scary dream world with my fists nervously balled up, and I just wanted it to stop.

I started stumbling through the streets trying to make out people's faces in the hopes that I would see someone I knew who could give me a ride home, but they were all jumbled and disfigured to me. The situation was so dire that I started laughing as a reflex to it, as if the recesses of my brain were trying to keep me from losing my mind. I started laughing maniacally and loudly. Pedestrians looked at me like I was some crazed vagabond who had just stepped away from huffing paint thinner to find a bush to take a dump in. My eyes were tearing up from the savagely cold winter wind bombarding me, and the wetness was starting to freeze to the side of my face.

Maybe I should start walking home; I could make it in a couple of hours. What the fuck was I thinking, smoking that much. Mike, you are never smoking weed ever again. I still don't know whether I was thinking that or talking out loud to myself.

"Mikey, what are you doing wandering around here? Your lips are purple. How long have you – wait, how fucked up are you?"

By the grace of some unexplainable cosmic convergence tipped in my favor, my best friend Timmy was standing in front of me on the sidewalk. He was en route to go grab a coffee, and we somehow managed to run into each other. Before that moment, I hadn't seen Timmy for over a week. I don't know what I would have done if I hadn't run into him that night. To this day, this moment in time is one of the reasons why I classify myself as agnostic and not as a stalwart atheist.

"I am tripping. It's bad. I'm too fucked up to talk. The guys went to the bar and left me out here. I don't know how long I've been out here. I can't see your face. I can't see anyone's face. Get me the fuck out of here. Do you have food?"

We got into his car and started driving to his parents' house. My stiff, frozen hands subconsciously massaged the heating vents in the dashboard as I filled Timmy in on the night's events as they unfolded in my head, and he just laughed at me. I didn't understand what was so funny about what had happened, but I didn't argue. The ethereal glowing contrails produced by oncoming headlights in the opposite lane distracted me from all rational thought and conversation for the rest of the ride.

Once inside Timmy's place, I consumed an entire box of oversized Cheez-Its, and promptly passed out sitting up on his couch with my winter coat zipped up and my shoes still on.

When I woke up the next morning, I was still extremely stoned, albeit at a level that was significantly more manageable than the night before, and could be driven home without fear of my mother thinking my brain was permanently damaged due to an undetected radon leak in our house. It did take me a few days to feel normal again, though.

It's been twelve years since I was a regular pot smoker, and I'd be lying if I said I didn't miss it sometimes. I'll be at a friend's summer barbeque or New Year's Eve party when a bowl full of the latest and greatest Canadian super strain gets passed around, and feel left out when somebody gestures to hand it my way, and I shake my head no. There's a social aspect to smoking weed that's a lot like smoking cigarettes. People who share the experience also share a largely unspoken bond with each other, and while smoke free folks aren't necessarily deemed as "Outsiders" (I never felt that way when I'm around my smoking friends), I've found there is a slight, barely perceivable disconnect between those that do and those that don't.

Anytime I entertain the thought of what it would be like to rejoin my ilk and accept that blunt the next time it's handed to me, I'm immediately nauseated. It's like when a father catches his underage son smoking cigarettes, and makes the boy huff down an entire carton at once to teach him a lesson. That's how weed is for me as a thirty-four-year-old man, regardless of how thoroughly I was groomed for it (ironically enough, almost all the smoking members of my father's side of the family have also given it up at the time of this writing). Most pot smokers associate the act with relaxing after a long day of work, as a social lubricant or as a ritual performed before a large, intricate meal. I unfortunately associate it with scrambled human faces, bathroom tiles scurrying around under their own propulsion, and firing half chewed gobs of bile soaked Chinese food out of my nose, and so I am forever cursed to live among the non-Irie.

POST SCRIPT: The aftermath of Micah's pot party is noteworthy enough to mention, as the colossal amount of pot we smoked in his bathroom was sucked up through the steam vent above the shower, and managed to make all three floors of his apartment building smell like Willie Nelson's tour bus. Several of his neighbors complained about it the following day. Micah narrowly escaped an eviction notice, but ended up moving into a nice house just outside of town in Kittery, Maine, where he could smoke without fear of reprisal. Rumor has it that to this day, if you turn the vent fan on in that old apartment's bathroom, it still smells like a little dwarf is smoking a little dwarf spliff in the exhaust pipe.

The Etymology of KungFu Mike

—ɯ—

THE FALL LEAVES CRUNCHED UNDER our ratty skate sneakers as Seth and I stepped out of his brother's maroon '87 Jetta, war-torn skateboards in hand.

Every Friday afternoon when we were fifteen, we would hit Seth's brother up for a lift to the Hong Kong Ramps; a secret skate spot we built in the parking lot of an abandoned factory. The factory sat behind Hong Kong Express, a less than sanitary Chinese restaurant. Young skaters fashioned the park together out of stolen and scavenged wood from construction sites. Ramps were held together with as many screws as we could afford with our collectively saved lunch money. The majority of the ramps and boxes we built were anything but sturdy, patches of grass had forced their way through gaping cracks in the aging pavement, and you could only skate as long as the sun offered illumination.

The city of Portsmouth was just beginning to enforce its long-ignored ban on skateboarding. This left the local kids who couldn't drive to legitimate skate parks with two options; either skate in the street and risk getting their boards confiscated by local fuzz, or skate at the Hong Kong Ramps, which were completely hidden from Big Brother by trees and empty commercial property. It was less than perfect, but it served its purpose as a sanctuary for youth being persecuted for participating in a sport that elderly town officials refused to acknowledge as legitimate.

The Hong Kong Ramps were empty that afternoon, save for a group of several unfamiliar guys and girls. They looked like they were roughly our age, and were wearing classic New England fall clothing; sweatshirts, fleece vests, jeans and light jackets. They didn't quite look like jocks, but they weren't exactly skate punks or wiggers. They looked like kids in high school that just blended in with everyone else in the hallways. They were sitting on one of the better-constructed grind boxes, not a skateboard among them.

Seth and I were a little confused as to how people we didn't know managed to infiltrate our secret skate lair. We went about our ritual warm up, rolling up and down the ramps until we felt confident enough to really kick it up, and decided how we were going to position ramps so we could execute new tricks we had been working on in our driveways during the school week. Every time I skated by the group of strangers I would take a quick look at them, taking care not to be noticed. Fights broke out at Hong Kong Ramps pretty frequently. Two of us and seven of them weren't great odds if a scrap broke out over something as small as a perceived shitty look.

The second or third time I looked over I noticed there were actually eight of them, and a grungy homeless looking man was also among their ranks. I also noticed that there were a few cases of Natural Ice resting on one of our grind boxes. Putting two and two together, I deduced that the homeless guy bought the kids beer, and they were hanging out at the park so they could slug them back in relative privacy. A few more passes by the group led me to believe they were all pretty drunk, partly from the stench of shitty beer wafting off of them, partly because the lion's share of their words were slurred.

I was practicing nollie backside heelflips on a forty-five degree bank, and Seth was angrily pushing back and forth by the kids on the box, hoping they would move so he could use it for what is was intended for. Seth wasn't the kind of kid that would just go up to people he didn't know and ask them for something and I could see the exasperation in Seth's face. I totally understood it. There's nothing more annoying than people sitting on shit you're looking to skate on or over. The fact that we only had a couple hours of useful daylight before it got dark made this particular skate spot etiquette infraction obnoxious, but tack on the fact that total strangers were blocking us from using ramps we built, and it became downright unbearable. I kept on skating, Seth kept on pushing, and the group of strange kids kept on drinking.

An hour into our session, Seth and I ended up at the top of a ramp together for a smoke break. Back then, we would share a pack of Marlboro Reds that we stole from a local convenience store. We would smoke maybe one or two cigarettes a weekend at most, so the pack would last us a month, maybe longer. I pulled a bent cigarette out of the tattered hard pack, and lit it using a book of matches. Seth and I whispered to each other under heavy, labored breath about the weird kids at our park.

"Who the crap are these goons, Mike? Do you know them?" Seth grabbed the cigarette from my hand and took a drag. I was the most social in the group, and Seth was home schooled. It was a valid question. The kids got louder and more animated as we talked.

"I sure don't. Don't they have somewhere else to drink? If the cops close the ramps down because those guys are being idiots, I'm going to be piss—"

That's when we both saw the homeless man turn around, cock his arm back, and punch one of the girls right in the face.

She fell, knocked senseless enough that she didn't even bring her hands up to stop her head from hitting the pavement. The homeless man immediately jumped on top of her. The drunk kids made a half circle around the melee, frozen in terror. Seth and I were frozen too. Sure, we saw plenty of fights growing up, but this was different. This was a grown up beating a child; a little girl no less, right in front of us. We were just a couple of little dudes with skateboards.

The girl was dazed. She didn't scream at first. Her arms lazily fought off the homeless man, who was tearing at her clothes, and forcing his hands up her sweatshirt. Her nose was bleeding. The kids standing around the girl and the homeless man yelled and screamed at him to stop and to go away. They would have overpowered him if all seven of them swarmed him at once, but they didn't. I could see it in their eyes; nobody wanted to be the first one to get hit. The homeless man was at least twice the size of everybody at the skate park. The girl started crying, then she started screaming. We built the Hong Kong ramps in that location was so nobody could hear us and kick us out. Nobody could hear any of her screams. Everything was in slow motion. We all stood there and watched.

"Seth, we have to do something. We can't just stand here. Dude, what do we do?" My muscles felt like they were going to rip through my skin and I could feel my asthma kicking in.

"I'm not doing anything. I'm staying right here."

"We can't...you can't..." I looked at him and saw the fear in his eyes. It was the same fear he saw in mine. I was currently paralyzed by it.

"I'm not going anywhere near that, dude. I'm leaving. We need to get out of here and find help."

"NO! DON'T! Don't leave, dude. Don't leave. Please."

There was no way that Seth was going to find an adult quickly enough. By the time someone got there, it would have been too late. One of the drunk kids tried kicking the homeless man. He got him right in the ribs. The man looked at the kid, and the kid vanished into the trees that surrounded the park. The bum continued to wrestle the girl, intermittently rubbing his crotch to get hard when she would pause, exhausted.

"Stay right here. If I start getting fucked up, come and get me."

"Um, yeah. Sure." The way he said it, I knew Seth wasn't going to come get me.

I ran over to the fray with my skateboard raised above my head. The girl and the homeless man were rolling around on the ground, and I couldn't get a clear shot in. The last thing I wanted to do was wail that poor chick in the face with my deck. I stood there for what felt like an hour, waiting for the perfect opportunity. I could hear the kids behind me screaming. "HIT HIM! COME ON, MAN! OH MY GOD!!! WHAT ARE YOU WAITING FOR?! FUCKING HIT HIM!!! PLEASE!!!"

I looked down and I didn't know if I even had it in me to hit the guy. I knew what he was doing was wrong and I knew he needed to be stopped, but I doubted my ability to make that happen. I've never been so scared in my life.

What am I doing? If I don't hurt this guy bad, I'm going to get my ass kicked at the very least. This guy could kill me. He's a homeless dude. He could have a knife, a broken bottle, anything. He's going to kill me if I try anything. What would I do against that? Maybe Seth is right. Maybe we should get help. I'm just a kid.

The bum rolled on top of the girl one more time, exposing his back to me.

Do it. Do it now.

DO IT NOW.

CRACK!!!

I held my skateboard by the trucks, swung the board over my shoulders, and drove it into the homeless man's upper back as hard as my little arms could. Instead of the hollow thud I expected to hear, a loud cracking noise followed. The man arched his back in pain, and let out a gurgling, silent scream, the only sound you can really make when the wind has just been knocked out of you.

He got to his knees, his arms flailed behind him in an attempt to reach the spot on his back that my skateboard connected with. The girl was still between his legs, wiggling her way out slowly. I struck again, this time swinging my skateboard like a baseball bat right into his lower back. The man collapsed onto his side and the girl got up and ran to her friends.

I positioned myself over to the man and plunged my deck tail-first into the side of his head like a jackhammer. Stunned, the bum covered his head with his hands and curled into a fetal position. I knew I had to keep hitting him. I couldn't let him get up. If I did, we were all fucked.

This is the part that I really don't remember too well. I remember crushing my skateboard into his back over and over again. Every third or fourth hit, I would hear that snapping sound again. I don't remember how many times I hit him. Everything just kind of went white. I remember the man trying to crawl away, seeing everybody looking on and screaming, but I don't remember what they were screaming. I definitely remember not knowing where Seth was, and abandoning my skateboard for a rusty dirt shovel laying by the entrance of the park and beating it against the man's head. He kept trying to crawl towards the trees and I kept hitting him. He was bleeding out of his head, back, arms and hands.

Finally, he sprung up in a last ditch effort to escape, and leaped into the trees that blocked us from the main road, disappearing from sight. I stood there for a while staring at the hole in the trees that he bolted through, still gripping the shovel. I finally turned towards Seth. He hadn't moved an inch from the ramp we were standing on.

I walked up to the group of kids. The girl was in the middle of them with her arms wrapped around herself.

She was staring at the ground and kind of swaying from side to side. Wet and dry blood matted the area underneath her nose. Her friends just stared at her, not even knowing what to do. I took off one of my t-shirts (I always wore two, so one of them would mop up my pubescent armpit stains), moistened it with the only drink I had - a bottle of Snapple pink lemonade - and cleaned her face up as best as I could.

"Are you OK?"

"I think so. My nose hurts a lot, but that's the worst of it, I think."

"Yeah, it might be broken. I'm not sure, though."

"What's your name?" The girl finally lifted her head up and looked at me. I remember her being pretty.

"I'm Mike. My friend over there is Seth. This is our skate park. How did you guys find this place? Are you from around here?"

The girl looked down again. Everyone else in her group looked around, anywhere else but at me directly. After a few seconds, the girl finally looked up at me and answered.

"We're from the Odyssey House."

The Odyssey House is a halfway house for troubled teens. Back then, it was in the town of Hampton which is about ten miles away from downtown Portsmouth. I remembered hearing stories about bad kids from school getting sent there and never coming out. It was like a black hole for bullies, depressed drama club cutters, and idiots with angry parents that couldn't do the bad shit every other kid their age did without getting caught. Moms and dads would drop the name of the Odyssey House when threatening their kids over doing their homework, or taking out the trash. Everybody knew what the Odyssey House was. I always pictured Odyssey House residents to look like Edward Gorey characters. These kids looked almost completely normal, besides them being drunk and one of them covered in blood.

"How did you get out?"

One of the group, a guy around my age with red hair and freckles, stepped up to answer. "We snuck out early this morning, yo. It's really not as hard as everyone makes it out to be. We hit the train tracks and just started walking until we ran into that bum. He said he would buy us beer if he could drink some with us. We didn't think he would ever..." He trailed off as he thought about what happened. I think the gravity of the situation was just starting to offset his shock.

"Alright, what are you guys going to do? Are you going to keep running or are you going to go back? Either way, she needs to see a doctor."

"We want to go back, dude. We just want to go back. We didn't think that anything like this would happen if we got out. What should we do?" Everyone nodded their heads in unison.

I handed the girl my shirt so she had something to blot her nose with, slung her arm over my shoulder and carried her a mile and a half to the Portsmouth Police Station. Seth and the Odyssey House runaways trailed a few steps behind. Once there, I waved goodbye and left. I didn't want to stick around for a two reasons, one of them being that I didn't know what the cops would say about me beating up a homeless man with a skateboard, the other being that I didn't want to be the one who led the cops to the Hong Kong Ramps. Being a teenager was tough enough without being a narc. Seth and I walked back downtown and hung out until his brother picked us back up.

I was riding home on the school bus the following week, when a kid that lived on my street in Stratham scooted down towards the back of the bus to talk to me. He was younger than me and went to the junior high. He and I didn't speak regularly.

"I heard about what you did last weekend."

"What?" I took a break from melting the back of a bus seat with a lighter. "What are you talking about?"

"You know, with that bum. You fucked him up big time."

Oh no, no no no. This isn't good. How did this happen? I'm in fucking Stratham. That's 10 miles from Portsmouth. "Um, how do you know about that, dude?" I could already picture what my room was going to look like at the Odyssey House; gray slate walls with white fingernail scratches around a barred windowsill.

"My dad's a big shot at the Portsmouth Police Department. Those kids mentioned your name to the officers on staff that night."

"...I'm in trouble, aren't I?"

"Nah! They were psyched. My dad wants to talk to you and give you some kind of award or something. You heard they caught the guy, right?"

"WHAT?! IS HE OK?!"

"Yeah, they found him lying on the sidewalk in front of Rite-Aid a few minutes after you dropped those kids off at the station. You broke a bunch of ribs in his back and his head was all fucked up. He couldn't walk or breathe too well. They say he's probably going to do a bunch of time." Rite-Aid was directly across the street from Hong Kong Express. I guess he didn't make it too far.

"How's the girl?"

"She's fine. They treated her at the hospital and then they all went back to that nut house. But yeah, you should stop by tonight and see my dad."

"Yeah, sure. Thanks for the heads up, man." I sunk into my seat and stared out the window as we neared my street, trying my best to take everything in.

I never ended up going to see that kid's dad, though. I didn't need any makeshift junior hero's award / generic ribbon with a fill-in-the-blank designation on the back that they were going to hand me for doing what any normal person should have done. I felt good enough as it was. The girl was OK, and the homeless guy was in the hands of the law. Even better, I wasn't in trouble, and the Hong Kong Ramps were safe. What a great ending to it all.

A few weeks later, Seth and I were walking around downtown with our skateboards, when a bunch of the older, tougher kids in town walked up to us. One of the biggest ones, Bobby, came up to me and shook my hand. I was nervous.

"What's up, little dude? I heard you wailed on some piece of shit rapist beggar with your skateboard the other day."

"You did?" I was just glad he didn't want to beat me up. Bobby was not only a huge, scary Greek guy who ran with the toughest crowd in town, he was a local legend, and well known for dispensing street justice with his gigantic fists. Smartly, Seth stared at his own feet.

"Yeah, everybody knows about that shit. That was awesome! You're alright."

"Thanks, man. It's no big deal. Anyone would have done the same thing if they were there."

"No way, dude. You fucking wrecked that guy. You're a tough little guy! You're name's Mike, right?"

I couldn't believe he knew my name. "Yeah! That's me."

"We're going to start calling you Karate Mike or something. Karate Mike; the toughest little skate rat in town!"

Anytime I saw those guys in town after that, they screamed "KARATE MIKE!" at me. It started to stick after a couple of weeks. Even my best friends started referring to me as Karate Mike instead of using my real name, the name they'd been calling me our entire lives, to differentiate me from other Mikes. "Which Mike is coming to the party? Oh, Karate Mike? Sounds good."

One day Bobby the Greek slipped up and called me "KungFu Mike" instead of Karate Mike, and ever since, I've been forced to tell this story at parties when drunk people inevitably ask me to do a spinning crane kick off the back deck into the pool.

POST SCRIPT: Six months after this incident, I ran into the girl from the Odyssey House at a local bowling alley. She gave me a huge hug and thanked me for doing what I did that day. She was living at her parents' house and going back to school again. She told me that the incident at the Hong Kong Ramps scared her straight. I was really glad to hear that. I have no idea where she is now, but I hope she's staying away from train tracks and Natural Ice.

An Even More
Unfortunate Halloween

—m—

MY ADULT LIFE HAS BEEN shaped largely in part by a need to compensate for things I didn't have growing up. I can easily connect the reason I regularly binge on unhealthy food to making up for Mom skipping the sugary kid cereals for Weetabix and All-Bran as a child, and the years in Wisconsin when I went without pretty much everything. I dress like a sixteen-year-old skateboard punk at thirty-four because I couldn't afford to dress like I wanted to when I was actually sixteen, and now that I can afford to create my own wardrobe (and because I work from a home office), I can regularly be found in a backwards hat, neon colored t-shirt and jeans instead of turtleneck sweaters and wrinkle-free Brooks Brothers button ups. It's not that I'm regressing back to a period when life was carefree and innocent as you would expect. These sophomoric cravings never had the chance to lose their luster for me, and I actively seek them out to fill a void most people my age aren't afflicted with. Of course, with that comes a level of scrutiny from the outside world that I can understand, but don't necessarily appreciate or wish to change myself because of.

The same can be said about my perpetual need to be showered with attention. Growing up as an awkward, friendless wonder until my early teens, I was deprived of childhood friendships, sleepovers and normal adolescent socialization that helps condition your average adult's behavior in social interactions. Once I got a taste of what is was like to be genuinely liked by my peers, I became addicted to it and did everything in my power to garner more of it. I began using humor to compensate for any physical, financial or social deficiencies a young adult spends so much time obsessing over, and it worked. Humor came easily to me and was something I learned to refine as a defense mechanism when faced with social anxiety. I quickly became the class clown, which I found made it possible to bridge the gaps between teenage cliques and become a quasi-diplomat that was able to gain acceptance from jocks, nerds, hippies, thugs, drama kids and any other caste within the walls of my high school. Everybody likes the funny guy.

Popularity through humor earned me friendships and relationships with women past college and early adulthood, gave my family something to focus on at holiday meals other than squabbling with each other, fueled my foray into the blogosphere when MySpace was still a thing people used and ultimately shaped my career as a writer, which is one of the most gratifying facets of my life. While I'm relatively happy with who I am as an adult and I'll shamelessly use the quote "if you like where you are on the mountaintop, don't hate the path that took you there" to justify the means, it is impossible to deny the fact that my wanton use of humor to ceaselessly draw attention to myself has also gotten me into a lot of trouble over the years.

When I was in my 20s, I used to wear silly hair metal costumes for Halloween. So easy - wig, tight jeans...it's the easiest low-budget get-up going, and girls somehow found it attractive. Well, at least drunk girls at a Halloween party found it attractive. If I got out of control drunk and started breaking furniture, I wasn't being an asshole; I was in character and method acting. It just worked. Back then, if I had to pray to a God, I would have prayed to the one that made sure women my age had big sisters with Mötley Crüe posters smeared with lip gloss above their beds growing up.

I was laid off from my job as an actuarial recruiter in October of 2005, and I was at home leisurely cruising around the Internet looking for a half-decent Kip Winger wig when I saw it - a vivid, clear-as-day picture that popped into my head out of nowhere that had me laughing so hard that the laughing turned into spastic coughing. The vision was glorious; it was perfection. I could barely contain myself as I started putting the pieces of the costume together in my bedroom. I didn't even notice the cardboard crust on the bargain basement generic frozen pizza burning in my oven. All I could think about was the costume. There would be no wig. There would be no spandex. There would be no Adidas high top wrestling sneakers. This year was going to be different. This year I was going to go as a special needs child.

Helmet? Check.

Undersized short sleeve button down shirt? Check.

Pants up to my nipples? Check.

As the deadline came closer, I kept coming up with new additions to the ensemble. I managed to save enough money before getting the axe so that I had a little cushion in the bank. The job market sucked and I was sick of shooting finely tailored resumes to unresponsive human resource departments. This was fascinating - not just the costume itself, but the thought of what people were going to think when they saw me in it. I had nothing against people with special needs, of course. This was more of a social experiment than anything else. Were they going to freak out and scream to me about their little special needs brothers and sisters at home? "THAT'S NOT FUNNY, MAN! MY BROTHER HAS TO WEAR A HELMET!!!" Would they burst into laughter and buy me shots? Would I be beaten half to death? At that point I didn't care. I was so deeply entrenched in the self-depreciating world of the young and unemployed, even the promise of an emergency room visit beat filling out mandatory state unemployment work search logs by a landslide. *I was going to feel like an unemployed degenerate, I might as well play the part with gusto.*

Teddy bear? Check.

Corrective shoes? Check.

Kiddie leash? Check.

The night of Halloween, I met up with Seth to go to a costume party at a local bar called Bananas that was going to close its doors permanently the following day, so the party was assumedly going to be wild. He took one look at my costume and fell over on the sidewalk laughing. He was scared that he wasn't going to be able to hook up with girls all night because of how I looked, and it took some convincing for him to walk down the street with me, let alone be seen with me at a bar. I had to stand on the sidewalk and persuade him to go through with it while pedestrians gawked and rushed their children past me.

As expected, Bananas was packed to capacity. Slutty nurses, slutty school girls, the occasional white guy in a lame pimp costume with accompanying lame felt pimp hat, slutty whores, a pair of meatheads dressed up as the Boondock Saints...picture any lame - o, unoriginal office Halloween party filled with lame - o, unoriginal coworkers. Now pick it up and move it into a dimly lit club setting. Voila; you're there with me.

I started getting noticed while I was plowing my way through the sea of store bought costumes towards the bar.

"Holy shit, that is hysterical!"

"What the fuck? Is he fucking serious?!"

"Man, fuck that kid. That shit is mean."

Their comments spanned the entire possible gamut before I had even gotten the bartender's attention. I asked for the strongest drink they made. I was so proud of my costume that I just had to celebrate.

Before long, Seth and I were annihilated. I had a new drink bought for me by a random stranger every time I put my glass down, and I only had time to drink them between high-fiving every third person that walked by and threatening anyone who dared look at me disapprovingly with John Basedow flex poses.

A random guy walked over to me during this point in the night and said, "Whoa brother, your costume is great! The more you drink, the more you're in character!"

That's when it hit me - this costume actually had the same benefits as the rocker costume. ***I was invincible.***

"I don't know about you, Seth...but I'm dancing. Yeah, let's dance the fucking shit out of these people."

Five minutes later, the once packed dance floor was all but cleared, and only a pack of Asian women remained in the corner huddled together. Seth and I, flailing around to the beat of some awful techno like a set of bath salt smoking whirling dervishes, inched our way closer and closer to the unsuspecting group while everyone on the sidelines pointed and laughed at us. Without warning, I started dry humping them. I was not even dancing at this point - I was literally pounding my crotch

against the ass of one of them with no rhythm whatsoever. They turned towards us, screamed and ran off of
the floor - all of them but the girl I was pantomime air
fucking - she stayed, and she backed that shit up.

She never looked at me; she just gyrated her cute
little Asian ass. She took my hands and began rubbing
them all over her hips, slowly moving up to her tiny
breasts. For a split second, I forgot why I was on the
dance floor in the first place, partly due to the crowd
having gone nearly silent with anticipation. We were
both grinding to the beat of the same awful techno
song, I was kissing her neck and she started slipping
her hands behind her into the front of my pants. That's

when she turned around. A look of breathless disgust spread across her face like a BP oil spill before she screamed and ran off into the bathroom, never to be seen again. I watched my tiny dancer sprint away and tried to conceal my partial erection while the laughter from the crowd erupted and roared over the music. I was a fucking hero.

Seth and I quickly abandoned the newly vacant dance floor for some socializing. After spooking The Joy Luck Club out of the bar, I began taking shots and high fiving my new adoring fans. I was beyond drunk; my vision was rapidly becoming a problem and I was starting to slur words. I was wearing at least two complimentary shots on my shirt because they failed to find my mouth. The night was starting to take its toll on me.

"Oh my God, you are KungFu Mike, aren't you?!"

A very attractive blonde girl approached me. As it turned out, she was an avid reader of a column I wrote for the local newspaper, which I had been fired from for being too risqué for the tastes of the bluehairs that made up the majority of the subscriber base. Her name was Tracy.

"So what brings you to this place?" Tracy leaned in closer to be heard over the DOOSHDOOSHDOOSH of the house beat.

"Can you babysit me?" I responded, leaning in to both be heard and get a better look down the front of her shirt.

"Huh?"

"I said, CAN YOU BABYSIT MEEE?!? DURRRR!!!"

I strapped the business end of the kiddie leash onto Tracy's arm and started dancing with her. Staying in character, my dance was an inebriated hybrid between the Heathcliff Huxtable shuffle and a photosensitive seizure. She laughed, and we chatted. The night continued on like this until the music stopped and a man's voice boomed on the PA system. It was the voice of the whiter than white DJ.

"Is ayeeone havin' a good time tonight? I saaaaaaid - is ayeebody havin' a good time tonight?!*people screaming*

I can't heaaarrrr youuuuu!! ***more people screaming***
Aiight, we 'bout to keep it poppin' off Halloween style
wif a costume contest, ya heeeearrrdddd. If y'all entered in n' shit, step on ova to da line next to da dance
flo. Holla!"

A line of about twenty or so people started forming by
the dance floor, which was now lit up with a man standing in the middle of it with a microphone. Contestants
walked out to the man one at a time, and he would ask
them why they thought they should win the contest. They
would say something to the effect of, "because I'm a
naughty police officer and you need a spanking" or some
tired shit and walk off, leaving the audience screaming
for another salacious Halloween whore to pander to
them.

I thought about jumping in line for a quick second,
and that second quickly came and went - the painful
thought of standing in a line for God knows how long
without being able to leave to get a drink or take a piss
was akin to that scene in Hard Candy where the guy gets
castrated – positively unbearable.

Tracy wanted me to do it, and was begging me to
get in line. Then Tracy's friends all started to chime in.
Then Seth began screaming at me to join the contest.
Then passing strangers that happened to witness the
dance floor incident started harassing me about it. They
just wouldn't take no for an answer, no matter how much
I resisted. Out of nowhere, two girls I hadn't yet spoken

with that night grabbed me by both arms, pulled me over to the registration table, signed me up and shoved me in line with a fresh drink. I would probably be involved in a lot more things if I had two girls like that working for me as Assistants. Things like fitness. And possibly church.

Slutty beer wench. Slutty Playboy bunny. Slutty nurse. Slutty toddler. Aaaaand I'm up.

I sauntered into the center of the dance floor clutching what was left of a Red Bull and vodka and a lit cigarette trapped between my fingers. As I made my way over to the announcer, I heard a woman gasp "Oh my God, I cannot believe that handicapped boy's parents let him drink alcohol. Someone should call the police!"

The announcer took one look at me and disapprovingly shook his head. Besides my ridiculous costume, my face told the tale of a man that had poured ten too many.

"Well now, what is your name?" The announcer boomed before *bringing the microphone to my face.*

"Mahhhhh name es Mikoww. Es Mikowww."

"Excuse me?" The announcer's brow furrowed as he brought the microphone even closer.

"Mikowww, Mikowww...mah name es Mikowww."

The announcer frowned and brought the microphone back to himself. "Ok, I guess. Now what makes you think *you* should win –"

Without even thinking about it, I snatched the microphone from the announcer's hand.

"G G G A A A R R R B B B B H H H H ! ! !
WINNNNUUUHHH!!! WINNNUUUHHHH!!! I AM
DEE WINNNUUHHHHH!!!"

Three hundred people went silent. My gibberish silenced a nightclub completely packed to capacity. You could hear a cell phone vibrate from across the room. The crowd just stood there slack jawed, staring at me. Ten seconds went by before a few nervous laughs sounded intermittently as I gave the microphone back to the announcer and shuffled off of the dance floor. If I once commanded the affection of the entire club with my eccentric antics, that affection was now long gone.

When I walked back to my table, Tracy grabbed me by the kiddie leash and demanded that I come with her to an after party a few blocks away. Not asked, told. I was far too drunk to be able to gauge facial expressions and tones of voice, so I wasn't sure if it was because I had just embarrassed her to the point that she felt she needed to leave or if she actually wanted to fuck me. Or maybe she wanted to fuck me so I would stop embarrassing her. Either way, it was getting close to last call, so I accepted.

As I was being led out of the door by my leash, I noticed Slutty Policewoman taking first prize in the costume contest. "FFFFFACK YOUUU, SHLUTTY COP!!! I AM DEE WINNUHHHH!!!! BLLLAAARRGRHH!!!" Tracy yanked me out the door by my kiddie leash, and I was gone.

The after party was pretty quiet. A handful of people from the bar and a few others hanging out in a living room were drinking cheap champagne and firing up a joint when Tracey and I walked through the front door. Everyone laughed when they saw my costume. As soon as I began to introduce myself, Tracy pulled me into another room by my kiddie leash and shut the door.

There I was; dressed like a special needs kid, getting a blowjob from an unfamiliar woman in a dimly lit room literally seconds after I walked in the door of a stranger's house. All I needed to do was turn towards a camera and give it a thumbs up to turn the entire night into a Mentos commercial.

I was pulling my pants back up when Tracy left the room. I imagined she was probably rinsing her mouth out, or maybe she was sobbing silently in the corner of the bathroom because it finally hit her that she just sucked off a strange man wearing a helmet. I heard people talking in the adjacent room and I saw a light peeking out from under the closed door, so I figured I would try to at least be sociable.

The living room was empty, save for a guy and a girl. The girl was blonde with bad hair and worse skin, and the guy was, well, he was your stereotypical Masshole; Italian looking, black t-shirt, short gold chain with a cross dangling over it and a manicured 5 o'clock shadow. Both of them looked like they caught the first chairlift of the morning on Sinus Snowstorm Mountain.

I said hello, sat down on the couch and poured myself a drink from the scattered bottles on the coffee table. It seemed as though the other guests had either taken off for the night or were hanging out in a different part of the house. Tracy was a smoker, so I put two and two together and came to the conclusion that everybody was in the backyard getting stoned and I was sitting in the McDonald's antisocial binge cocaine user's Play Place. I decided to hang out with them and wait for Tracy to come back so I would have a comfortable place to sleep, wake up and deposit my penis into her once more before walking home.

Me and the two greasy looking cokeheads made conversation about what we did that night, what local bars we liked and what was on TV; innocuous shit. Well, it was more like I was talking about all of those things while Cokey Roberts and Coke-a-Dile Dundee fidgeted in their reclining chairs, looked nervously around the room and cringed every time the crushed Aspirin taste of their post nasal drips hit their tongues.

The girl left the room to go to smoke a cigarette, leaving me and the guy behind to chat. Not being a fan of awkward silences, I kept the conversation going.

"So, where are you from?"

"Lowell." the guy responded. I wasn't surprised at all.

"Ah, gotcha. How do you like it there?"

"It's ok, except for the niggers and the spics."

I just looked at him with a half-smile, waiting for his poker face to break and tell me he was kidding, but he never did.

"They're everywhere. They ain't human, guy."

And there it was. I had gone from horrifying 500 people in a nightclub, to ejaculating in a strange girl's mouth, to having light conversation with the Aryan Brotherhood. Deliberate, casual racism was something I would normally get riled up about, but I was in a strange place and there wasn't a familiar soul in sight. It's funny how your initial fight/flight instincts change when you're all alone.

"So why don't you move away from Lowell if you hate minorities?"

"No fucking way, guy. I'm not leaving my fucking family with those fucking animals. I'm going to kick all of those filthy niggers and spics out of Massachusetts. Leave the commonwealth to clean white people, you know?"

I could hear the hammerlock of a handgun click in my head when he finished that sentence. I can deal with ignorance to a point, but only if I have something to gain from it, like breakfast, or another blowjob. Maybe the booze had something to do with it, but I just couldn't listen to his shit for another second. I stood up, still garbed in full special needs regalia, and let him know exactly what I thought about his Aryan ideals. His female companion came back into the room just in time to witness the end of my tirade.

"I think it's time that you left."

"Yeah, I think you're probably right. Thanks for the hospitality, though."

"Get the fuck out of here, you motherfucker." The guy bolted out of his chair, teeth clenched and fists balled up.

I quickly walked out the door, down the steps of the front porch and onto the street. I looked at my cell phone. 3:00 a.m. The street was completely dark except for one lamp attached to a telephone pole casting long, fingerlike shadows from a tree branch bending in the brisk fall breeze. No lights were on in houses, no cars driving by, nothing. Silence.

I heard the screen door swing open behind and bash against the side of the house. It was the guy from inside.

He raced down the stairs of the porch and started after me.

"You laughin' at me? Huh?! You laughing at me, guy?!"

My instincts told me to start walking backwards quickly "No, I was walking home, dude. Relax."

The girl came out of the house, screaming for the guy to come back inside. I sized him up as he was walking towards me. He was about my size, maybe a little more built, but I definitely didn't want it to come to blows; not when I was with a bunch of strangers on a deserted street at 3:00 am.

The guy continued on his tirade. "I'll fuckin' cut you, faggot! GO GET ALL YOUR NIGGAH FRIENDS!!! I'LL CUT THEM TOO!!!"

This is where he whipped out a knife. Not some Webelo-issued two-inch locking knife - a fucking twelve-inch bowie knife. It looked like something Ted Nugent would use to skin a stray cat in his backyard. He held both of his arms outstretched in the universal "come at me bro" pose, knife in his right hand as he got closer. I started to backpedal with my arms out.

"Dude, put that fucking thing away. It's just you and me; there is no need to bring a knife into this. Just relax."

It came at me like a flash. The knife darted toward my head and I threw my hands up in the only way I could feasibly guard my face from getting cut. The blade grazed my forearm and retracted for another strike.

That's when I stopped backpedaling, turned around and sprinted for my life. I glanced back to find him running just a few paces behind me. I could see the knife gleam in the light from the street lamp every time his arm made an upstroke. I turned around, put my head down and ran harder. Faster. I had to run faster. I could see the well-lit intersection that I needed to be on to get back to my apartment about a hundred yards away from me; I just had to make it there. My arms pumped furiously, my strides were long but I was barely breathing. I was too scared to breathe. The closer I got to the intersection, the further away my assailant trailed me. By the time I had hit the intersection and hooked a right, he was long gone.

I slowed my pace down to a trot about a block after I turned, checking behind me every five or ten seconds. After a bout of panting, wheezing and spitting, I lit up a cigarette to calm my lungs and resumed walking. Miraculously, my forearm only had a small gash in it, nothing serious. I took my button up shirt off and covered the cut so I wouldn't draw attention to myself. Then I started laughing because I realized I was still dressed up in my special needs costume; helmet cocked to the side, one of my teddy bears missing and my zipper still all the way down from my earlier encounter with Tracy.

I got home around 3:30 am, changed into some pajamas, cleaned up my arm and began filling out mandatory state unemployment work search forms with a genuine, focused zeal they'd never witnessed before. The scare and the run had sobered me up significantly, and despite the hour, I was determined to find a job and resume a normal schedule; a normal life. Most people my age were several years into their respective professions after graduating from college, settled down in long term relationships and were even buying cute little pastel starter homes together in cute little pastel coastal neighborhoods, where the man would let a neighbor borrow the weed whacker on a Saturday morning and start wearing button-down shirts to backyard barbecues, and the woman would half complain, half gloat about her status as a golf widow at the monthly girl's night wine and cheese parties she despises hosting. I was a twenty-five-year-old unemployed college dropout who had been gallivanting around town wearing a deliberately insensitive Halloween costume in what was really nothing more than a despicable attempt to garner attention, blowing what little savings I had left on poorly mixed well drinks, having unprotected oral sex with an unfamiliar woman in an unfamiliar house, and risking my life with knife-wielding racist Massholes while the pastel families slept. Compared to your run-of-the-mill homeless person I was sitting pretty, but compared to the bulk of my peers, I was a fucking degenerate. I was disgusted with myself for even entertaining the idea of allowing myself a mental vacation when my life was in shambles, let alone following through with those insensitive, largely irresponsible plans to that degree.

It took the chest-knotting self-loathing that only comes in the moments after I realize I truly fucked up for me to make the conscious decision to shed another twenty pounds from the coffers of my ingrained emotional need for attention. This is the reoccurring pattern in my life, but hey, if you like where you are on the mountaintop, right?

Whiskey and Cannibalism

—∿—

AN AUTHOR NAMED TUCKER MAX puts some events together called Tanked for the Troops, to send our troops overseas cool stuff like porn and playing cards (I would later go on to manage Tucker's book tour for I Hope They Serve Beer in Hell and work with him at his entertainment company Rudius Media, but we had yet to meet when this story took place). Micah and I decided one year that we were going to fly from New Hampshire to Philadelphia to attend one of them. That winter was unusually brutal in New England, and we needed to escape, if only for the weekend. Southwest was running an obscenely low priced $89 round-trip package from Manchester, New Hampshire to Philadelphia, so we purchased our tickets online, and made plans with my sister to spend the night at her place just outside of the city.

As soon we got off the plane, my sister Gen and her buddies took us to Fado, a cookie-cutter chain Irish pub. We managed to run up a $500 tab worth of Jameson shots before last call, which was a bargain because we were $1,000 worth of drunk. I stood on my table, gyrating my hips and screaming Journey lyrics at people in line for the bathroom, and Micah took shots with a gaggle of Lane Bryant models sitting next to us, all the time with a predatory, "One of these girls definitely digs me" grin on his face. Everybody hated us. That is what happens when you give an unending supply of whiskey to men in their early twenties, and it's never good.

We eventually made our way back to my sister's friend's apartment for more booze and some bong action. My sister's hot friend was asking me where Micah was because she wanted to hook up with him. I went downstairs to give him the good news, and found him sleeping face first on the dining room table, snoring and drooling. When I went back upstairs, my sister was curled up around the toilet like a cat, emptying her guts. Both of my sister's friends were sleeping on top of each other, one of them still holding the bong in their hands. I slapped Micah awake, grabbed my sister, and directed everyone out so we could sleep comfortably.

The first thing that I noticed when we walked into my sister's apartment was her little Buddhist altar in the living room. Once everyone else left, I decided to take a closer look. It had a bunch of weird Asian crap all over it, and in the center was a cabinet that held some kind of tapestry with Chinese calligraphy. I assumed that it was some kind of silly chanting sheet music. I saw a little black lacquered box on the table, and I asked my sister what it was while she brushed her teeth in the bathroom. *"Oh, that's just Dad's ashes. They came in the mail the other day."* This was the first time I had seen them since he died a few months before.

I lifted the box up, and all that was there was a little brown burlap baggie. I was kind of disappointed that they didn't put the ashes in an urn or anything; I didn't even know that a burlap sack was something you were supposed to put human remains in. Different strokes for destitute folks, I guess.

I picked up the baggie to examine it further. It was pretty light. I gave it a little squeeze and it gave a kind of a light, whiny crunch, like when you step in the ashes of fresh campfire. Micah told me I was crazy for even touching it. I feigned playing hacky sack with it to freak him out. He laughed, I laughed, and then I raised the bag to my face, and pretended to wail it off of my forehead like a soccer ball to make Micah even more uncomfortable. The bag accidentally tapped my hairline, and a little, tiny, almost unnoticeable sprinkling of dust sifted out of the bottom of the bag and into my mouth.

Oh my God. I just ate Dad.

My eyes welled up. My first instinct was to barf. No, actually, my first instinct was to cry. *What the fuck was wrong with me? Why did I have to do that? Why did I always mask my emotions with humor? Was I trying to prove something to myself and everyone around me by pretending I wasn't fazed by my dad's death?* My whisky sodden brain tried to wrap itself around all of those questions as the ashes mingled with my saliva, creating a paste on my tongue.

I quietly put the baggie down, and slid the black box back over it like nothing happened. Micah didn't even notice; he had already flipped over to face the couch and sleep right as it happened. I couldn't say anything. I mean, how do you tell someone you just ate a piece of a dead person? How would I break it to my sister? She was wasted. I could just picture her bursting into tears and raining girly punches on my head and shoulders for desecrating her shrine by committing cannibalism, before rifling Micah and I out of her place in the middle of the night, shamefully shitfaced in a strange city and without any resources to rectify the situation.

I slowly walked into the bathroom, shut the door behind me and puked as quietly as one possibly can after a night of heavy drinking. I vigorously washed my mouth with a hydrogen peroxide solution I found under the bathroom sink, scoured my teeth with baking soda, and drank a liter of Smartwater before lying down on the couch with drunken, guilty tears in my eyes long after everyone fell asleep.

When we woke up the next day, both of us were suffering from different levels of alcohol poisoning. Micah couldn't even make it to Tanked for the Troops, as his eyes had turned a jaundiced yellow and he couldn't stop vomiting. I walked to the event by myself, paid the cover charge to get in, bought a beer, and survived maybe five minutes before I had to rush back to our hotel room and lie under the covers with the shiver sweats until our flight home the next day.

Doot Doot Doot

—◇—

SHORTLY AFTER MY SIXTEENTH BIRTHDAY, my mother sat me down and told me I would have to get my first real job. I was on school vacation and was planning on spending the time skateboarding around town with my friends, but the concept of earning a steady income and not relying on the occasional low-paying odd job around the house was enough to keep me from complaining about it too much. The local water park was hiring seasonal workers en masse, so my mother helped me type out a resume, forced me into an ill-fitting button up and tie, and drove me to fill out an application.

The water park was situated on the main traffic corridor that cuts through my coastal New England hometown. Complete with dozens of water slides, a wave pool and a smattering of urine-warmed kiddie wading areas, it would tempt thousands of people through its gates every day during the summer, which in turn forced the family who owned and managed it to hire a small army of minimum wage-worthy students to properly staff the park every year. Even though all the season's positions were already filled by the time I arrived, I was able to sneak in for an on-the-spot interview with the hiring manager, who was so impressed by the fact that I hadn't worn shorts and a t-shirt like the rest of his applicants that he brought me on board as a "loader."

On the ladder of professional respect at the water park, the top rung was reserved for the family who owned the place, a group of born-again Christians who, to the dismay of their nervous attorneys, seized every opportunity to shove a funnel down someone's throat and glug their religion into it. Their evangelism ranged from the seemingly innocuous, such as holding after-work prayer sessions and private parties for hand-picked employees, all the way to the deliberately insidious, including going out of their way to carve Biblical passages and iconography in the cement walls of a kiddie wading area tunnel too small for discerning parents to enter, but just the right size for their small, tractable children. They closed the park to the public so their church could have free reign of the place at no charge. Those they deemed to be unrepentant nonbelievers or poorly performing employees during their leisurely strolls through the park were fired on a whim and replaced daily, forcing exhausted employees to straighten their backs and smile disingenuously as they passed. Consciously or not, they created an "us vs. them" working climate that favored the saved with bonuses and promotions. They were the combination of wealthy, power wielding and outwardly religious normally reserved for megachurch televangelists and successful businessmen who took Jesus into their hearts after deciding He blessed them with money because they were more worthy of Paradise than their fellow man. On the first day of work, employees were taught to recognize members of the owning family, and to drop what they're doing and do whatever they may ask of them without question.

The next rung down was the site managers, typically teachers needing reliable work on summer break, who were each in charge of their own team of employees and ran the portions of the park they were delegated to. Below the site managers were the on-site EMTs and assorted maintenance staff in charge of keeping people alive. One more rung down was for guest relations, who took care of customer complaints, answered phones and handled a wide variety of administrative duties. Descending from guest relations was a rung dedicated to the parking lot attendants and janitorial staff, who would normally be at the bottom of any organization chart, if not for their freedom to roam the park on electric golf carts with virtually no supervision. Travelling further down the ladder, lifeguards were tasked with standing at the bottom of water slides and blowing their whistles at guests who thought it would be a good idea to stand directly in front of the mouth of the slide and receive the next guest's feet in their face at thirty miles-per-hour. Lifeguards went through special training, and were often the most likely to be promoted to the guest relations rung due to their perceived acceptance of added responsibility.

And now we arrive at the loader; padded from the rock bottom rung only by the pimple-faced fry cooks and unrepentant white trash that filled the ranks of food service. The main function of the loader was to stand at the top of every water slide, help guests into their rubber rafts and guide them into the mouth of the slide until the flow of water and gravity took over. Warm summer sun, fresh air, the sound of people laughing and enjoying themselves pervading the experience; the job doesn't sound so bad until you factor in the human condition. Overfull diapers would come into contact with water and explode. Elderly people would accidently lacerate your calves with their razor sharp, yellowing toenails. Guests from Massachusetts would berate you in Spanish for not letting them go down the slide with a plate of fried dough and a lit cigarette. Entitled, waspy mothers and fathers demanding their family go down the slide in succession of each other despite their place in line. Fist fights. Public sex acts. The theft of sandals and sunglasses. Adults vomiting on the stairs due to a combination of heat exhaustion and alcohol sickness. Children shitting in their bathing suits and leaving hundred foot brown skid marks that resulted in the slides being closed and sanitized before further use. It all happened, and for reasons unknown it happened on top of the water slides more than anywhere else in the park.

Out of the thousands of water park guests that came every day, many were overweight adults and overpowered gravity with the friction of their calloused rhinoceros asses on the slide bottom. They just lay in the shallow entrance pool like a beached manatee, genuinely curious as to why they didn't float as gracefully as the thirteen-year-old girl in front of them, and looking at you as though it was your fault. This prompted a loader to grab hold of the guest's tube handle, pull them toward the mouth of the slide with all their might until the suction of their gluteal anchors gave way. If one was so big they got stuck halfway down the slide, which actually happened with alarming frequency, a loader typically sent an equally big person down to dislodge them. In summation, a loader's job was to drag fat people across a five-foot expanse, over and over again, for eight hours a day in the baking summer sun. While most employees of the water park stayed employed there all the way through school and sometimes all the way through college, loaders typically lasted one season before heat exhaustion an and overall sense of unhappiness sent them to greener pastures. I lasted five years as a loader before being promoted to a management position, and made it two more years after that, until dwindling funds finally forced me into the grey, drab, adult workplace.

While many waddled into the park positively brimming with Totino's pizza rolls and glee, many more arrived in peak physical condition, and confidently bounded around wearing little to hide their bronzed and sexually resplendent bodies. Unlike high school where the women were covered up to meet dress code regulations, female guests of the park revealed their athletically toned legs, and virtually spilled out of their bikini tops upon splashing into the catch pools at the bottom of each slide. It was enough to give an inexperienced sixteen-year-old boy a throbbing case of priapism, and prompted an early introduction to learning the importance of dark sunglasses during the summer months, out of fear of being caught ogling a musclebound man's girlfriend and thrown over the railing of a fifty foot tall waterslide tower.

Not only were guests filling the safety deposit boxes of my teenage spank bank, employees of the water park also contributed to the youthful, sexually charged atmosphere. While a loader's uniform consisted of a boring t-shirt and khaki shorts, female lifeguards wore white tank tops over red one-piece bathing suits, and most of them were athletes in high school and college. I remember sitting down to one of the first couple of morning meetings after being hired, and looking around at my attractive coworkers in bathing suits, all sitting Indian style in a circle while our site manager went over the agenda, and thinking "I don't care how many fat people I have to pull down these slides. I'm never quitting." It was at one of those morning meetings two years after I was first hired later as an eighteen-year-old that I laid eyes on Amber.

I already knew Amber from high school. We were casual acquaintances and chatted occasionally when our paths crossed at work, but I'd never seen her in anything as revealing as a bathing suit before. At school she wore outfits assembled from a modest wardrobe that reaffirmed her tomboyish attitude and aspirations; sneakers, loose fitting jeans, hooded sweatshirts and t-shirts typically bearing some kind of field hockey message on them. Nothing about her gait, conversation or appearance gave any hint of Amber's hidden femininity, but her water park uniform betrayed her by offering her athletic ass, flat stomach and full breasts to the staff at the morning meeting. Amber, as it turned out, was secretly hot.

I was flabbergasted by Amber's hotness, almost to the point that it offended me. I wanted to scream "WHY WOULD YOU HIDE THIS FROM THE WORLD?!", but was unable to mouth the words. I couldn't understand why somebody would prevent the public from knowing about their positive assets, especially when they would clearly be received with fanfare. I likened it to coming home after a long day of work at an Indonesian sweatshop, drawing the shades and beating a computer at chess seventeen times in a row before going to bed. Why not embrace your incredible skill? Why would you keep America from standing up and applauding your killer rack?

Because the secretive nature of Amber's attractiveness made her somehow seem more obtainable, my confusion ultimately led to conspiracy, and I decided I wanted Amber's mystery tits for myself, so when she invited me to come along with her and several other water park employees to a Third Eye Blind / Eve Six concert being held at a large outdoor venue upstate, I agreed without hesitation.

In 1998, Third Eye Blind and Eve 6 were incredibly popular bands and dominated the music video channels, radio stations, movie soundtracks and Strawberry's sales charts. You couldn't walk five feet down the street without hearing Third Eye Blind's "How's It Gonna Be" or Eve 6's "Inside Out" blasting out of someone's car stereo. Being a huge fan of gritty underground hip hop and brutal death metal, the oversaturation of soulless, sugary pop rock on the airwaves drove me to the brink of madness. If I was going to spend money on a concert, it would be to see Kool Keith at the Asylum in Boston, or to get punched in the mosh pit watching Cannibal Corpse play at Worchester Palladium. If anybody else in the world asked me to go see a Third Eye Blind and Eve 6 concert, I would have laughed at them. If anybody else in the world asked me to PAY FOR TICKETS to a Third Eye Blind and Eve 6 concert, I might have kicked them in the shins. But this wasn't just anybody. This was Amber, and I was a teenage boy willing to compromise my still developing integrity for a chance to touch a boob, so I crammed into a rusty pickup with her and four Bible thumping lifeguards who wanted nothing to do with a lowly loader, and drove up to the Meadowbrook to see what I considered to be the worst two bands to ever grace a stage play live.

Eve 6 was well into their set by the time we arrived, found parking and secured a spot on the lawn of the Meadowbrook. The crowd was thick; backwards visors and puka shell necklaces as far as the eye could see. As expected, the music blaring through the Meadowbrook's massive speakers was terrible, the lanky ginger front man crooning "SUCKING ON MY BRAIN – YOU'RE THE TEACHER, I'M THE STUDENT." Throngs of men in bowling shirts and women wearing bikini tops and JNCO jeans swayed back and forth, giving the crowd a tidal effect.

As we all stood and watched the show, I reached into my backpack, pulled out a can of beer and opened it. The hiss and crack turned the heads of my holy coworkers toward me, each face dripping with shock and disgust.

"What do you think you're doing?"

"Um, I'm drinking a beer."

"We're at a concert."

"…I know."

"And you're not twenty-one."

"Also true."

"I don't think that's a good idea."

"Look dude, I'm at a fucking Third Eye Blind concert. Either give me a beer or give me a cyanide pill."

They then turned around and mumbled to each other something I couldn't hear over the music, but I assumed it had something to do with my eternal soul being forever tainted by Budweiser.

Amber, not aware of the conversation we just had, was enthralled with the band. I watched her sing along to the songs and dance by herself, and slugged back the rest of my beer, trying to muster up the courage to stand next to her.

Eve 6 eventually packed up their gear and gave way to Third Eye Blind, who rifled out each and every one of their spineless gumdrop rock songs in such a quick progression that it made me clench my teeth. It was awful. Everything about the concert was awful; the music, the people I came with, the crowd full of American Eagle and Abercrombie and Fitch, the fact that I couldn't bring myself to talk to Amber because I was too damned scared of rejection to take the initiative with girls that other guys displayed freely. *This music is killing me. I feel like punching one these holy rolling lifeguards in the face. Why did I agree to go to this? WHY CAN'T I JUST WALK UP AND START DANCING WITH HER?!* Everything terrible about the night intermingled with my social anxiety to make a thick gruel of shittiness that eighteen-year-old Mike couldn't wade through. I stood by myself, watching the band play and loathing my inability to man up and take control of the situation.

Almost as if timed to tip me over into blind rage, Third Eye Blind broke into their overplayed smash single "Semi-Charmed Life," and the crowd erupted, singing along to the insipid lyrics so passionately you could barely hear Stephan Jenkins belt them into his microphone. I stood before a roiling sea of idiots, all of them jumping up and down in unison and screaming "DOOT DOOT DOOT – DOOT DOO DOO DOOOOOOOT" as loudly as their vocal chords would allow.

A space cleared near the front of the stage, and shirtless college guys began prancing around in a circle, shoving each other and cheering each other on.

Are they? They aren't. Oh my fuck, they are. They're trying to start a mosh pit…at a Third Eye Blind concert.

That was it. That was what my teenage mind fixated on and focused its insecure, self-depreciating anger toward. I barreled toward the clearing with my teeth clenched. I shoved people this way and that until I broke into the clearing, and started swinging my fists like I would have done at any respectable heavy metal show. *How DARE they mosh to this music.* I kicked and shoved and leaned back into the people who lined the clearing, expecting them to brace my fall and throw me back into the pit so I could continue my onslaught. The people, clearly not aware of mosh pit etiquette, allowed me to fall backwards into the mud.

I sprang back up and launched myself back into the fray, knocking a frat boy over and connecting a fist with another guy's head. They scrambled to their feet, one of them quickly exiting the mosh pit. When I danced near someone, they held their hands out to keep me from colliding with them. I was a perfectly violent cyclone of punches and kicks fit for the thickest of hardcore pits, not moshing because I loved the music, which is the catalyst for most moshes, but because I hated the music. I hated the people dancing to the music. I hated that I spent the last two years working as a human pack mule. I hated myself for not having any confidence with girls, and it was much easier to hate everything around me than to hate myself, and hate came freely when DOOT DOOT DOOT – DOOT DOO DOO DOOOOOOOT.

When their show-closing song ended, I stopped swinging and realized I was the only person left in the mosh pit. The people lining the outside of it stood pensive and slack-jawed. The gravity of how my emotional outburst must have looked to those people started to sink in, and just as I was about to walk back to my coworkers and Amber, the crowd erupted in applause. Not just for the song, but for me. People clapped me on the back and shook my hand. A guy I punched in the head handed me a beer in a clear plastic cup. They congratulated me. I couldn't understand it.

"Let's hear it for the guy in the mosh pit who just went crazy! Damn!"

That wasn't the guy who handed me the beer. That wasn't the guy that shook my hand. That was Stephan Jenkins, the front man for Third Eye Blind and boyfriend of a then relatively unknown Charlize Theron, pointing at me from center stage.

It all made sense to me then; a sickening, dreadful sense.

Everybody here thinks I'm Third Eye Blind super fan number one.

Instead of reacting honestly and extending two disgusted middle fingers back at the crowd and Stephan Jenkins, I felt a strange, gracious exhilaration that's typically reserved for when a famous person – famous for making terrible music or not – pays direct attention to you. I smiled and waved like a pandering asshole, and gracefully backpedaled out of the pit and scurried off to meet my coworkers, who were packing things up and getting ready to head back to the truck.

Amber sat next to me on the quiet ride home, and despite how badly I wanted to, I didn't attempt to hold her hand. Suffering through one more defeat that day would have left me gibbering in the corner of a state-run sanitarium.

Born to Die

—m—

I STRUGGLED AWAKE THAT MORNING, still wearing the same clothes from the day before. There was a half-smoked cigarette jutting from between the fingers of my right hand.

I sat upright and reached for my alarm clock to find the time, only to discover that I was on the kitchen floor and not in my bed. The kitchen was an absolute disaster; pizza boxes, beer bottles and empty plastic jugs of cheap booze littered the countertops and floor, and the refrigerator door had been left open all night.

Standing up, clutching my head and wiping the drool from my cheek, I realized the front door to the apartment had been left open as well. My vacuum cleaner was upside down on the ground, its attachments strewn all over the hallway. A foot still in a shoe dangled from the arm of a couch in the living room.

Shuffling forward, I saw a handful of people had spent the night instead of braving the roads and the brutal DWI checkpoints the Portsmouth Police had inevitably set up on that Saturday night. Bodies littered the couches, and the carpet next to the couches. One person was using a stained tablecloth as a blanket. Another was using a pile of Xbox games as a pillow.

It was the morning of June 5th, 2005, and this scene was pretty common for my apartment on any given weekend morning during the summer. I lived right in the heart of downtown Portsmouth, directly above a bar called the State Street Saloon, that would serve you until you were rendered blind seven days a week, pay you out under the table on the video poker machine, and allow you to score a laughably low quality bag of cocaine in the men's bathroom. My friends would use my apartment as a pre-game watering hole, post-game speakeasy, free hotel, and love nest any time one of them was lucky enough to convince a girl to fuck them in my bathroom, which was really the only room that afforded any privacy.

It was a small apartment in an incredibly run down building owned by a notorious slum lord who was too busy getting arrested for shoplifting at T.J. Maxx, or stealing the security deposits of enlisted tenants who were being shipped to Afghanistan to keep the building up or answer any voicemails demanding repairs. It was an absolute shithole of an apartment, but I was in my mid-twenties with no real direction in life, so it was *my* absolute shithole of an apartment.

I took a closer look at who was in my house, only because the door was open and I wanted to make sure it was actually my friends, and not a gaggle of homeless people strung out on huffing keyboard cleaner.

Timmy was passed out on the couch face first and snoring like a rusty chainsaw. Tim's friend Nick, who was dating Tim's girlfriend's sister at the time, was the one using the stack of Xbox games as a pillow. Nick was young, and as we did with all young people we took into the fold, we hazed the shit out of him all the time. As soon as I saw his face, the hazy recollection of someone demanding he turn the vacuum up to full power and attach the hose to his penis drifted into center vision. I remembered his watery cry for help when the suction took hold being drowned out by our merciless, alcohol amplified laughter. I laughed out loud just thinking about it. While this might sound like Abu Ghraib-quality enhanced interrogation protocol, this was par for the course on a night out with the boys.

Evan was using the tablecloth as a blanket, and had somehow ended up cuddling with the wall. Evan was one of my oldest friends; a Volkswagen obsessed gearhead (which was odd from a historical standpoint considering the fact that he was approximately 140% Polish) and a granite pillar in my group of best friends on the planet. He was extremely close with his family, and was always ditching us for random dinners and parties they would throw for themselves. I regularly gave him shit about how their get-togethers were really pierogi-fueled V.C. Andrews-esque incest orgies, but I was honestly fascinated by how close Evan was with his family, especially because my family was anything but. He was living with his parents at the time, another fun fact we gave him endless shit about, and would sleep over regularly so he wouldn't have to deal with the "Are you drunk? Evan are you drunk?" late night mom-in-a-nightgown conversations I think every one of you reading this has had to suffer through at least once in your life.

Evan was also incredibly obsessive compulsive to the point that some people mistook it for Asperger's. He would spend hours picking out the best two t-shirts to wear on top of each other, ruin the nights of waitresses with perpetual meal order changes, and possessed the uncanny ability to be able to rattle off every statistic about every 80s rock band, every sports team and every German car ever produced on the spot, and always be right. Above all else, Evan loved getting hammered, he loved having fun, and he was a valued member of our band of bastards.

"Wakey wakey, eggs and bakey" I announced to the room as I grabbed the strangely sticky TV remote and clicked on some Comcast Music Choice, which happened to be Van Halen's "Ain't Talkin' 'Bout Love". The troops slowly started groaning and rubbing the sleepies out of their eyes.

"Dude, why are you up right now? You're fucking killing me." Tim's eyes were hilariously bloodshot. He stuffed his hand down the front of his jeans, scratched his balls and then brought his hand back up to smell it; a habit he had no problem executing in private or public.

"I'm too hungover to sleep." I sat down on the couch he was lying on, and cleared off some room on the coffee table to put my feet up. "Also, this place reeks of stale beer and cigarettes. It smells like your grandma's kisses. I'm fucking starving. Let's get breakfast."

"Uuunnnghhhhh." Evan let out the grunt of a rhinoceros drunk on fermented fruit as he peeled himself off the wall and joined the conversation. "Dude, let's go to Molly's."

"Jesus Christ, are you serious?" Tim turned to Evan. "You're ready to get back in the saddle already? You're an episode of Intervention on two legs."

"Fuck it. It's Sunday. We'll just grab some food and have a couple mimosas – a COUPLE mimosas – and take off. I can't get too hammered today. I have shit to do with my family today."

I couldn't pass up the opportunity. "Yeah guys, Evan can't get too hammered today. If he can't get it up at the family picnic, they make him drink a bucket of potato vodka and make him swear allegiance to Hitler."

"It's Molly's brunch. Nobody walks out of Molly's brunch sober. It's those god damn BobMosas." Tim sat up on the couch and continued. "Dude, I used to be a bouncer there, and the brunch crowd was worse than the Saturday night crowd. People barfing on the sidewalk and getting into fights just as church is letting out type of shit. Let me repeat what I just said; I used to have to work as a bouncer – at brunch."

Tim wasn't lying. Molly Malone's was an Irish pub in downtown Portsmouth, and it was the kind of place you'd stop in once every other bartender in town had shut you off – if you were a townie (tourists were never given the same level of service there, which was another reason why we liked Molly Malone's so much). After local establishments stopped serving Irish Car Bombs due to reports of customers cracking their front teeth or ingesting broken shards of shot glass, Molly Malone's refused to buckle to the pressure and was the only place in town you could an Irish Car Bomb served to you. If you liked getting hammered and loud, Molly's was the place to be, even for brunch. Especially for brunch.

Every Sunday morning, they would host a full Irish themed brunch spread in their upstairs dining room, deceptively decorated to instill in the casual observer a sense of innocent elegance, complete with pressed white tablecloths, fresh flowers and beautiful table settings. An employee, typically male and rather large, would stand by the door to the dining room during the event, but didn't escort people to their tables or bring them their hash benedicts and black puddings. That was because he wasn't a host or a waiter, but a bouncer. The bouncer would casually check IDs and survey the room during the early hours of brunch, doing his best to enjoy the calm before the storm, and watch the catalyst of the storm being poured into pint glasses, set on trays and passed around the room by waitresses to thirsty yet still well behaved customers.

The drink in question was called the "BobMosa", a legendary concoction created by a local man named Bobby Powers, whose main priority that day was to turn a standard breakfast drink into a nuclear warhead. It was a regular mimosa, but with the addition of Stoli Orange and a Grand Marnier floater. This seemingly wretched combination of unrelated alcohols somehow managed to mingle together in a way that both completely masked its generous alcohol content and became entirely too refreshing to the customers buying them, who were already dehydrated from all the drinking they had done Saturday night. It was the con man of breakfast drinks, in how it would be just quenching enough to sneak past your lips and convince your brain to order another, before your common sense could kick in and make you order a glass of water instead. "Oh, I'll have just one BobMosa," was the equivalent of saying you would have just one Pringle, or one dose of heroin. One BobMosa would become two, two BobMosas would become four, and before you knew it, you spent $6 on breakfast and $50 on drinks...and it was only 10:00 am.

The once polite, civil morning brunch would quickly devolve into a closed-fist-around-a-fork-shoveling-food-in-your-mouth, booming-laughter-inducing, fist-fight-ridden, bouncer-throwing-you-out-by-the-scruff-of-your-shirt, puking-on-the-sidewalk unholy Sabbath melee. The BobMosa would openly mock all the hard work your body put in to purging last night's alcohol from your bloodstream, bring you right back to the level of drunkenness you were at before you passed out eight hours earlier, and then King Leonidas kick you over the ledge and into a pit of blubbering, staggering uselessness.

"BobMosas sound pretty good right now," Evan and I both said at the same time, turned to each other and started laughing.

Tim laughed along with us. "I wouldn't mind one, but I absolutely cannot get hammered today. I have a ton of errands to run."

Evan nodded in agreement. "Yeah, I have family shit to do today. I can't be too fucked up for that."

"Don't worry, man." I put my arm around Tim and gave him the most sensible, respectable look I could muster given my fragile, hungover state of being. "We'll just have one with breakfast, and then we can all go our separate ways and do all sorts of responsible Sunday shit. Drinks or no drinks, I need some food to soak up the hot booze sloshing around in my gut right now."

Before Tim could refuse my idea, Nick's head fell off the stack of Xbox games and fell on the floor with a muffled thud. "Ungh. My dick still kills."

The room burst into laughter, and we started getting our shit together to leave the apartment.

"Get up, dude." Tim nudged Nick with his foot. "We're going to get some food."

We walked into to Molly Malone's at 10:00 am.

When we walked back out onto the sidewalk, it was 12:00 pm, and each and every one of us was irreversibly shitfaced.

"What the fuck happened to us?" Nick squinted in the bright sun.

"I'm pretty sure I just spent $80 on drinks for myself" I croaked as I popped a cigarette into my mouth.

We were drunk. Very drunk. Definitely far too drunk to be in public on a gorgeous, sunny summer Sunday afternoon. Parents walking around with their kids, tourists were snapping pictures of the ancient Victorian architecture, and songbirds crooned the soundtrack to a picture perfect New England postcard of a day. The contrast between the wholesome setting that surrounded us and our greatly intoxicated, newly depressed group was stark and immediate. I felt genuinely uncomfortable. The day was too perfect for us to even be in it.

A little boy and his undoubtedly high maintenance mother walked by us, and I accidentally blew a lung full of cigarette smoke into their faces. The little boy coughed like a tuberculosis patient, and the mother gave me a glare that smacked of *I hope you get cancer for making Baby Preston uncomfortable for three seconds.* This made my level of discomfort blast through the roof like the puck breaking the bell in one of those sledgehammer strongman carnival games.

"Maybe we should walk around for a while," I suggested while dropping my cigarette on the street.

"This isn't good." Tim rubbed his eyes and checked his watch. "I'm so drunk. We're so drunk."

Nick, ever the optimist, chimed in. "Maybe we can walk it off. Let's just take a loop around town and get some fresh air."

"I don't think we're going to be able to walk this one off, guys. None of us can drive, so that's out. If we stop drinking now, we're going to pass out, get sick or both. I think we have to accept that the day is ruined for productivity." I honestly had nothing important to do that day (read: any day), so I didn't mind keeping the party rolling.

"Dude, I had stuff to do today." Despite how drunk he was, Tim was not having a good time coming to my conclusion.

"Well, what do you have to do today?" I asked.

"I have to go to Michael's and get those stupid decorative balls you put in a bowl and leave on the mantelpiece. My girlfriend is going to kill me if I forget."

"My mom and dad are going to kill me if I show up for dinner like this." Evan donned a pair of sunglasses and took a drag from Nick's cigarette. "This was a bad idea."

I got us walking down the sidewalk and began what I hoped would be the winning argument for Operation Day Drunk.

"Alright, this is how I see it. We can't drive, and won't be able to for a while. That means we can't get our errands done. I'm also going to barf or get a massive headache if we abruptly stop drinking. Those are just the facts. We also know we can't just hang out here in daylight like this. We're too fucked up to be in public place, people are freaking me out, and I feel like I'm going to be placed in protective custody if a cop walks up to me right now. For me, the only solution for us that makes sense right now is to keep drinking. We don't have to black out drunk or anything, but sip on a beer in a dimly lit, air conditioned hole in the wall until we can figure out a better plan."

When everyone nodded in agreement, I thought I delivered the most genius oration of all time and that I should have been a lawyer. In reality, I was shitfaced and made no sense at all, and to say we made a conscious decision is an insult to decision makers everywhere. We were drawn to the open door of State Street Saloon like iron filaments to a Wooly Willy magnetic pen.

My plan to nurse a drink until we were able to craft a better plan, as well as everybody's anxieties about

Sunday's chores, flickered out of existence almost immediately. We were ordering shots of whiskey after our first beers were finished, and were transferring from beer to mixed drinks shortly after that. The threshold between functional drunk and dysfunctional drunk had not been merely crossed, but sprinted over. A handful of normal looking families with children and some elderly people were eating lunch at tables scattered around the bar, and most of them scurried away after being subjected to horrifying conversations like "Which girl had the worst smelling pussy?" or "describe the biggest dump you've ever taken, and how you think the food you ate prior to taking the dump helped make it a monster."

Any customers brave enough to hold on to their stools and withstand our guttural, subhuman discourse were slowly recognized by us, and then we made it a game to see how quickly we could force them to pay and leave by pumping $20 bills into the jukebox and playing the absolute worst music we could find. A handful of tunes from The Chipmunk's Christmas Album, Thompson Twins and Foreplay later, and we succeeded in evicting the last sentient customer in the entire bar.

We cheered, and the bartender cheered along with us, high fiving us for our efforts. We were buying enough drinks, over-tipping and entertaining as fuck compared to the people suffering through their BLT's, so he gave us free reign to drink and act like savages, and we heartily accepted.

Evan, in what would become a regular occurrence during the course of his life, became so drunk that he was nearly catatonic, before anyone else. Slurred speech, eyes half closed, impaired motor skills – essentially to the point where it becomes difficult to get a bartender to pour him another drink, even one who thinks we're God's gift to a boring Sunday afternoon. He pulled up a bar stool next to Timmy and almost fell over trying to sit in it.

"Timmy, I want to get a tattoo."

Tim looked at him and rolled his eyes. "Yeah, sure thing."

"No, seriously. I want to get a tattoo."

This was true. Evan *did* want a tattoo. I can count a thousand nights where we sat together, drinking malt liquor and listening to Evan drone on and on about *the* tattoo he was "definitely going to get" from Tim. It was always the same design; a graffiti-altered Audi logo, but with Volkswagen logos inside each link in the Audi chain. One night, Tim went as far as to grab a pad and pencil and sketch out the design exactly the way Evan wanted it, with Evan sitting next to him, draining his forty, and giving him pointers on the specific dimensions. Once it was done, Tim offered to ink it on Evan free of charge, but Evan would find an excuse and back out every single time. "I'm tired." "I'm hammered." "I want to think about it more." Evan getting hammered and wanting Tim to tattoo him, only to baby out became so common at our parties that we would just laugh at him and change the subject.

"You always say you want me to tattoo you, and you never go through with it. We've had this conversation a thousand times. Just drink your Jack and Coke and relax." The bartender, in an effort to slow down Evan's spiral into unconsciousness had poured him a Coke and Coke, a fact Evan didn't seem to notice.

"Tim, I want you to tattoo me right now. Like, right now. Let's do this. I'm ready."

Tim and I looked at each other, and had to say nothing to understand what each other was thinking. It really wasn't about the tattoo, either. This was about helping Evan overcome what we saw as a legitimate phobia. He was afraid of disappointing his parents. We knew Evan's parents and knew they were massively accepting and wonderful people. Mrs. stuffed us full of homemade pierogies and kielbasa at every chance, and Mr. always plopped a glass full of Grey Goose in our hands and asked us how our lives were going, genuinely caring about what our answers were. These weren't the overbearing parents we imagined when we spoke with Evan, and we knew his deep-rooted fears of parental unacceptance were wildly unfounded, even if he didn't. This was a chance to help Evan over the hump, and take a plunge he might never take again, and we absolutely had to capitalize on it.

Tim, seeing how drunk Evan was and realizing he was never going to have a chance to actually pull off tattooing Evan again, paid all of our tabs after sucking down two consecutive Mountain Dews for a caffeine boost.

"EVERYBODY, PILE INTO MY CAR. WE'RE GOING TO MY PARENTS' HOUSE."

The four of us shuffled down the street. Nick, the most lucid of us, handed out sticks of gum in order to mask our scent. I donned a pair of sunglasses I'm not sure I even owned. Upon making it to the parking lot, we all piled into Tim's Toyota Echo. Despite Tim being a gigantic specimen of human being and despite the Toyota Echo Being the Shriner's clown car of road legal automobiles, we all managed to fit, not wasting any time to bitch about it.

A quick stop was made to buy some beer, and minutes later we were at Tim's parents' home, a nice ranch style house in a quiet, suburban neighborhood filled with other nice ranch style houses. We fell out of the Echo and onto the driveway, walked through the open garage, and down to a set of stairs. Tim opened the unlocked door, and we were immediately in a full tattoo studio set up in the bathroom basement. Dentist's chair, professional tattoo equipment, sterilization tools, the works. Tim built the studio as a way to make some extra money on the side after he finished an apprenticeship at a tattoo parlor in Keene during his late teenage years. When I turned eighteen, I was the first person Tim tattooed. They came out terribly and are the butt of many jokes in my adult years, but Tim continued to work as a professional tattoo artist, and became incredibly good at it.

We all sat down on a couch in the basement and flicked the TV on. Knowing time was of the essence, as the more sober Evan got the greater the chance of him famously backing out, Tim began sterilizing equipment, sanitizing surfaces, and mixing inks.

"Oh hey, guys. What are you guys up to?" Tim's mom came halfway down the spiraling metal staircase leading to the basement to see what we were up to. I instantly froze. *Once she realizes what we're doing and how drunk we are, there's no way she's going to be cool with us doing this. What mom would possibly be cool with us tattooing somebody this drunk?*

Tim's response was maddeningly honest. "Evan's hammered, and he asked me to tattoo him, so I'm going to do it."

Tim's mom just smiled. Not an ignorant smile, but a knowing, intelligent smile. "Oh you boys are just crazy. We were going to order some pizza. You boys hungry? You want some pizza?"

Tim's mom went upstairs to dial Papa Gino's, and I finally began breathing again. The planets were truly aligning. The Universe was harmonizing with our desires. All that laws of attraction new age bullshit in The Secret wasn't completely bullshit after all. We were going to tattoo Evan.

"Alright man, so what do you want for a tattoo?" Timmy was almost ringing his latex gloved hands in anticipation.

Evan took a leisurely slug from his beer. "I want to get the dumbest thing in the world tattooed on me."

Tim, Nick and I turned to each other at the same time, instantly recognizing the goldmine that was Evan's statement and doing our best not to smile. Not only did we get him drunk enough to break through his OCD barriers and finally get the tattoo he secretly desired, but he was demanding to get the dumbest thing he could think of permanently inked on his skin.

Tim looked away and struggled not to laugh. "OK, what is the dumbest thing in the world?"

Evan paused. Not because he had to think about it, but for dramatic purposes. What he was about to tell us was something he had been thinking about for some time. In a world brimming with stupidity, coming to a conclusion about the dumbest thing in it isn't something you casually spitball guesses at.

"Born to die."

We chuckled, and then the chuckle became laughter, and then the laughter became an uproarious, beer spilling cackle. The more we thought about it, the more perfect "*born to die*" became in our heads. It truly was the dumbest phrase any sentient human had ever thought of, but what made it even more special was the fact that you could totally picture some heavy metal guy saying it into a microphone with a straight face, or a road weary biker scooting up I-95 North to Bentley's Saloon with a threadbare "*born to die*" embroidered patch adorning his leather vest. Much like the movie Ski School, "born to die" was so terrible that it was absolutely amazing. As drunk as Evan was, his tattoo concept was brilliant.

Tim composed himself while he finished prepping the studio. "OK, we'll do that. Where do you want it?"

Evan lifted his shirt with one hand and pulled his pants down with the other, until his left butt cheek was exposed. Everybody laughed except for Tim. "No. No nonoNONONO. There is NO WAY I'm tattooing your ass."

"What do you mean?" Evan put his butt cheek away and made a sulking face as if Tim offended him. "That's where I want it."

"I'm not touching your ass, dude. I'm not touching a dude's ass." At several times throughout our friendship, Tim attempted to make the argument that masturbation made you gay because you were touching a dick, so touching another man's ass in order to tattoo it was definitely off the menu for him.

"Why don't you get it somewhere else?" I did my best to reason with him, although knowing Evan as well as I did, little to no reason would sift through the wall of drunk and reach his brain's synapses. "You know, in a place that's less effeminate, like your arm or back or something."

"No. I want it on my butt. It has to be on my butt."

"Evan, why does it have to be on your butt?" Nick asked. "Why would you want to hide something so awesome?"

Evan took another sip of his beer, filling the room with silence as we waited for an answer. I was frustrated; partly because my booze fueled, sleep deprived brain wouldn't allow comprehensive logic to run its course, but mostly because I was watching this incredible chance slip through our fingers, and there was nothing I could do about it. It wasn't like we just dropped the ball either; we rushed him out of the bar and into a tattoo parlor (albeit illegitimate) in order to make this happen.

"Oh shit, you want to get the tattoo on your butt so your mom doesn't see it!" It seemed like it fell out of Tim's mouth more than he actually said it, but there it was. Laugher and pointing and jeering filled the room as Evan, unable to deny the accusation, finished his beer and rummaged around the coffee table for an unopened one.

"If I can't get it on my ass, I'm not getting it." Evan found another beer – a warm Heineken – and popped the cap off with his lighter. "I'm not kidding."

It was all falling apart. The giddiness we felt as we sped through the streets to Tim's house, the years we coaxed Evan to go through with a tattoo, the buzz of Tim's machine as he ran a needle through sanitation fluid in preparation – all of it was crumbling away. Evan was toppling from his drunken Clydesdale and was about to hit the pavement of cold, sobering reality, and there was nothing we could do about it. There was --

"I'll do it." I said the words before I was able to pull them back in and reformulate them into a sentence that made sense. "If I get the tattoo on my arm, will you get it somewhere other than your ass, like your arm or back or something?"

"I don't know, man."

"Yeah, I'll get it too, dude." Nick chimed in. "We'll all get it. You'll get it too, right Tim?"

Tim laughed and nodded in agreement. He was already covered from head to toe in tattoos, so a couple of letters didn't exactly send him screaming.

I turned back to Evan, eyes glimmering with hope. "We'll all get 'Born to Die' tattooed on us if you pick a different place to get tattooed. What about your back? What about your lower back?"

Seconds passed, and then finally "Fine, my lower back. Just do it and get it over with."

The applause was deafening. Beers were pounded. Men hugged men. Delivery pizza was accepted and appreciatively mowed down.

"Well we can't just all get 'born to die' tattooed on us. I'm hammered. I'm going to screw all of those letters up." Tim's admission of drunkenness was disheartening, but honest enough that we were glad he gave it. The last thing any of us needed was some drooping scribble looking like a codeine addled toddler's scrawlings permanently injected into us.

We thought about it for a moment, before we somehow turned it into an acronym. "Born To Die Crew" or "B.T.D.C." seemed even more hilarious than just "Born to

Die" by itself. Adding "Crew" to the end made us sound like some kind of low rent street gang that would hassle Eddie Winslow on an episode of Family Matters. Carl would be all like "Eddie, you know I told you not to be messin' with those boys in the Born to Die Crew. They're nothin' but trouble."

Tim, in a flash of brilliance uncharacteristic to our collective blood alcohol content, immediately tattooed B.T.D.C. on his own wrists in order to ensure Evan's compliance. "No backing out now, motherfucker." Nick also had his done on his wrists. Landing somewhere on the spectrum in between absolutely 'batshit insane' and 'disappointingly conservative', I chose to get my B.T.D.C. on my tricep.

Evan sighed in surrender, and sprawled out on the couch in a way that allowed him to guzzle beer, while Tim tattooed B.T.D.C. on his lower back like a tramp stamp. His face winced out of reflex, but the half closed eyes revealed he wasn't actually experiencing any pain. Ten minutes later, he was up and walking around.

We did it. We finally got Evan to get a tattoo. Sure, we may have totally taken advantage of him while he was inebriated, but we still did it. Mission accomplished.

We cleaned up Tim's basement, applied bacitracin to our fresh tattoos, and made our way back to the State Street Saloon to celebrate our success. Evan managed to get one drink down before the bartender smartly cut him off for the night, and I had to carry him fireman style up the three flights of stairs to my apartment above the bar, where he spent the night on the floor next to the couch in the living room. A couple hours later, I went to bed myself. Dreamless sleep came to me within seconds of my head hitting the pillow.

"AAAHHHHHHHHHHHHH!!!"

I rolled over in my bed and squinted when the light filtering through the shades hit my eyes. I checked the alarm clock. 8:19 am on Monday morning. I decided the scream must have been residual from a dream I was having right before I woke up, and resigned myself to falling back asleep for another hour or so, before waking up and making a pot of coffee.

"AAAAAAAAAAAAAAAHHHHHHHHHHHHH HHHHHH!!!"

Apparently that was a real life scream, and it was coming from my apartment. I bolted out of bed and made a beeline for the living room, where Evan was struggling to sit up. His eyes bulged out of his head and his face was a study of human panic. His shirt was lifted up, exposing the fresh tattoo on his lower back. He would touch the tattoo with his fingers, bring the fingers to his face and let out one of his screams. I watched him do this several times before I asked him if he was OK, because I really wasn't sure what was going on. I finally settled on the theory that he was blacked out the entire day yesterday, and was just now registering the fact that he had a tattoo. *A tattoo his mother would surely see and be disappointed with.*

I immediately felt awful for putting Evan through the ringer like we had the day before. Sure, we all thought his anxiety about getting tattooed was completely unfounded, but they were Evan's anxieties alone, and nobody had the power to shut those off but Evan, and not until he was ready to shut them off. We knew he was hammered, and we took advantage of him. All of the sudden, our plan didn't seem as glorious as it did the day before, and I knew Timmy and Nick would have felt the same way if they were in that room with me.

"I take it you don't remember getting that last night." I said with the most sympathetic voice I could muster and plopped down on the couch next to where Evan was lying.

"I don't remember anything past brunch. What the fuck happened to me? Is this a tattoo?" You could see in his eyes and hear in the way he talked that there was nothing funny about this incident. He was losing his shit, and the brutal hangover he had to be experiencing couldn't be making it any better. My guilty stomach knotted.

"You begged Timmy to ink you. You demanded that he leave the bar and tattoo you right away, so we all drove to Timmy's house and he did it there." At that point I didn't know whether I was trying to make him feel better or make me feel better.

"I WAS HAMMERED!!! YOU KNEW I WAS HAMMERED!!! WHY DID YOU LISTEN TO ME?!?" Evan's frustrated voice erupted out of nowhere, and then immediately settled down again. "This is fucked. I'm fucked. This is totally fucked." Over and over again, like his circuits were overloading. If he wasn't experiencing a panic attack, it was going to become one very soon.

"We were all really, really fucked up. You came up with the idea, and we figured we'd never get another chance like that again, so we rolled with it. We definitely didn't want to upset you. I'm sorry, man."

"I can't even really see it." Evan struggled to crane his neck around trying to get a peek at his lower back. "It looks like a handful of letters. What does it say?"

"It says 'B.T.D.C.' 'Born to Die Crew.' You came up with it. We all have them now, not just you."

I rolled my t-shirt sleeve, showed him my arm and he stopped touching his tattoo. You could almost see a flicker of remembrance kindle in his eyes. He actually smiled, and then he laughed with the note of exhausted relief you only really hear not when things get better, but when you realize other people you know are suffering right along with you.

"Everybody?"

"Tim and Nick tattooed their fucking wrists, man. You and I got off easily. At least we can hide ours."

We both laughed, and I felt a million times better after seeing how Evan woke up moments before. He obviously hadn't completely accepted the events as they took place, or forgiven us for what can only be described as his friends' "Well intentioned yet deliberate collusion", but he was well on his way to doing both, and I could live with that.

Besides, what choice did he have? We were officially a fake street gang, and you can't get jumped out of a fake street gang.

Born to Die Crew 4 Lyfe.

POST SCRIPT: Evan's mom didn't end up seeing his tattoo for five years. When she did see it, she didn't care. She actually thought it was funny.

Micah, after finding out we didn't include him when getting our new tattoos, launched an incredibly successful smear campaign against the Born to Die Crew. I spent several years having to convince people at parties that we weren't gay, and that B.T.D.C. didn't stand for "Born To Drink Cum".

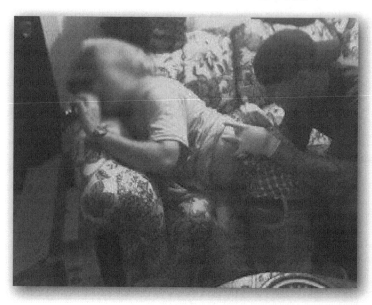

Baked Potato

—〰—

NEW MESSAGE. RECORDED ON TUESDAY, April 29th at 3:37 p.m.:

"Mike, it's Julie. I just wanted to let you know that, well...my period stopped yesterday" - - *click*

My phone hit the bed before I even hit "end". The robotic voice muffled by my comforter rattled off options to save or delete my new message as immediate, acute panic set in; the kind of panic that would send you climbing up the walls of an impossible crevice you've just fallen into, fully well knowing that you're going to tear every one of your fingernails out in the process. The fear caused my heart to beat erratically. My breathing became irregular and the newly familiar signs of an impending anxiety attack ravaged my consciousness; tunnel vision, the whole shebang.

I am not ready for this. I am not ready for this at all.

—〰—

I started hanging out with Julie back in 2008, the month after I moved back home from California. She moved to Portsmouth from out of state a few months prior and had nobody to hang out with, which is understandable because it's hard to meet anybody here during the winter unless you're out at a bar doing the standard seasonally affected New Englander "forget juice shuffle." She found me on Myspace (back when Myspace was actually a thing), struck up a conversation, and figured out that we lived on the same street, literally three doors apart from each other.

We quickly made plans to have a drink and chat in person, and I was stunned when a ridiculously hot little Greek/Brazilian girl answered the door. For the first time in the history of the Universe, somebody was actually hotter in person than in their pictures online.

Julie and I became fast friends. She worked as a waitress by day, and danced at strip clubs a few nights a week. In a past life she'd been an esthetician, but after being in a major car accident that left her with massive brain trauma, and the resulting mild insanity and a mountain of hospital bills robbed her of the profession.

Julie didn't think like regular people anymore. She thought, acted and talked more like a wildly eccentric artist, waxing about her acid-fueled, gothic electronica-scored glory days, and would blow money on a $60 fleece shark puppet before stocking her fridge with food or paying bills. Her worldly possessions consisted of a bag of clothes, stacks

and stacks of spiral notebooks used as hastily scrawled jour-
nals, and a talkative Siamese cat aptly named "Pussy." Julie
was crazy, good-natured and immensely entertaining, and
that's why I loved spending time with her. She was so different from the people I was exposed to on a daily basis; a
breath of fresh air. Correction; a breath of fresh hurricane.

I guess you could call Julie my quasi-"friend with
benefits". When Julie and I drank around each other, we
fucked. It was inevitable. Sober? We didn't lay a finger on
one another. Three drinks into the evening? Our clothes
were scattered across New Hampshire, and we were making wet spots on my sheets. We didn't plan it out like that;
it just worked out that way. At first I was kind of weirded
out that we only had sex under the influence. I didn't understand why I was waking up to awkward morning-after
conversations instead of good morning blowjobs, partly
because I love being woken up with enthusiastic fellatio,
but mostly because I felt like a piece of meat, as effeminate as that sounds.

Although I'd prefer to say otherwise, my ego typically demands stoking via being sought before, during
and after casual encounters and this whole pump-and-
dump operation was playing Jai-Alai with my emotions.
I definitely wasn't looking for a girlfriend in Julie, but I
did feel like I wanted to be ... well, *wanted* - on or off the
wagon. *What the fuck? I'm awesome; when did I become dispos-
able?* Strangely enough, excellent pussy clouds a young
man's convictions, and I ended up abandoning the whole

Troll King from Labyrinth mentality for pinker pastures. Quick, somebody call Ripley's Believe it or Not.

Julie spent the night that Friday after a three-hour round of post-bar, rapid position switching, dirty talking coitus, before she hopped on a Greyhound to her hometown to dance and waitress at a strip club in Connecticut. The next morning we woke up, looked at each other, and asked the same question almost simultaneously.

"Did we use a condom last night?"

—✺—

After finally digesting the news, I frantically dialed Julie over and over again, getting nothing but voicemail. I pictured myself ten years into the future, T.V. dinner gut slumped over the counter of a gas station with my name embroidered on a short sleeve button-up, and a stack of pay stubs stamped with red letters spelling "GARNISHED" sitting on the ripped seat of a rusty 1977 Toyota Starlet in the parking lot. My hopes, dreams and aspirations were sitting in a microwave, and the Devil was reaching for the "baked potato" button. After ten tries, I threw the phone back onto the bed and stared at my feet.

As I stared at my feet waiting for my Herbie Hancock ringtone to shock me out of panicked, obsessive thought, I speculated on how the situation would play out. Seeing as though she was a dancer and not ready for kids in any way, she would probably want to 86 our Miracle Baby of the Immaculate Conception as soon as possible. But what if she didn't? What if she wanted to keep it for some insane reason? What would I do? How would I explain it to my mother that I got a GreekZilian stripper pregnant without her jumping out of a moving Prius? I could barely take care of myself (if you consider my Monday through Friday diet of Lean Cuisine, Cliff Bars and Newcastle Brown Ale "Sustenance"), so how was I supposed to support a rug monkey?

I mean, I would do the honorable thing and be there for my little Antichrist, but what would I have to *give up* in order to *man up?* Going out and getting drunk? Definitely, that costs money. Travel? Out the window. Writing? I made a pittance at my seasonal gig, and my website didn't generate enough traffic to make my checks capable of supporting anything above a Ramen noodle habit. I would have to go out and get a real job, probably back in the sinister, soul-sucking world of energy trading. Seventy/eighty hour workweeks would demolish my ability to write coherently. After time, I would probably abandon writing altogether because I'd be too focused on making enough scratch for braces, school clothes, and whatever I need to baby-proof the skuzzy studio apartment I'd undoubtedly have to live in. The life I envisioned for myself would be put on hold for eighteen years. Who knows if I would ever get it back after that kind of time? That's the part that scared me the most.

Just as I got off the phone with Planned Parenthood to get some blood work after my adventures in raw dogging, the screen on my cell phone lit up.

Call from: JULIE, CELL

"JULIE! WHAT THE FUCK IS GOING ON?!?"

"I don't know. My period stopped three days into it. I'm kind of nervous."

"Kind of?! I'm losing my fucking mind over here." I rummaged through my desk drawer for a stale pack of Parliament Lights I reserved for when I was extremely drunk or something terrible happened. "What should we do?"

"I don't know, Mike. This has never happened to me before."

"Yeah, me neither. I mean, I was too drunk to cum on Friday night. How did this happen? Isn't it impossible to get pregnant when your tin roof's rusty?"

"I think it's possible, but just really rare. Why don't you Google it?"

I spent the next twenty minutes looking up every possible Boolean combination of "Sex, period, and pregnant" while on the phone with Julie. Every website, forum and blog all echoing the same sentiment; it's not impossible to get pregnant, but there was only a very, very slim chance that it could happen.

"It says that it's next to impossible, so that's good. It also says that your flow can be interrupted if you have sex during it. That could also be it." My voice didn't sound relieved in the slightest.

"That's true, I never thought about that." Julie's voice didn't sound relieved in the slightest either.

"Well, what...what should we do, Julie?"

"Look Mike, chances are it's nothing, but just in case it isn't nothing...I'm not keeping it. Don't worry. I'm going to go to the store and grab a Plan B."

The tension left my body immediately upon hearing Julie say that.

"OK, phew! You have no idea how worried I was about that very thing."

"I figured as much. I just need to figure out how to get to the store. I have no car down here. I might have to borrow my friend's van, but it's not registered, inspected or insured."

The tension re-entered my body with all the grace of a serial rapist gorilla. A new vision emerged; Julie with a big fat mom stomach behind bars. Another vision overlapped that one; me with big bags under my eyes, sipping a McDonald's coffee and staring off into the distance as my seed held the other children in the Play Place hostage with a Lunchables spork.

"Honey, just be careful." I didn't want her to drive that van, but I didn't want an heir to my throne either. "Drive slow."

"I will, don't worry. Hey, you should totally write about this."

"I am buying a pallet worth of condoms after this. I'm going to drop them everywhere like Hansel's bread crumbs so I'm never without one again."

"Don't bother. We're not having sex anymore. The next time we get drunk and horny around each other, I'm just going to suck your dick."

"I guess that works too."

Magic Sunglasses

—⚹—

JUST BEFORE I LEFT LOS Angeles to move back to New Hampshire, I started talking to a girl on MySpace named Jess. She was a friend of a friend, and while I was creepily stalking her profile, I noticed she lived in Boston and listed the Coat of Arms in Portsmouth as her favorite bar. The Coat has been a second home to me for well over a decade, so that coupled with the fact that she looked really cute in her pictures made me send her a creepy stalker unsolicited friend request.

She responded to it with "Why do you want to be my friend? Because I like the Coat of Arms?"

My response: "If the Coat of Arms is really your favorite bar, I will put a ring on your finger."

It was a terrible line, but apparently it worked. We started talking, and discovered we had a lot in common. She grew up in New Hampshire, she was very familiar with Portsmouth and she also attended to UNH. Her sense of humor was very similar to mine, and we laughed easily about a thousand topics.

We graduated to texting each other after a while. At the risk of coming across like some kind of socially mal-adjusted basement dweller, writing each other from our phones somehow seemed more personal than the cold, stark letters on a computer screen. We would send each other at least two or three dozen texts a day. What started out as my feeble attempt to get into a girl's pants ended up being something fairly meaningful, albeit distant. This went on all the way until I boarded a plane with little more than my clothes on my back and headed back east.

The day after I arrived, Jess asked me if I wanted to finally meet her in person. I was staying at my mother's apartment in Beacon Hill, which was only a furlong, ten rods, anything but a stone's throw from her shared apartment in Southie. I was really excited to meet her and hang out (and hook up. What? I'm a dude.), but I had just moved home after a fairly emotionally traumatic experi-ence back in California, and I desperately needed to take some time to figure my shit out before I jumped back into the dating game. Also, I was broke. Dead broke. I was driving my recently dead grandmother's '92 Pontiac Grand Am, and while it only had a few thousand miles on it, the car was in rough shape and I was almost posi-tive that it was haunted. The radio would regularly turn on and the volume would go up and down without me pressing any buttons, enough to make the hair on the back of your neck stand up. I wasn't exactly in a position to wine and dine a girl, no matter how much I liked her. I delayed meeting Jess for as long as humanly possible, and we continued to text each other.

A couple weeks later, I moved back to Portsmouth and into the spare bedroom of my friend's apartment until I could land my own one bedroom in town. Finally, after a long conversation on the phone, Jess accused me of not really wanting to meet her because it had been so long since we first started talking, but she was coming up to my area to try on a dress for her best friend's wedding, so we decided on short notice that she would stay with me in Portsmouth. She arrived on a Saturday afternoon, wearing a herringbone coat and had her hair in a ponytail. She looked better than she did in her pictures, and I mentally high fived myself as soon as I laid eyes on her. We sat on the couch and talked for a long time, with the TV on in the background. I wanted to impress her by making chicken Parmesan for dinner, but I ended up setting off the fire alarm because I used olive oil to fry the breaded cutlets. Later that night, I took her out in Portsmouth for drinks, and she ended up spending the night.

It wasn't like some easy one-night stand with Jess that night. We had been talking for so long before we finally met in person that it almost felt like two teenagers getting ready to consummate their months long relationship on prom night. I was as nervous as a teenager, that's for sure. I really liked her.

Jess and I didn't settle into each other easily, like some couples do. Another thing we had in common was that we were both incredibly stubborn, and that lead to some blowouts early on in our courtship. We clearly liked each other and loved each other's company, but neither of us were very good at giving in, and a trivial little disagreement regularly bloomed into a full on scream fest. It got so bad at one point that we parted ways for a few months after a heated argument on the phone.

I spent that three months dating here and there, but nothing serious ever came of it. The girls that succeeded Jess just didn't inspire me like she did. I know it sounds corny, but I remember sitting through meals at restaurants, shuffling food around my plate with my fork and wishing it were Jess in front of me and not someone a friend set me up with or a fan of my writing who was so doe-eyed she didn't notice how bored I was with her. I burned through girl after girl like a heavy smoker trying to quit by buying a pack of ultralight cigarettes.

The only girl I dated for an amount of time worth mentioning had a full spectrum of control issues that ranged from not allowing herself to orgasm to running so much that her body started falling apart to inevitably being hospitalized for acute anorexia. After that one took off to chase down an old flame she still had feelings for, I looked at the fifty-something sleazebags at bars hitting on twenty year olds with jealousy instead of the usual disgust. *Fuck it. I'm just going to give up this meaningful relationship stuff and be a creepy old fuck. I'm going to have a grey Justin Bieber haircut and convince girls thirty years younger than me to suck the liver spots off of my useless old man dick. Fuck it.*

Later in life I would accuse myself of subconsciously sabotaging my love life during this period because I didn't want things to work out with anyone other than Jess, which confused the fuck out of me because I hadn't had a relationship last longer than six months in my entire life and I honestly liked it that way. I liked girls, I liked sex and I liked the company of a female, but I didn't like how they complicated things, or at least that's what I told myself. The more I thought about it, the more I realized I liked her *because* she complicated things in the right way. She wasn't an easy fuck or a superficial conversation to breeze through while thinking about something else. She challenged me and commanded my attention, and I liked that. *Am I in love with this girl? Is this what it's supposed to feel like?* I honestly had no idea.

My writing wasn't even coming close to paying the bills at the time, so I took a job doing mosquito control to make ends meet. If you've ever been to New England in the summer, you know how brutal our mosquitoes are. It was a grueling job that consisted of wearing rubber hip waders and a fifty pound backpack filled with poison, and stomping around humid swamps and salt marshes in blazing sun and hundred degree heat all over southern New Hampshire. The owner of the business was a curmudgeonly middle-aged woman who owned a pack of awful little Schipperkes that would draw blood from your ankles any time you crossed the baby gate that separated the office from the garage to punch in or out. The pay was mediocre and the work was incredibly physically demanding, but overtime was occasionally offered and I had never been more tan or in better shape. I thought I looked so good that I commissioned a professional photo shoot of myself because I wanted to memorialize the sexiest moment of my life and maybe even use one of the headshots above a little about the author blurb, if ever got my shit together and finished writing the book I was always telling people was "*THIS* close to being done."

One day a coworker and I headed out to Jess's hometown of Londonderry, New Hampshire to treat catch basins and any other standing water we came across, and I decided to break the three months of silence by texting Jess to let her know where I was, and to ask her where a good place to eat lunch in the area might be. She told me about a decent sandwich about a mile away called the Wrap Shak, and then asked me what street I was on. We were both amazed to learn that I was compelled to text her while standing on the street she grew up on. Coincidence? Fate? The hands of God mashing two people together like a little boy playing with G.I. Joes in the backyard?

She picked me up at my apartment that Saturday, and we spend a few hours sunning ourselves on a picnic blanket at the local park. We talked about how our lives were going, and what events took place during the months we didn't speak. She'd dated a couple guys in Boston, and was actually still in the middle of seeing one of them, a co-worker at the financial firm she worked for. We talked about what I was up to, how my writing was going, and the hilarious string of failures I was then calling my dating life. It was a good talk; not forced or strained in any way, just two intelligent people who genuinely cared about each other catching up and enjoying each other's company.

Jess got up to use the bathroom facilities at the other side of the lawn we were parked on. I rolled over on my back stared up at the perfectly blue sky through my chunky Oakley sunglasses and thought about our conversation. *Was I acting cool? Did I seem nervous? Oh shit, did I wear deodorant?!* I was in the middle of smell checking my armpits when she walked out of the bathroom and across the sunny lawn. I was all at once entranced by her, and everything slowed down. The way the sun hit her brown hair and tanned skin, the feminine way her little black dress moved around her body as she walked, her graceful stride; they all worked to paralyze me in a star struck way I'd never experienced before. It was amazing and terrifying all at once, and for the first time in my life, I knew I was in love. Not selfish high school love where you say you love someone because you want to get laid, or needy adult love where you say those three words because you're afraid of losing someone you're comfortable with if you don't, or implausibly flawless soap opera love that has no basis in reality, but real, stomach sickening, throat closing, anxiety sweat producing, thought erasing, mouth drying love. When I'm on my death bed and my life flashes before my eyes in that quintessential mortal PowerPoint everybody talks about, that pure, perfect, exquisite moment in time when my Jess walked toward me through the lawn of Prescott Park on that perfect summer day is the last slide I want my mind's eye to see before I blink out of existence.

We stayed there for another hour or so before she dropped me off at my apartment. When we were parked, we both agreed that we wanted to give our relationship another chance, and we kissed. It's a good thing I was wearing those sunglasses, because I probably would have scared her off with what I can only imagine were the wide, glassy, idolizing eyes of an emotionally unbalanced celebrity stalker.

A few weeks later, Jess called me up and invited me to a huge annual Labor Day weekend boat party on Lake Winnipesaukee, where people congregate in the middle of the lake, tie their boats together to create a giant flotilla and throw a boozy rager on it. I was excited to go, as I grew up dirt poor and my only real experience with boats was watching them from the shore, but I was definitely nervous about meeting Jess's parents for the first time. I can get pretty socially anxious in certain settings, but I've always been good with people's parents. I have friends who can't charm a mom or dad to save their lives, and that always made me laugh. I mean, there's really not that much to it. Agree with everything they say, compliment them on the flowers in their garden/tools in their garage and ask if you can help with anything while they make dinner, even though they say no 99.99% of the time, right? It was different with her parents because I loved her, and I wanted to make the best first impression I possibly could. Instead of just going with the flow, I was forcing myself to be "On", which in turn cranked my anxiety meter to code red. Nevertheless, I told my boss I was sick in order to get the time off, packed a small bag and drove up with Jess to the lakes region.

We arrived at Weirs Beach just before noon. The sidewalks to the left were filled with a strange mix of out-of-state summer people in their expensive Tommy Bahama button up shirts and Nantucket reds, biker guys in t-shirts and black leather vests signifying their respective clubs and regular old local folks who kept their heads down as they walked past the crowded bars and speared their way through the barbaric insurgents who invaded their otherwise quiet fiefdom every year. The unrestrained summer sun dappled on the surface of Lake Winnepesaukee, which was to our right as we drove down the main thoroughfare of Weirs Beach. I could see right away why so many celebrities and wealthy tycoons bought houses up here. The view was absolutely breathtaking.

We parked the car, grabbed our bags and made our way toward a busy boardwalk pier that was peppered with unattended children wandering in an out of the arcade on it. Jess's mother and stepfather (it would be a few more months before I met her biological father for the first time) had their boat docked at a marina that was situated underneath the pier, giving it a rather handy roof that protected boats, gear and people from the elements. Instead of paying for a hotel, people would either sleep in their docked boats or set up camping tents right on the pier next to them.

"You made it!" A cheerful woman's voice chirped from a picnic table situated at the end of the marina as soon as we made it down the stairs. When we reached the picnic table, I discovered the voice belonged to Jess's mom Sue. She was dressed casually as you would expect most people to be while on vacation, wearing a short-billed Castro cap, tank top and jeans. She gave Jess a hug, and then turned to me.

"You must be Mike. It's nice to finally meet you!" I mentally prepared to start into my tried and true *mom talking routine*, which would consist of casserole recipes and discussion about the top 10 episodes of Everybody Loves Raymond.

"You want a Jagerbomb?"

"Uh…" I wasn't ready for that kind of curveball, especially at 11:30 in the morning. Say yes and you're drunk before noon in a strange place where you know nobody. Say no and you run the risk of insulting Jess's parents before you've even had a chance to get to know them. "Absolutely, I'd love one."

Jess turned to me, gave me a wry grin and a nod that insinuated go for it, and put her bag down next to Steve's boat, a spacious Four Winns cabin cruiser, which rocked gently in is slip.

"Where is Steve, anyway?"

"Who knows? He's probably still in the cabin of the boat doing God knows what. He wasn't feeling very good when we drove up here."

"Oh no?" I slammed my Jagerbomb and handed her my red Solo cup for a refill. "What's wrong with him?"

"Maybe it's the flu or something. We're not quite sure. He's been taking some weird pills that seem to be helping."

I took the refilled cup from Sue and prepared my stomach for another salvo of booze missiles. "Oh, like Tylenol or something?"

"No, I wish. Apparently he found an old bottle of pills inside a wall at his house in New York. It's so old that the label was unreadable, so we have no idea what's in it or how old it is. Whatever they are, he's having a blast taking them, but they're making him sweat like a pig."

No sooner did she speak those words than Steve's bald head poked up out of the boat's cabin like a gopher. "Suzie, get me another beer, will ya'?" He stood up straight, revealing a large, stout build covered by worn jeans and a grey t-shirt riddled with sweat stains.

"Is this that Mike character you've been yapping about?" He climbed out of the boat, shook my hand and took a fresh can of beer from Sue.

"Hey Steve, it's nice to meet you. Sorry to hear you're not feeling well." I watched him guzzle about a third of his beer in one sip.

"I'm fiiiiiiiine." Steve extended his "I's" in "fine" like the people in northern New Hampshire are known for. "I was feeling a little under the weather on the way up, but I've been taking these pills and now I feel great. They must be Quaaludes or something." Giant beads of sweat rolled down the sides of his face like translucent boulders.

I downed my second Jagerbomb. "Yeah, Sue said you found a bottle of pills in the – "

I turned to my left to casually regard Sue as I was speaking about her, and found her firing up yet another drink for herself; the third in the thirty minutes I had been there. I couldn't even finish my sentence; I was absolutely floored. On one side I had Sue, who was draining Jagerbombs like a sorority girl on Lake Havasu, and on the other side I had Steve, who was crushing beers and eating expired pain medication *he found inside of a wall.*

I immediately felt silly for spending so much time worrying about what Jess's parents were going to be like. They were super nice, and they could obviously party harder than any other set of parents I've ever encountered. They were fucking incredible.

After setting our two-person tent up next to the boat slip, Jess and I had a few more drinks at the marina and decided to venture out with the parents to a few bars for food and more booze. The next ten hours after this is a block of time in which my memory became compromised by alcohol, but what I do remember was Sue and Steve knowing EVERYBODY, no matter where we went. We'd walk into one bar, and not only would seventeen patrons come over to hug Sue and slap Steve on the back. We'd walk into another bar, and the owner of the place would come out and pour them free shots. These guys weren't just well known locals; they were full-fledged local celebrities. If Camelot was Weirs Beach, Sue and Steve were Jackie Onassis and John F. Kennedy. I guess that made Jess Caroline Kennedy, because everybody knew her too. Before everything went kind of grey, I specifically remember thinking how great all these people were. Jess, her parents, the people from the lake. They were all just so friendly and genuine; very much unlike the people back home, who were always about three words away from "go fuck yourself." There was no awkward conversation where you could tell the person on the other end was just waiting for you to shut up so they could talk. These people looked you in the eye when you spoke, they were actually listening and they actually cared about what you said. The night became a blur of loud music, laughter, clinking glasses and occasionally making out when we would sneak outside for cigarettes.

Bright morning sun turning my closed eyelids a hot magenta on the inside, unbearably hot camping tent air and the cawing of lake birds woke me. I pried one bloodshot eye open to see the sun was filtering right through the transparent screened top of the tent. We never bothered using the rainfly, as we were underneath the boardwalk. I blindly ran my hand along the crinkly tarp floor until I found my Oakleys, which were lying on top of one of my flip-flops. The other flip-flop was still on my foot. I slid my sunglasses up the bridge of my nose and groaned in relief, after which I clasped my hands behind my head and basked in my hangover. This woke Jess up, who was curled up like a cat underneath the sleeping bag we brought with us. She rolled over, rested her head on my chest and wrapped an arm around me. We lay like that for a while before she playfully slid her hand down underneath the sleeping bag and wrapped her cold fingers around my morning salute. Before I even had time to register what was happening to me, she kissed me, right before her head followed her hand underneath the covers, and all rational thought process abandoned me.

There I was; a twenty-seven year old college dropout with a pile of debt and no career, future or options even worth mentioning, lying outdoors, mere inches from the waters of Lake Winnipesaukee lapping up against the support beams of a marina filled with extremely expensive boats on an absolutely gorgeous summer morning...receiving a phenomenal blowjob from a beautiful girl. I stay in my reclined position staring up through the translucent mesh of the tent's roof, listing to the birds cooing in the rafters of the boardwalk thinking all I needed was a bottle of Champagne and "Mo Money, Mo Problems" to start playing and the scene would be complete. My brain was drunk with pleasure and its synapses were only allowing snippet of ultra-positive, almost New Agey inspirational blurbs to pass between each other. *Going from awful Los Angeles to this? My life is really turning around. Things are really looking up for me. I'm –*

"OH. That's nice."

Standing black against the bright summer sun filtering through the tent's window was Steve's bald head, looking in at us. I bolted upright. Jess pulled her head out from under the sleeping bag, scrambling to cover herself with it. "STEVE, WHAT THE FUCK?!"

Steve laughed so hard and for so long he started coughing. "I was just walking by the tent, for Christ's sake. You were the one giving blowjobs right out in the open."

Jess looked over at me and I was frozen in terror. I stared back at her with wide, fearful eyes. "Oh my god. Oh my god. Ohmygodohmygod." I whispered while pulling my shorts up.

"What's all the racket out there?" Sue climbed out of the cabin of the boat with a confused look on her face.

"I was just walking by the tent, and Jess was giving ol' Mike over here a hummah!"

When I heard Steve say that, my heart sank. In less than 24 hours, I met her parents for the first time and managed to get caught defiling her. Crazy, panicked scenes screamed through my head; Steve barreling into the tent and beating me into a life of catheters and Gerber bananas, Sue throwing my clothes into the lake and demanding I stop seeing her daughter, Jess being so crushed by the incident she ended things with me herself. Electric pangs of anxiety and embarrassment raced up and down my body. Sweat beaded up on my brow and moistened the underarms of my t-shirt as I began putting my clothes back into my bag. That was it. I ruined everything. I had a great thing, and I threw it in the trash by acting like an idiot. Par for the course. Jess asked me why I was packing up my things and tried to get me to stop.

"Are you crazy?!" I hushed toward her. "Your stepdad just caught us...you know! There's no way I'm going to be able to stay here. He probably wants to kill me, and your mom...oh Christ. I can't believe this is happening."

Just as I was about to unzip the tent and make a break for the car, Sue and Steve starting bellowing laughter together. Steve's was the loudest.

"Suzie, it was awesome. He was just lying there with his hands behind his head...wearing those sunglasses... he looked like a fucking rock star. It was the greatest thing I've ever seen." Sue was shaking her head in disgust, but laughing all the while.

I unzipped the tent's door and stepped outside while Jess put her clothes on, arms up and hands facing out as if I was surrendering in the middle of a bank robbery. "Guys, I'm so, so, so sorry." I refused to make eye contact and half braced myself to be fly tackled by Steve, or have Sue start windmilling cat claws at my guilty face.

"Jesus, Mike. You don't have to say you're sorry." Steve looked at Sue and bent over laughing again. "You're a fucking rock star! You're Keith fucking Richards!" He then laced his fingers behind his head, closed his eyes and made a theatrical orgasm face. My eyes darted nervously from Steve to Sue, not knowing what to do next. My heart was beating out of my chest. *Do I leave? Do I stay?*

Without even really knowing it was happening, I started laughing. It kind of just fell out of me, like holding back vomit and running to the bathroom, only to have it launch out of you inches from the toilet. The situation was just so awkward and emotionally charged (at least for me), and I was either going to laugh or suffer an aneurysm. I laughed, and the more the anxiety melted off of me, the harder I laughed. By the time Jess emerged from the tent, all of us were doubled over laughing at the absurdity of it all.

Steve spent the rest of the day recounting every lurid detail of the story for his legions of friends and fans, and pestering Sue to buy him a pair of "M*agic* sunglasses" for home use.

And that is the story of how I met my in-laws for the first time.

POST SCRIPT:

* Shortly after this incident, the magic sunglasses fell off of my head while enjoying a boat ride on Baxter Lake near Rochester, New Hampshire. I can only hope there's a lucky fish down there reclining back with his fins behind his head and a stupid look on his face.

* To this day, Steve is still begging Sue for a pair of "Magic" sunglasses. Sue still refuses. He has tried on several pairs, but he tells me none of them have had the same effect.

Acknowledgements

—⟋⟍—

I FEEL LIKE IT'S KIND of pretentious to create an acknowledgements section for your very first book, isn't it? I mean, who am I? A virtual nobody who self-published because he couldn't convince anybody in the publishing industry to touch a male memoir. Yet here I am, blathering on in an acknowledgements section of my own creation, as if there's no doubt in my mind about my readers being desperate to know about the people behind this project.

Even though this makes me feel like an actress giving a long winded thank you speech at the Academy Awards despite the music trying to play her off stage, there are some good people I want to sincerely thank for helping make this book a reality. I say this without a shred of sarcasm; without them, there would be no book, and quite possibly no me at all.

I'd like to thank Tucker Max, who took a young idiot under his wing back in 2002, showed him the ropes, gave him work, and compelled him to make each story he wrote better than the last. I'd also like to thank Nils Parker, Erin Tyler, and everybody else with the old Rudius Media gang while I'm at it. You've always been good friends and mentors to me, and I wish you all the success and happiness in the world.

The editors of this book took on the heroic task of slapping sense into me when needed, and painstakingly transforming my sloppy manuscript into something you wanted to buy and read. Chris Elliott and my wife Jessica, you are both the wind beneath my wings, and I am forever indebted to you. If this book sells a million copies, I'll buy each of you a pony.

Next up is Cara Langevin, for her masterful artistry in painting what would become the cover of this book. Her painting was inspired by a photograph of me taken the night before Born to Die Crew took place. It was a late night, and I'd just pried myself off the bathroom floor after having won a Fireball chugging contest when the flash went off. How Cara managed to make such a moment look as beautiful as she did will forever be beyond me.

Mon Petit Studio was in charge of converting Cara's painting into a book cover, as well as designing my website and countless other things I'm not smart enough to create myself. Not only are they the photographers we used for our wedding, but they also create all of the book covers for the short stories I sell on Amazon. They're an incredibly talented couple, and we're lucky to be able to call them close personal friends.

Of course, this acknowledgement section wouldn't be complete without thanking the people who appear in these pages. Timmy, Evan, Zach, Micah, Seth, Matt, Brendon, Pete, Teddy, and all of my friends in Portsmouth, New Hampshire – you are the family I chose, and every day I remind myself how lucky I am that you guys chose me in return. Born to die, forever.

To my sisters Gennie and Chrissie, my brothers Brendan, Emmett and Martin, my cousins, nieces, nephews, aunts and uncles, you guys mean the world to me. Life and distance have kept us from seeing each other as often as we'd like over the years, and I sincerely hope we can make that change in the years to come.

Mom, you are an amazing woman. We've been through a whole hell of a lot together, but we've made it through to the other side, and the other side is pretty damned good, isn't it. Thank you for taking care of me when times were tough, for putting up with me through what I'll refer to as my "extended adolescence", and for keeping me alive long enough for you to pass the torch of responsibility on to your daughter-in-law. I love you.

I save the last acknowledgement for Jessica, the woman tasked with the incredible responsibility of being my wife, and the main reason you are able to read these words today. Jessica, you are the most important thing in life that my mind is capable of recognizing. You are everything and anything that matters. You are the Nutella to my strawberry, and the Baxter to my Molesley. I love you more than I'll ever be able to say or show. Let's grow old and weird together.